The Law of Prescription

and

Limitation of Actions

in Scotland

The Law of Prescription
and
Limitation of Actions
in Scotland

by

DAVID M. WALKER

C.B.E., M.A., Ph.D., LL.D., Hon.LL.D., F.B.A., F.R.S.E.,
F.S.A.Scot., F.R.S.A.,
One of Her Majesty's Counsel in Scotland,
Of the Middle Temple, Barrister,
Regius Professor Emeritus of Law in the
University of Glasgow

FIFTH EDITION

EDINBURGH
W. GREEN & SON LTD.
Law Publishers
1996

First edition	1973
Second edition	1976
Third edition	1981
Supplement	1984
Fourth edition	1990

ISBN Paperback 0 414 01135 x)

A catalogue record for this book is available from the British Library

Typeset by Trinity Typesetting, Edinburgh
Printed and bound in Great Britain
by Butler & Tanner Ltd, Somerset

PREFACE

THE first edition of this book was prepared very hastily while the Prescription and Limitation (Scotland) Act 1973 was going through its legislative stages and it had to be so written that the major part of it could be reprinted as the print of that Act with annotations contained in *Scottish Current Law Statutes 1973.* For the second edition it was completely rewritten in the light of further study of the subject and to present the law in a more rational form, though it is still necessarily largely an explanation of and commentary on the statutes which bear on the subject, particularly the 1973 Act, as interpreted in case law. Parliament has, however continued to amend the 1973 Act and the courts have had to cope with numerous problems of interpretation, while the Scottish Law Commission issued early in 1989 Consultative Memorandum No. 122—Prescription and Limitation of Actions (Latent Damage and Other Related Issues), so that further change is possible. In this edition I have extensively revised and partly rewritten the text and tried to take account of all developments to this date.

I have sought to state the law down to September 30, 1995.

D.M.W.

School of Law,
University of Glasgow,
Glasgow, G12 8QQ.
October 1, 1995

CONTENTS

TABLE OF CASES

TABLE OF STATUTES

CHAPTER 1

THE CONCEPTS OF PRESCRIPTION AND LIMITATION

THE concepts of prescription and limitation of actions are both concerned with the effects of the passage of time on a person's rights but are of different natures and have different applications and effects. The concept of prescription as understood in Scots law itself takes several forms with different effects.

PRESCRIPTION

The concept and name of prescription originated in Roman law.[1] Under imperial enactments the concept of *longi temporis praescriptio* gave the holder of property a defence against another claimant after the lapse of 10 years if parties were present in the same province or 20 years if they were not.[2] Under Justinian prescription became a means of acquiring title and the period for moveables was three years and 10 or 20 years for immoveables.[3] In the later Empire there appeared *longissimi temporis praescriptio*; it was enacted that 40 years possession, whatever its origin, should complete a right and extinguish contrary rights; in at least some cases this was later cut to 30 years. Justinian enacted that a bona fide buyer who held a thing for 10 or 20 years acquired good title thereto, but if the former owner did not know of the acquisition the time was 30 years.

Actions might also be barred by lapse of time. Though the civil law admitted this in a few cases only, many praetorian actions were limited to an *annus utilis*. An extension of time was recognised if the claimant were under age, and the period was interrupted and must begin again if the debtor gave any acknowledgment. These ideas reappear in Scots law.

Prescription was introduced into Scots law "after the example of the Romans ... though under different limitations as best suited the genius and constitution of the several states."[4] It is "the common extinction and abolishing of all rights".[5] "Prescription is a legal presumption of abandonment or of satisfaction, and so extinguishes the debt."[6] The underlying principles are the presumption that after the lapse of a substantial time a person entitled to challenge or to make a claim has determined not to do so, and the desirability of rights being settled and not open to challenge or claim indefinitely.

There is no authority for prescription of rights by common law. "By our ancient custom, there was no place for prescription in any case, which hath been corrected by our statutes, both as to long and short prescription."[7]

---

[1] Stair, II, 12, 1.
[2] Bruns, *Fontes Iuris Romani*, no. 87.
[3] *Dig,* 41.3; *Inst:* II, 6.
[4] Ersk., III, 7, 1. *cf.* Stair, II, 12, 9. The Prescription Act 1617 expressly invoked the civil law in its preamble.
[5] Stair, II, 12, 1.
[6] Bell, *Prin.*, § 586. See also § 605.
[7] Stair, II, 12, 12.

1

DEVELOPMENT OF PRESCRIPTION IN SCOTS LAW

In Scots law the rules as to prescription developed in rather haphazard fashion over a long period, with little uniformity of terminology, nature or effect, in a large number of statutory provisions enacted and amended at various times. While the general concept was that certain claims or rights were extinguished after the lapse of a fixed period of time, prescription assumed three forms in Scots law. The first was the positive prescription of heritable rights, whereby after the lapse of, originally 40, later 20, and since 1970, 10 years, an *ex facie* valid title to certain classes of heritable property became unchallengeable, all contrary claims and pleas being barred and excluded by law from being stated, save only the pleas that the title founded on was not *ex facie* valid or that it had been forged. The effect was to validate certain possibly challengeable titles and establish them as unchallengeable.

Positive prescription was introduced by the Prescription Act 1594 (c. 214); A.P.S. IV, 68, c. 24, and restated by the Prescription Act 1617, (c. 12); A.P.S. IV, 543, c. 12, which, as interpreted, provided that 40 years' possession, continually and peaceably, without interruption, founded on a charter or disposition followed by sasine, should confer an unchallengeable right. The period was reduced to 20 years by the Conveyancing (Scotland) Act 1874, restated by the Conveyancing (Scotland) Act 1924, and the period further reduced to 10 years by the Conveyancing and Feudal Reform (Scotland) Act 1970.

The second was the group of so-called "short" prescriptions, traditionally known from their durations as the triennial,[8] quinquennial,[9] sexennial[10] and vicennial prescriptions,[11] which did not, after the lapse of their respective periods, wholly extinguish the kinds of obligations to which they severally applied but merely altered the onus and method of proof and required proof that the obligation still subsisted undischarged to be given by the creditor, and to be made by either the writ of the debtor or by his admission on oath. Provided proof in such a way could be given the obligation subsisted till extinguished by the long negative prescription.

The third was the group of extinctive prescriptions which after the lapse of their respective periods wholly extinguished the obligations to which they applied. These included the triennial prescription of spuilzies and ejections,[12] the triennial prescription of actions of removing,[13] the septennial prescription of cautionary obligations,[14] the decennial prescription of tutors' and curators' accounts,[15] and, most importantly, the long negative prescription,[16] originally of 40 and later of 20 years, which all, after the

---

[8] Prescription Act 1579 (c. 21), A.P.S. III, 145, c. 21.

[9] Prescription Act 1669 (c. 14), A.P.S. VII, 561, c. 14; Prescription Act 1685 (c. 14), A.P.S. VIII, 471, c. 14.

[10] Bills of Exchange (Scotland) Act 1772. This was probably, in nature, a limitation rather than a prescription provision; it is so treated by Bell, *Prin.*, § 594.

[11] Prescription Act 1669 (c. 14), A.P.S. VII, 561, c. 14.

[12] Prescription (Ejections) Act 1579 (c. 19), A.P.S. III, 145, c. 19.

[13] Prescription Act 1579 (c. 20), A.P.S. III, 145, c. 20 (repealed by Statute Law Revision (Scotland) Act 1964).

[14] Cautioners Act 1695 (c. 7), A.P.S. IX, 366, c. 7. This also was probably, in nature, a limitation rather than a prescription; see Bell, *Prin.*, § 586, 600.

[15] Prescription Act 1696 (c. 9), A.P.S. X, 35, c. 9.

[16] Prescription Act 1469 (c. 4), A.P.S. II, 95, c. 4; Prescription Act 1474 (c. 9), A.P.5. II, 107, c. 9; Prescription Act 1617 (c. 12), A.P.S. IV, 543, c. 12.

lapse of their respective periods, wholly extinguished the kinds of rights and obligations to which they severally applied.

All the statutes and sections of statutes mentioned have been repealed, nearly all by the Prescription and Limitation (Scotland) Act 1973.[17] The only pre-1973 provision dealing with prescription still standing is the presumption that 13 years' possession is sufficient to support a churchman's right to any subject as part of his benefice, though he can produce no title in writing to it. This is based on the common law maxim *decennalis et triennalis possessio non tenetur docere de titulo.*[18]

All these statutory provisions were interpreted and applied in numerous cases. The 1973 Act has not only repealed all these statutes, and thereby rendered obsolete large numbers of cases, but considerably simplified the law by establishing a new positive prescription generally on the lines of the 1617 Act (positive portion), and a new short negative prescription, and a new long negative prescription generally on the lines of the 1617 Act (negative portion). As the first and third of these are founded on the same general principles as the former positive and long negative prescriptions some of the cases decided under the former statutes are still useful illustrations. The second is wholly new in that it does not alter the onus and mode of proof but extinguishes the obligations to which it applies.

Accordingly the subject of prescription must be dealt with in chapters[19] dealing respectively with the positive, short negative, and long negative prescriptions. Special provision is made for prescription of obligations under the Consumer Protection Act 1987.[20]

LIMITATION OF ACTIONS

The concept of limitation of actions is not one native to Scots law but derived from English law. The basic principle is that after the lapse of a set period of time a claim founded on a stated ground of action is to be no longer maintainable or actionable. Limitations bar the remedy and not the right. "Limitation is a denial of action ... after the lapse of a certain time, without regard to the actual subsistence of the debt ..."[21] Statutes of limitation were passed in England from 1623 onwards but were mostly replaced by the Limitation Act 1939 which was amended and replaced by the Limitation Act 1980. The policy underlying statutes of limitation has been said to be that long dormant claims have more of cruelty than justice in them,[22] that a defendant might have lost the evidence to disprove a stale claim,[23] and that persons with good causes of actions should pursue them with reasonable diligence.[24] Limitation is accordingly procedural; it neither establishes nor extinguishes a title, nor a ground of action, but provides that after the lapse of a period of time an action cannot be brought in court

---

[17] 1973 Act, Sched. 5, Pt. I.
[18] Stair, IV, 24, 4.
[19] Chaps. 2, 3 and 4, *infra.*
[20] Chap. 5, *infra.*
[21] Bell, *Prin.*, § 586.
[22] *R.B. Policies at Lloyd's v. Butler* [1950] 1 K.B. 76, 81.
[23] *Jones v. Bellgrove Properties Ltd.* [1949] 2 K.B. 700.
[24] *Board of Trade v. Cayzer Irvine & Co.* [1927] A.C. 610.

to enforce a claim. The claim may still exist but is legally unenforceable. The distinction between prescription and limitation "is grounded on a real difference in principle; and although it may seem unimportant, it enters into all arguments on the more nice and difficult questions in this department".[25]

The plea that a limitation period has run is a defence. The onus of averment and of proof is accordingly on the defender.

Various limitation provisions were introduced into Scots law by various statutes in the nineteenth century, the most noteworthy being the Public Authorities Protection Act 1893 which limited the time for bringing actions against "public authorities" to six months.

A major extension of the principle of limitation was made by the Law Reform (Limitation of Actions, etc.) Act 1954 which repealed the 1893 Act and certain other later but similar protective provisions and enacted that actions of damages where the damages claimed were or included damages or solatium for personal injuries or death had to be commenced within three years of the act, neglect or default giving rise to the action. Defects having become apparent in this provision it was amended by the Limitation Act 1963.

Numerous other specific limitation provisions applicable to particular kinds of claims only were also enacted at various times.

The law on limitation, accordingly, like the law of prescription, had got into a very unsatisfactory state in that it was scattered over many statutes. The 1973 Act simplified the law a little by repealing[26] but re-enacting the limitation provisions relating to claims for damages for personal injury or death, but these proved so difficult to interpret and unfair in their application that they were replaced by new provisions under the Prescription and Limitation (Scotland) Act 1984. The other specific limitation provisions still stand.

Limitation of actions has accordingly to be dealt with under the heads of Limitation of Actions for Damages or Solatium,[27] Limitation of Actions under the Consumer Protection Act 1987[28] and Other Statutory Limitations.[29]

DIFFERENCE BETWEEN PRESCRIPTION AND LIMITATION

The difference in nature and effect between prescription rules and limitation rules is material. "Limitation is a denial of action on an instrument or document of debt, after the lapse of a certain time, without regard to the actual subsistence of the debt; as in holograph writings, bonds of caution, bills and notes. Prescription is a legal presumption of abandonment or of satisfaction, and so extinguishes the debt; as in the long negative prescription, the decennial, quinquennial, and triennial prescriptions. This distinction is grounded on a real difference in principle; and although it may seem unimportant, it enters into all arguments on the more nice and

---

[25] Bell, *Prin.*, § 586.
[26] 1973 Act, Sched. 5, Pt. II.
[27] Chap. 6, *infra.*
[28] Chap. 7, *infra.*
[29] Chap. 10, *infra.*

difficult questions in this department."[30] "The principle clearly emerges that the non-enforcement by a creditor of a contractual right for the prescriptive period infers an irrebuttable presumption that the right has been abandoned, and therefore that the correlative obligation has been extinguished, the doctrine of prescription being in this respect in contrast with the doctrine of limitation which merely denies certain rights of action after a certain lapse of time."[31]

A prescription rule is a rule of substantive law which provides that after a stated period of time particular kinds of rights, such as the right to challenge another person's title to heritage or to claim a payment, or damages for a breach of obligation, are wholly extinguished and cease to exist as legal rights; the right is not merely rendered unenforceable; it is extinguished and no longer exists. The plea of prescription is one which it is *pars judicis* to take, and a decree for a prescribed debt, even one admitted to be unpaid, would be a legal nullity, there being in law no longer any debt.

A limitation rule on the other hand is a rule of procedural law which provides that after a stated period of time particular kinds of claims are legally unenforceable and cannot be founded on in actions. But they are not wholly extinguished and continue to exist, at least as moral claims, so that if a plea of limitation is not taken timeously a decree for the sum claimed would be competent and valid,[32] and a payment made *ex gratia* thereafter would be irrecoverable as one morally and equitably due though not exigible by legal process. The plea of limitation can moreover doubtless be waived by a defender.[33]

By the Prescription and Limitation (Scotland) Act 1984, s. 1, the extinction of obligations to make contributions between wrongdoers, originally enacted as a limitation provision by section 20 of the 1973 Act, was reclassified as a prescription provision and added to the 1973 Act as a new section 8A.

Distinct from statutory limitations are limitations of actions by convention, as where an obligation is stipulated to be binding for a certain time only and ceases to be enforceable after that time has elapsed, such as a guarantee for a year only. These depend entirely on contract and are not further discussed in this book.[34]

DISTINCTION IN INTERNATIONAL PRIVATE LAW CASES

The distinction between a prescription rule and a limitation rule may be very important in a case raising an issue of international private law. The distinction is that a statutory provision which finally creates or extinguishes a right after the lapse of a stated time (prescription provision) is a matter of substantive law and the Scottish statutory provisions are applicable to all cases where Scots law is the appropriate *lex causae*, whether the case is brought in Scottish or foreign courts, but a statutory provision which limits

---

[30] Bell, *Prin.*, § 586.
[31] *Macdonald v. North of Scotland Bank*, 1942 S.C. 369 at p. 373, *per* L.J.-C. Cooper, citing Bell, *Prin.*, § 586, 605.
[32] *cf. Rodriguez v. Parker* [1967] 1 Q.B. 116 at p. 136; *Seabridge v. Cox* [1968] 2 Q.B. 46.
[33] *cf. Lubovsky v. Snelling* [1943] 2 All E.R. 577
[34] Bell, *Prin.*, § 587–588.

the time within which a claim of a particular kind may be made is procedural in nature and the Scottish rules are applicable, as part of the *lex fori*, only where the case is brought in the Scottish courts.[35] Thus if an Englishman buys tweed in Scotland, making a contract regulated by Scots law and, the tweed being defective, sues the seller in the English courts five and a half years after the sale, having served the writ at the seller's London office, he can be met by the plea that by Scots law (*lex causae*) the right of action for breach of contract is extinguished after five years. If the same Englishman is personally injured in England but for reasons of jurisdiction has to sue the wrongdoer in the Scottish courts and delays to do so, he can be met by the plea, that by Scots law (*lex fori*) the right of action for personal injuries is unenforceable after three years, though not extinguished.

In drawing this distinction between prescription provisions and limitation provisions and determining in which category a particular provision belongs, complete reliance should not be placed on the name of the relevant statute, the headnote of the section, or even on whether the word used is "prescribe" or "limit" or variants thereof, or words translated as one or the other of these. The real question is of the effect of the rule; does it finally establish or wholly extinguish the right, or merely bar a claim therefor? If of the former kind the right must be taken as subject to the inherent qualification imposed by the system which created it; if it is held to be of the latter kind the right may become unenforceable sooner, or be enforceable longer, in the jurisdiction in which action is brought than it would in the jurisdiction in which the right itself arose.

A judgment obtained in one jurisdiction of the United Kingdom and registered in another is treated as a judgment of the country of registration, so that a defender cannot plead that the debt in respect of which the judgment was obtained would be irrecoverable in the country of registration by reason of lapse of time.[36]

Thus if a Ruritanian has a claim against a Scot for breach of a contract the proper law of which is Scots law, and fails to pursue his claim for five years, his claim will be rejected by a Scottish court, having been extinguished by prescription.[37] If he can found jurisdiction against the Scot in a Ruritanian, or even an Arcadian, court, the Scot can still plead that by the proper law of the contract his liability is extinguished, and this plea should be upheld, notwithstanding that in Ruritania claims on contracts may subsist for 20 years and in Arcadia for 50 years. If on the other hand an Arcadian, by careless driving, injured a Ruritanian in Scotland and the latter sues the former in Scotland, he must do so within three years[38] even though if he had sued the wrongdoer in Ruritania he might have been able to do so for 10 or 20 years, as may be competent by the law of Arcadia. If a Scot while in Arcadia injures a native, or a Ruritanian, he cannot plead in an action against him in the courts of either of these countries that his liability is

---

[35] *Dundee Harbour Trs. v. Dougall* (1852) 1 Macq. 317; *Westminster Bank Ltd. v. McDonald,* 1955 S.L.T. (Notes) 73; *Stirling's Trs. v. Legal and General Assurance Society Ltd.,* 1957 S.L.T. 73.

[36] *Re Low, Bland v. Low* [1894] 1 Ch. 147 at p. 162.

[37] Prescription and Limitation (Scotland) Act 1973, s. 6 and Sched. 1, para. 1 (*g*).

[38] *ibid.,* s. 17.

limited to three years, because that is a matter of Scottish procedure. But he can rely on any time limits for suing prescribed by the Ruritanian Civil Procedure Code or the Rules of the Arcadian Supreme Court as the case may be.

While, accordingly, the principle is that a right acquired under one legal system carries with it into a foreign court any period of prescription to which it is subject under that legal system, but that a right enforceable in one legal system is subject to the limit of time applicable to the enforcement of such rights in the courts in which it is invoked and pled, the classification of qualifications as extinctive or remedy-barring, as substantive or procedural, as matter of the proper law or of the *lex fori*, may be difficult. Thus it has been held[39] that the rule in the English Fatal Accidents Act 1846, s. 3 (now replaced), that a plaintiff's claim for pecuniary loss caused by the death of a related person must be commenced within twelve months of the death, was a rule of substantive law as much as was the statutory right of action conferred by section 1 itself, and that the right was inherently qualified and restricted thereby, and was not enforceable thereafter in any jurisdiction; this was not merely a limitation rule limiting the time for suing thereon in an English court. It was a qualification, in effect a one-year prescription of the right.

The complications of prescription and limitation provisions in cases involving private international law gave rise to section 4 of the Prescription and Limitation (Scotland) Act 1984, which introduced a new section 23A into the 1973 Act, providing in substance that where a Scottish court has to apply the substantive law of another territory it has to apply any relevant rules of law of that country relating to the extinction of the obligation or the limitation of time within which proceedings may be brought to the exclusion of any corresponding rule of Scots law, unless that would be incompatible with the principles of public policy applied by the court. In effect a Scottish court must now take a rule of foreign law subject to its qualifications, whether these are of the nature of prescription or limitation, and it is not now necessary to discover whether a foreign provision is a prescription provision or a limitation provision. But a foreign court may still have to inquire whether a Scottish provision is of the nature of a prescription or a limitation.[40]

THE CHANGES IN PRESCRIPTION AND LIMITATION EFFECTED IN 1973

The Scottish Law Commission included the subjects of prescription and limitation of actions in their First Programme of Reform of 1965 and in 1968 issued their memorandum No. 9 containing their provisional views on the matter. Having considered the comments and representations made thereon they published in 1970 their proposals for reform (Scot. Law Com. No. 15, 1970). Their conclusions were, briefly, that the existing law was complicated and confused, largely contained in very ancient statutes of

---

[39] *McElroy v. McAllister*, 1949 S.C. 110; *cf. The Harrisburg* (1886) 119 U.S. 199. This interpretation is questionable.
[40] For England, see Foreign Limitation Periods Act 1984 which enacts for England provisions generally corresponding to s. 23A.

uncertain application, and on many matters uncertain and productive of doubt and litigation, and that it was desirable that the general rules of positive and negative prescription should be restated in amended and modernised form in a single statute, that the various shorter prescriptions affecting mode and onus of proof should be abolished and be replaced by a single short extinctive prescription, and that the general limitation provisions of the 1954 Act, as amended, should be consolidated in the same Act. The Prescription and Limitation (Scotland) Act 1973, very largely gave effect to these recommendations. It repealed all the existing statutes containing generally applicable prescription provisions and restated them in modern form, replacing the old "short" prescriptions by a new short negative prescription applicable to a wider range of cases and having extinctive effect, and re-enacted with verbal changes the limitation provisions of the 1954 Act, as amended. It accordingly rendered obsolete large numbers of cases interpreting one or another of the repealed statutes, and most of the commentary thereon in the institutional writers and later textbooks, though as the general principles of the new statutory positive prescription and long negative prescription are generally the same as obtained under the former Acts some of the older cases are still useful as illustrations, and as the limitation provisions of the 1973 Act were very substantially re-enactments of sections of the 1954 and 1963 Acts cases decided on these Acts were still authoritative.

The 1973 Act did not, however, consolidate or affect the large number of statutory provisions which affect particular kinds of rights and obligations only, nor did it abolish, as the Scottish Law Commission recommended it should, the rule of *decennalis et triennalis possessio*, nor affect the plea of *mora*. The Limitation (Enemies and War Prisoners) Act 1945 relaxed the requirements of certain prescriptions and limitations in favour of the necessary parties to an action or arbitration or parties to an obligation who were enemy, as defined, or detained in enemy territory. The Scottish Law Commission recommended that the principle of this Act be retained but that its provisions be re-enacted in the proposed comprehensive statute on prescription and limitation. This was not done, but the 1945 Act was amended.

In view of the wide scope of the 1973 Act most questions of prescription or limitation of actions now turn on the interpretation in the circumstances of sections of the 1973 Act and they must be the core of exposition of the subject.

While in many respects the 1973 Act restated principles long accepted in the Scottish law of prescription and of limitation, and, accordingly, cases decided under now-repealed statutes are frequently still of value as guides to interpretation, it is necessary to emphasise that the 1973 Act, to a substantial extent, both in principle and in language, makes alterations to the law, and that the major question must always be whether a particular provision applies and, if so, what it prescribes, and that interpretation of the words of the Act should not be controlled by decisions reached on the wording of superseded legislation. The 1973 Act "re-wrote the law of prescription in Scotland. The old law, in whatever form it took, was replaced by statutory provisions, and it is to these that we must look for the answer, not to the pre-existing law. The one exception to that is provided in section 14 of the Act".[41] The 1973 Act was intended to enact a comprehensive new code for prescription and is to be regarded as laying down a positive rule to be interpreted and applied on its own terms.[42]

DEVELOPMENTS SINCE 1973

The Scottish Law Commission continued to consider the subject of prescription and limitation of actions. In April 1980 it published a consultative memorandum (no. 45) and in July 1980 a consultation paper on prescription and limitation in private international law. The English Law Commission also published in 1980 working paper no. 75 on classification of limitation in private international law and subsequently published a report (Law Com. No. 114) thereon. In 1983 the Scottish Law Commission published Scot. Law Com. No. 74 – Prescription and the Limitation of Actions: Report on Personal Injuries Actions and Private International Law Questions. This recommended various changes to simplify the law and eradicate some obvious defects and annexed a draft Bill designed to achieve its objects.

In December 1983 Mr. Alexander Eadie, M.P., who had won a high place in the ballot for private members' Bills, introduced a Bill based on the Scottish Law Commission's draft Bill. It received all-party support and in July 1984 became the Prescription and Limitation (Scotland) Act 1984.

The general principle of limitation remained unchanged; in the interest of justice and to protect defenders from being vexed by stale claims, claims should be brought within three years of the time when it was, or should have been, discovered by the party that injury had been sustained, but provision is made for extending that time-limit in particular cases, and the court continues to have a discretion to extend the time for suing where it deems it equitable to do so.

Further amendments have been made, notably by the Prescription (Scotland) Act 1987 and the Consumer Protection Act 1987.

The main Acts are referred to hereafter as "the 1973 Act", "the 1984 Act" and "the Prescription Act 1987" respectively. Particularly in chapters 5 and 7 the Consumer Protection Act is referred to as "the 1987 Act".

In view of the decision in *Pepper v. Hart*[43] that, where there is obscurity or ambiguity in legislation, reference to statements by a minister when the legislation was being debated in Parliament might be made to assist in interpretation, it may be helpful to record the references, on the Bills which became the Acts relevant to prescription and limitation, in the Parliamentary Debates (Hansard). These are:

1973 Act: H.L. Official Report, Vol. 341, cols. 418–425 and 1050–1051; Vol. 342, cols. 257–258 and 513–514.

1984 Act: H.C. Official Report, Vol. 46, col. 388; Vol. 49, col. 1112; and Vol. 56, col. 609.

---

[41] *British Railways Board v. Strathclyde R.C.*, 1981 S.C. 90 at p. 98.
[42] *G.A. Estates v. Caviapen Tr. (No. 2)*, 1993 S.L.T. 1045.
[43] [1993] A.C. 593; [1993] 1 All E.R. 42.

H.L. Official Report, Vol. 449, cols. 1179; Vol. 453, col. 1089; and Vol. 454, cols. 1241 and 1486.

Prescription (Scotland) Act 1987: H.C. Official Report, Vol. 112, col. 299; Vol. 113, col. 1398; and Vol. 114, col. 958.

H.L. Official Report, Vol. 486, col. 1421; and Vol. 487, col. 708.

Consumer Protection Act 1987: H.C. Official Report, Vol. 115, col. 51; and Vol. 116, col. 345.

H.L. Official Report, Vol. 482, cols. 233 and 1003, Vol. 483, cols. 715, 781, 818, 865 and 1463; Vol. 485, cols. 824, 840, 886, 1140, and 1519; and Vol. 487, col. 784.

It is unfortunate that as a result of these amendments the law is relapsing into a confusing mess, particularly as to limitation of actions, in which the time-limits apply to actions based on certain grounds, such as personal injuries, but not others, notably property damage. It is very far from being a simple or clear body of principles and it gives rise to many disputes and many difficult problems of interpretation. It is a pity that the concept of limitation of actions was ever introduced into Scots law.

Complicated as they are, the rules as to prescription and limitation of actions are important and they require to be known. Ignorance or neglect of these rules by a legal practitioner, resulting in loss to his client, can easily amount to professional negligence.[44]

Similarly in several cases where application has been made to the court under section 19A to extend the time for suing for personal injuries or death, in cases where it had expired, the court has indicated, when refusing the application, that the pursuer may have a claim against his solicitors for negligence in not having commenced the action within the time allowed.[45]

Loss of a right of action in this way is loss of a right of substance and damages would not be merely nominal but determined by an estimate of what the pursuer would probably have secured if he had been allowed to pursue his action in the first place, *i.e.* the value of his lost prospects of success.

---

[44] *Simpson v. Kidstons, Watson, Turnbull & Co.*, 1913, 1 S.L.T. 74; *cf. Fletcher & Son v. Jubb Booth & Helliwell* [1920] 1 K.B. 275; *Kitchen v. R.A.F. Association* [1958] 2 All E.R. 241; *Robertson v. Bannigan*, 1965 S.C. 20.

[45] *Henderson v. Singer (U.K.)*, 1983 S.L.T. 198; *Donald v. Rutherford*, 1984 S.L.T. 70; *Williams v. Forth Valley Health Board*, 1983 S.L.T. 376; *Whyte v. Walker*, 1983 S.L.T. 441; *Craw v. Gallagher*, 1988 S.L.T. 204; *Forbes v. House of Clydesdale*, 1988 S.L.T. 594; *Bell v. Greenland*, 1988 S.L.T. 215.

cf. Firman v. Ellis [1978] 2 All E.R. 851 at pp. 862, 865 and 868; *Thompson v. Brown Construction (Ebbw Vale) Ltd.* [1981] 2 All E.R. 296 at p. 303.

CHAPTER 2

POSITIVE PRESCRIPTION

THE function of the rules of positive prescription is to validate and ratify certain claims to property after the lapse of a stated period of time, and to exclude all contrary claims, to secure the title to an estate against anyone alleging a competing title, to determine the extent of an estate, the title to which is not challenged, and to effect consolidation by merging a title of property with the higher right of superiority.

FORMER LAW

Positive prescription was founded on the Prescription Act 1594, c. 24,[1] which enacted that though sundry of the lieges and their predecessors had been heritably infeft in land and annualrents and by virtue thereof had possessed these lands and annualrents for 40 years together, nevertheless the infeftments were sometimes challenged on various grounds, and for remedy thereof it was declared that none of the lieges might be compelled after 40 years to produce deeds whereby the present proprietors and their predecessors were in possession for 40 years together, and the lack thereof should be no cause of the reduction of the infeftments nor of questioning whatsoever of them after 40 years, where infeftments had taken effect by possession for 40 years.

This was followed by the Prescription Act 1617, c. 12,[2] the first branch of which,[3] after narrating the difficulties, provided that whoever of the lieges possessed lands and other heritages by himself or others, by virtue of heritable infeftments, for 40 years, continually and together following their infeftment, peaceably, and without lawful interruption for 40 years, were never to be troubled by any person claiming right to the same by virtue of prior infeftments, nor upon any other ground except falsehood, provided they could produce a charter of the lands with the instrument of sasine following thereon, or where there was no charter extant, instruments of sasine, one or more, continued and standing together for 40 years, either proceeding on retours or on precepts of *clare constat*, which rights the Act declares to be good, valid and sufficient rights.

The principle of the Act of 1617 was modified by the Conveyancing (Scotland) Act 1874, s. 34, which provided that "Any ex facie valid irredeemable title to an estate in land recorded in the appropriate register of sasines shall be sufficient foundation for prescription, and possession following on such recorded title for the space of twenty years continually and together, and that peaceably, without any lawful interruption made during the space of twenty years, shall for all the purposes of the [1617

---

[1] A.P.S. IV, 68, c. 24. See Stair, II, 12, 15.
[2] A.P.S. IV, 543, c. 12. See Stair, II, 12, 15; Ersk., III, 7, 3; Bell, *Prin.*, § 2002.
[3] The second branch dealt with the long negative prescription.

Act] be equivalent to possession for forty years by virtue of heritable infeftments for which charters and instruments of sasine or other sufficient titles are shown and produced ..., and if such possession ... shall have continued for the space of thirty years no deduction or allowance shall be made on account of the years of minority or less age of those against whom the prescription is used or objected, or of any period during which any person against whom prescription is used or objected was under legal disability."

The Conveyancing (Scotland) Act 1924, repealed section 34 of the 1874 Act, but by section 16 substantially re-enacted the passage above-quoted, adding that if possession continued for 20 years, no deduction or allowance was to be made on account of the years of minority or less age or legal disability of those against whom the prescription was used and objected. But there were excepted under both 1874 and 1924 Acts from the reduction of time the existing law relating to the character or period of possession, use or enjoyment necessary to constitute or prove the existence of any servitude or of any public right of way or other public right, which accordingly remained at 40 years.

The Conveyancing and Feudal Reform (Scotland) Act 1970, s. 8, provided that section 16 of the 1924 Act was to have effect, except in relation to any claim as against the Crown to the ownership of any foreshore or salmon fishings, with the substitution for references to 20 years of references to 10 years.

All these statutory provisions were construed in various cases and, though the statutory provisions have been repealed, cases decided on these provisions may still be helpful in the interpretation of the modern law.

THE MODERN LAW

All these provisions were repealed and replaced by sections 1 to 5 of the Prescription and Limitation (Scotland) Act 1973,[4] this part of which came into force on July 25, 1976.[5] While the wording is very different there is no ground for thinking that there was any parliamentary intention to change the basic underlying principle of positive prescription, namely, to make possession for the required time fortify and render unchallengeable the possessor's written title,[6] "a method of confirming and consolidating defective titles to property. "[7] There must be a written title, and possession referable thereto for the prescriptive period.[8]

This principle of rendering the possessor's title impregnable applies even against the Crown[9] and even where the title founded on was granted by one who was not the true superior, or the true previous owner,[10] or the grantor had no right to the lands in question[11] or the right was originally redeemable

---

[4] 1973 Act, s. 16 and Sched. 5.
[5] 1973 Act, s. 25(2)(*b*).
[6] *cf.* Ersk., III, 7, 2.
[7] Bell, *Prin.*, § 2002.
[8] *cf. Andersons v. Lows* (1863) 2 M. 100.
[9] *Lord Advocate v. Dundas* (1831) 5 W. & S. 723; 1973 Act, s. 24.
[10] *Glen v. Scales' Tr.* (1881) 9 R. 317; *Fraser v. L.A.* (1898) 25 R. 603.
[11] *Duke of Buccleuch v. Cunynghame* (1826) 5 S. 57; *Macdonald v. Lockhart* (1853) 1 Macq. 790; *Roxburghe v. Scott* (1891) 18 R. 8; *Young v. North British Ry.* (1887) 14 R. (H.L.) 53; *Duke of Buccleuch v. Boyd* (1890) 18 R. 1; *Fraser, supra.*

only.[12] Indeed it is the function of ratification by prescription to fortify bad or at least doubtful titles[13]; a good title needs no fortification by passage of time but even it gains the advantage that it cannot thereafter even be challenged or questioned. "Prescription operates not merely to secure the right of property, but to protect the title from question."[14]

"Nullity from extrinsic error is not a relevant ground of objection to a prescriptive title." "The positive prescription operates by excluding all inquiry beyond the forty years into the previous titles and rights to the lands." "All the prior history of the lands is excluded."[15] "I hold that it *is* the purpose of prescription to exclude all enquiry as to whether titles, habile in their form, on which prescriptive possession has followed, were in their original nature and constitution good or bad and specially the enquiry, whether the author from whom they have proceeded had power to grant them or not. When prescription has run, there is an absolute presumption that they are good."[16] "The positive prescription operates by excluding all inquiry, beyond the prescriptive period, into the previous titles and rights to the lands, so that it is not competent to inquire, and consequently cannot be known legally, whether lands possessed for forty years on good ex facie titles were ever forfeited or not."[17]

Good faith in the claimant is not required: "Even granting that the titles had been derived *a non domino*, still [the heir] is entitled to plead prescription, whereby any inquiry into that fact, or into *mala fides* is excluded."[18]

The only exceptions to this operation of prescription were and are the intrinsic nullity or forgery of the title produced.

APPLICATIONS OF PRINCIPLE OF POSITIVE PRESCRIPTION

This principle that possession for the prescriptive period renders a title unchallengeable applies to all kinds of interests in corporeal heritable property which may be held by written title and actually possessed,[19] and also to interests in corporeal heritable property, notably servitude rights and public rights of way which may be held by written title or grant but are frequently based only on possession by virtue of a fictionally presumed grant.[20]

FORTIFICATION BY PRESCRIPTION OF RIGHTS TO INTERESTS IN LAND GENERALLY

Section 1, as amended by the Land Registration (Scotland) Act 1979, s. 10,[21] enacts:

---

[12] *Chambers v. Law* (1823) 2 S. 326.
[13] *Scott v. Bruce Stewart* (1779) Mor. 13519, 3 Ross L.C. 334; *Duke of Buccleuch v. Cunynghame* (1826) 5 S. 57; *Lord Advocate v. Graham* (1844) 7 D. 183, 205; *Glen, supra,* 324.
[14] *Lockhart v. Duke of Hamilton* (1890) Millar on *Prescription* 11; *Ramsey v. Spence,* 1909 S.C. 1441.
[15] *Forbes v. Livingstone* (1827) 6 S. 167; 1 W. & Sh. 657.
[16] *Lord Advocate v. Graham, supra* at p. 205, *per* Lord Moncreiff.
[17] *Fraser v. Lord Lovat* (1898) 25 R. 603 at p. 616, *per* L. P. Robertson.
[18] *Duke of Buccleuch v. Cunynghame, supra* at p. 60, *per* Lord Balgray.
[19] ss. 1 and 2, *infra.*
[20] s. 3, *infra.*
[21] The amended section will be brought into operation by areas by statutory instruments: 1979 Act, s. 30.

Interests in land: general

1.—(1) If in the case of an interest in particular land, being an interest to which this section applies,—

(a) the interest has been possessed by any person, or by any person and his successors, for a continuous period of ten years openly, peaceably and without any judicial interruption,[22] and

(b) the possession was founded on, and followed

     (i) the recording of, a deed which is sufficient in respect of its terms to constitute in favour of that person a title to that interest in the particular land, or in land of a description habile to include the particular land, or

     (ii) registration of that interest in favour of that person in the Land Register of Scotland, subject to an exclusion of indemnity under section 12(2) of the Land Registration (Scotland) Act 1979,

then, as from the expiration of the said period, the validity of the title so far as relating to the said interest in the particular land shall be exempt from challenge.

(1A) Subsection (1) shall not apply where—

(a) possession was founded on the recording of a deed which is invalid *ex facie* or was forged; or

(b) possession was founded on registration in respect of an interest in land in the Land Register of Scotland proceeding on a forged deed and the person appearing from the Register to be entitled to the interest was aware of the forgery at the time of registration in his favour.

(2) This section applies to any interest in land the title to which can competently be recorded or which is registrable in the Land Register of Scotland.

(3) In the computation of a prescriptive period for the purposes of this section in a case where the deed in question is a decree of adjudication for debt, any period before the expiry of the legal shall be disregarded.

(4) where in any question involving an interest in any foreshore[23] or in any salmon fishings this section is pled against the Crown as owner of the regalia, subsection (1) above shall have effect as if for the words "ten years" there were substituted the words "twenty years".

(5) This section is without prejudice to the operation of section 2 of this Act.

Interpretation of Part I

15.—(1) In this Part[24] of this Act, unless the context otherwise requires, the following expressions have the meanings hereby assigned to them, namely—

"bill of exchange" has the same meaning as it has for the purposes of the Bills of Exchange Act 1882;

"date of execution," in relation to a deed executed on several dates, means the last of those dates;

"enactment" includes an order, regulation, rule or other instrument having effect by virtue of an Act;

"holiday" has the meaning assigned to it by section 14 of this Act;

"interest in land" does not include a servitude;

"land" includes heritable property of any description;

"lease" includes a sub-lease;

"legal disability" means legal disability by reason of nonage or unsoundness of mind;

"possession" includes civil possession, and "possessed" shall be construed accordingly;

"prescriptive period" means a period required for the operation of section 1, 2, 3, 6, 7, 8 or 8A of this Act;[25]

---

[22] See *Scammell v. Scottish Sports Council,* 1983 S.L.T. 462.

[23] As to prescriptive possession determining the extent of a barony title see *Luss Estates v. B.P. Oil Grangemouth Refinery,* 1987 S.L.T. 201.

[24] ss. 1–15.

[25] As amended by the Prescription and Limitation (Scotland) Act 1984, Sched. 1, para. 7.

"promissory note" has the same meaning as it has for the purposes of the Bills of
  Exchange Act 1882;
"trustee" includes any person holding property in a fiduciary capacity for another
  and, without prejudice to that generality, includes a trustee within the meaning
  of the Trusts (Scotland) Act 1921; and "trust" shall be construed accordingly;
and references to the recording of a deed are references to the recording thereof in the
General Register of Sasines.

(2) In this Part of this Act, unless the context otherwise requires, any reference to an
obligation or to a right includes a reference to the right or, as the case may be, to the
obligation (if any), correlative thereto.

(3) In this Part of this Act any reference to an enactment shall, unless the context
otherwise requires, be construed as a reference to that enactment as amended or
extended, and as including a reference thereto as applied, by or under any other
enactment.

GENERAL NOTE ON SECTION 1

Subsections (1) and (2) replace the provisions of the Conveyancing
(Scotland) Act 1924, s. 16 and the Conveyancing and Feudal Reform
(Scotland) Act 1970, s. 8, which respectively defined the basis for positive
prescription—"any *ex facie* valid irredeemable title to an estate in land"—
and shortened the prescriptive period, originally (1617) of 40 years and
then (1874) of 20 years, to 10 years (1970). The provision of the 1973 Act
is however wider in that it extends to interests in land other than servitudes,
and accordingly includes the interests in land of the creditor under a recorded
standard security, whose title is not "*ex facie*... irredeemable," though the
title fortified by prescription in such a case will be a redeemable title only
and not an irredeemable one.

The essential conditions for the validation of title by lapse of time are
possession and title and they are cumulative. Possession alone will not
suffice[26]; where one party could establish possession not referable to any
infeftment and the other to infeftment without possession, it was held that
prescription could not operate.[27] Nor will possession without infeftment
suffice. [28]

By subsection (5) section 1 is without prejudice to the operation of section
2; a proprietor may accordingly found on either section.

VERBAL COMMENTARY ON SECTION 1

*"in the case of an interest in particular land, being an interest to which
  this section applies"*

An interest in land is defined (section 15(1)) only as not including a
servitude. It is not defined positively, but may be explained as being the
aggregate of the rights which a particular person has in and over a tract of
land by virtue of his title thereto.[29] The main recognised interests in land

---

[26] *Fergusson v. Shirreff* (1846) 6 D. 1363; *Edmonstone v. Jeffray* (1886) 13 R. 1038; *Grant v. Henry* (1894) 21 R.
358; *Johnston v. Fairfowl* (1901) 8 S.L.T. 480; see also *Montgomery v. Watson* (1861) 23 D. 635; *Copland v. Maxwell*
(1871) 9 M.(H.L.) 1.
[27] *Andersons v. Lows* (1863) 2 M. 100; see also *Lick v. Chambers* (1859) 21 D. 408.
[28] *cf. Wallace v. St. Andrews University Court* (1904) 6 F. 1093.
[29] The phrase is defined positively in the Conveyancing and Feudal Reform (Scotland) Act 1970, s. 9(8)(*b*) and the
Land Registration (Scotland) Act 1979, s. 28(1) for the purposes of those Acts.

are those of the Crown as ultimate superior holding *dominium eminens*, of each subject superior who has a *dominium directum*, of each vassal who has a *dominium utile*, of joint proprietors and proprietors in common, of heirs of entail in possession, proper liferenters, tenants under recorded long leases, holders of rights in security over the land, parties in right of a grant of port and harbour,[30] a riparian proprietor's right to abstract water from a river,[31] parties in right of salmon-fishings.[32] A servitude right would normally be understood to be an interest in the servient tenement of land, but section 15(1) excludes servitudes from the definition of "interest in land," servitudes being dealt with separately in section 3. A right to obstruct an access from the street to various premises is not an interest which can be acquired by prescription.[33]

By section 1(2) this section applies to "any interest in land the title to which can competently be recorded" in the General Register of Sasines. This accordingly excludes the interests of tenants, other than those under recorded long leases, of occupiers at the will of the proprietor, of persons having a licence to do something on the lands, and other interests title to which cannot be recorded. But it includes the interest in land of the creditor under a standard security over land. The interests to which the section applies are not confined to irredeemable interests.

The right of the public to be at or on the non-tidal portion of a river for the purposes of navigation does not confer a right to fish for trout and no amount of possession can confer on them a prescriptive right.[34] Nor can persons not being a group or community acquire any right in property merely by possession or exercise of the right.[35]

The phrase is "can competently be recorded," not "has been recorded." Accordingly the title of the holder of a floating charge over heritage, which is valid though not so recorded, may be fortified by prescription.[36] But for this to happen such a holder must have possession, which must (section 1(1)(*b*)) have followed the recording of the deed, before prescription can operate. The section, as amended by the Land Registration (Scotland) Act 1979, s. 10, applies also to "any interest in land ... which is registrable in the Land Register of Scotland." What interests are registrable are set out in the 1979 Act, s. 2.

By section 15(1) "land" includes heritable property of any description. It comprises accordingly not only physical land and buildings but rights to minerals[37] and to salmon fishings,[38] but presumably excludes heritable rights in incorporeal objects of property such as an annuity, because the title to such a right cannot be recorded in the General Register of Sasines. But the creation over a registered interest in land of, *inter alia*, an incorporeal

---

[30] *Macpherson v. Mackenzie* (1881) 8 R. 706 at p. 715.
[31] *Pirie & Sons v. Earl of Kintore* (1906) 8 F. (H.L.) 16; *J. White & Sons v. J. & M. White* (1906) 8 F. (H.L) 41.
[32] *Ogston v. Stewart* (1896) 23 R. (H.L.) 16.
[33] *Stewart, Pott & Co. v. Brown* (1878) 6 R. 35.
[34] *Grant v. Henry* (1894) 21 R. 358.
[35] *Henderson v. Lord Minto* (1860) 22 D. 1126; *Breadalbane v. McGregor* (1846) 9 D. 210; 7 Bell 43; *Smith v. Denny Police Commrs.* (1879) 6 R. 858.
[36] Companies Act 1985, s. 462(5).
[37] *Lord Advocate v. Wemyss* (1899) 2 F. (H.L.) 1.
[38] *Ogston v. Stewart* (1896) 23 R. (H.L.) 1.

heritable right is registrable in the Land Register.[39] The creation of a right of annuity payable from registered land is therefore registrable and hence a possible subject for prescription. "Particular land" is presumably a particular piece of land.

"If ... the interest has been possessed"

"Possessed" is, by section 15(1), to be construed consistently with "possession", which is there defined only as including civil possession. Possession is either "natural," when exercised by a proprietor himself, or "civil" when held by others on his behalf, as by a vassal,[40] liferenter,[41] tenant, employee, factor or other intermediary.[42] For the creditor in a security right to claim fortification of his title by prescription he must have taken possession, either by agreement with the debtor or under a decree of maills and duties. Possession of heritage[43] means that it has actually been occupied, or at least that a claim of right to occupancy or exercise of the relevant heritable right has been made and any competing claim or attempted exercise of rights has been resisted. Land is clearly possessed when it is tilled, or occupied by one's animals, or shooting or fishing rights periodically exercised over relevant portions of it, or trespassers warned off or squatters removed, or buildings are occupied or used at least periodically. Possession means "possession of the character of which the thing is capable."[44]

Where there was an express title to minerals possession of the surface has been held sufficient, but where minerals are claimed as part and pertinent of lands the claimant must prove possession of the minerals themselves by working them.[45]

The sufficiency of possession proved must be judged *secundum subjectam materiam.*[46]

It is always a question of circumstances whether acts of possession each extending to something less than the whole of the subjects in dispute can together be regarded as justifying an inference that those acts amounted to an assertion of ownership of the subjects as a whole and whether any gaps in the course of actings were so substantial as to amount to interruption of possession. Some actions, such as extracting peat, moving a fence and having a survey carried out were referable to a right of ownership, but regular dumping of rubbish could be regarded as exercising possession, and shooting over land was a clear assertion of possession.[47]

---

[39] 1979 Act, s. 2(3).

[40] *Lord Advocate v. McCulloch* (1874) 2 R. 27; *Duke of Argyll v. Campbell,* 1912 S.C. 458. Contrast *Lord Advocate v. Hall* (1873) 11 M. 967.

[41] *Campbell v. Wilson* (1770) 5 B.S. 543; *Neilson v. Erskine* (1823) 2 S. 216; *French v. Pinkston* (1835) 13 S. 743; *Shepherd v. Grant's Trs.* (1847) 6 Bell 153. It is however otherwise in the case of the liferenter by reservation: *Marquis of Clydesdale v. Earl of Dundonald* (1726) Mor. 1262.

[42] *cf. Duke of Argyll v. Campbell, supra.*

[43] See Stair, II, 1, 10 *et seq.*; *Ersk.,* II, 1, 22; Bell, *Prin.,* § 2004.

[44] *Young v. North British. Ry.* (1887)14 R. (H.L.) 53 at p. 56, *per* Lord Fitzgerald.

[45] *Forbes v. Livingstone* (1827) 6 S. 167. See also *Lord Advocate v. Wemyss* (1899) 2 F. (H.L.) 1.

[46] *Ramsay v. Duke of Roxburghe* (1848)10 D. 661; *Stuart v. McBarnet* (1868) 6 M. (H.L.) 123; *Warrand's Trs. v. Mackintosh* (1890)17 R. (H.L.) 13; *Young v. North British Ry.* (1887)14 R. (H.L.) 53.

[47] *Hamilton v. McIntosh Donald,* 1994 S.L.T. 212; 1994 S.L.T. 793. Appeal to the House of Lords was abandoned. See also R. Rennie, "Possession: nine tenths of the law." 1994 S.L.T. (News) 261.

Where adjoining proprietors both had habile titles to include a disputed strip of ground the one who had used it for rough shooting was held to have had adequate possession to found a claim for prescription.[47a]

Possession may be of subjects expressly conveyed by the grant in question, or of subjects included in the grant only as parts and pertinents of the subjects expressly conveyed. "It must be shown that the possession is to be ascribed to the alleged title; and when the subject is not expressly described in the title, but is said to be included in a grant of pertinents, it is necessary to show that it has been in fact possessed, not merely along with, but as a pertinent of, the subject described."[48] The term "pertinents" is "of very potent and comprehensive meaning, and sufficient by Scotch law to pass every subject in connection with the land which usually goes to the vassal as accessory to the subject expressly granted."[49]

It has been well settled in older cases that the possession founded on need not be the actual possession of the person maintaining the right. The possession of a vassal may be founded on by a superior,[50] or the possession of an institute by a substitute. It is competent to look at prior writs outwith the prescriptive period to ascertain the nature of an occupier's possession and the character in which he obtained it.[51]

To be effective for purposes of positive prescription possession must be adverse, in that the party against whom it is pleaded must have been in a situation to oust that possession if his title was good.[52] Accordingly possession granted as custodier or tenant or liferenter cannot found a prescriptive claim to property against the owner because it is not inconsistent with or adverse to his claim of ownership but at least equally referable to the claimant's rights as custodier, tenant or otherwise.[53] To avail to fortify a title to any interest in land possession must be clearly and unequivocally referable to that title and not at least equally explicable on some other basis.[54]

A distinction is drawn between possession which establishes a new and adverse right in the possessor, in which case the maxim *tantum praescriptum quantum possessum* applies, and the extent of prescriptive right is limited by the proven extent of possession, and the prescriptive possession which the law admits to construe or explain, in a question with its author, the limits of an antecedent grant or conveyance, in which case partial acts of possession are much more readily admitted as evidencing proprietary possession of the whole.[54]

"by any person, or by any person and his successors"

It has long been accepted that, if the possession founded on was ascribed to charter and sasine, an heir or singular successor could competently prove possession for the prescriptive period by persons who can connect

---

[47a] *Bain v. Carrick*, 1983 S.L.T. 675.
[48] *Duke of Argyll v. Campbell*, 1912 S.C. 458 at p. 501, *per* Lord Kinnear.
[49] *Young v. North British Ry.* (1887) 14 R. (H.L.) 53 at p. 56, *per* Lord Fitzgerald.
[50] *cf.* Stair, II, 12, 16.
[51] *Duke of Argyll v. Campbell, supra.*
[52] *ibid.,* at pp. 477 and 502.
[53] *Houstoun v. Barr*, 1911 S.C. 134.
[54] *Lord Advocate v. Wemyss* (1899) 2 F. (H.L.) 1 at pp. 9–10, *per* Lord Watson.

themselves with the original title and with whom he can connect his title, whether by writs merely personal or by writs on which infeftment followed.[55] This principle is intended to be continued, so that the period of possession in question is counted from the first possession under a recorded title more than the prescriptive period back from the time when the question has arisen, provided that the possessor claiming that his title has been fortified by prescription can connect himself with that previous possessor as being the successor in title of that possessor.

A successor may be a singular successor, who has acquired right by purchase or gift or judicial title, or a universal successor who has acquired right to the interest on intestacy.

"for a continuous period"

As under the earlier acts the period must be "continuous" and not broken, nor interrupted legally.

In the cases, such as of shooting and fishing rights, which are exercised on occasions, questions may arise of whether possession has been had "for a continuous period of ten years."[56] It will probably suffice if the possessor exercise his rights on whatever occasions he chooses and also takes reasonably adequate steps to assert his right against others and to warn them off or prevent them seeking to assert a contrary right. In a case of the right to the foreshore it has been observed[57]: "It is, in my opinion practically impossible to lay down any precise rule in regard to the character and amount of possession necessary in order to give a riparian proprietor a prescriptive right to foreshore. Each case must depend upon its own circumstances... I think it may be safely affirmed that in cases where the seashore admits of an appreciable and reasonable amount of beneficial possession consistently with [the rights of navigation and of the general public] the riparian proprietor must be held to have had possession within the meaning of the Act 1617, c. 12, if he has had all the beneficial uses of the foreshore which would naturally have been enjoyed by the direct grantee of the Crown. In estimating the character and extent of his possession it must always be kept in view that possession of the foreshore in its natural state can never be, in the strict sense of the term, exclusive. The proprietor cannot exclude the public from it at any time, and it is practically impossible to prevent occasional encroachments on his right, because the cost of preventive measures would be altogether disproportionate to the value of the subject."

Possession may be continuous though exercised by acts of possession at substantial intervals; how many instances of possession need be proved is a matter for the court; moreover *probatis extremis praesumuntur media.*[58]

If the period of possession is "either voluntarily abandoned by the possessor, without any intention of resuming it, or is actually taken from him within the forty years, the course of the positive prescription is broken

---

[55] *Middleton v. Earl of Dunmore* (1774) Mor. 10944; *Caitcheon v. Ramsey* (1791) Mor. 10810; *Fraser v. Lord Lovat* (1898) 25 R. 603.
[56] Ersk., III, 7, 3, discusses the case of a right of patronage of a church and the possibility of only one presentation during the 40 years.
[57] *Young v. North British Ry.* (1887) 14 R. (H.L.) 53 at p. 54.
[58] Stair, IV, 40, 20.

with regard to him who has thus abandoned the possession, or been turned out of it; because the law hath said. That in order to establish a right by prescription, the possession must be constant and uninterrupted through that whole period. Though therefore the former possessor should recover the possession, he must enter upon a new course of prescription, to be computed from the time of that recovery."[59]

It has been held that a proprietor of a barony who had not an express grant of salmon fishings had not instructed a right thereto by establishing that the tenants of cottages on his estate had been in use to fish for salmon in the sea for their own behoof.[60]

"of ten years"

The period is that fixed by the Conveyancing and Feudal Reform (Scotland) Act 1970, s. 8. Possession must be for the whole of the statutory period; nothing less will do.[61] Much importance accordingly attaches to the rules for the computation of time.

It is apparent from the provisions that there must have been possession founded on and following the recording of a deed sufficient to constitute a title to the interest in question that the *terminus a quo* for the 10 year period is the date of recording of the deed in question,[62] or the date of the commencement of possession, if later than the date of recording.

Under the former law it was held that the prescriptive period commenced at midnight on the date of infeftment and was not complete until midnight on the same date in the same month the requisite number of years later.[63] This is consistent with section 14(1)(c).

The 1973 Act provides:

Computation of prescriptive periods

14.—(1) In the computation of a prescriptive period for the purposes of any provision of this Part[64] of this Act—

   (a) time occurring before the commencement of this Part of this Act[65] shall be reckonable towards the prescriptive period in like manner as time occurring thereafter, but subject to the restriction that any time reckoned under this paragraph shall be less than the prescriptive period;

   (b) [66]any time during which any person against whom the provision is pled was under legal disability shall (except so far as otherwise provided by subsection (4) of section 6 of this Act including that subsection as applied by section 8A of this Act) be reckoned as if the person were free from that disability;

   (c) if the commencement of the prescriptive period would, apart from this paragraph, fall at a time in any day other than the beginning of the day, the period shall be deemed to have commenced at the beginning of the next following day;

   (d) if the last day of the prescriptive period would, apart from this paragraph, be a holiday, the period shall, notwithstanding anything in the said provision, be extended to include any immediately succeeding day which is a holiday, any

---

[59] Ersk., III, 7, 42.
[60] *Lord Advocate v. Hall* (1873) 11 M. 967.
[61] *Fraser v. Grant* (1866) 4 M. 596.
[62] cf. *Duke of Roxburgh v. Don* (1734) 1 Pat. 126.
[63] *Simpson v. Melville* (1899) 6 S.L.T. 355; *Simpson v. Marshall* (1900) 2 F. 447.
[64] Part I (ss. 1 to 15).
[65] July 25, 1976.
[66] As amended by Prescription and Limitation (Scotland) Act 1984, Sched. 1, para. 6.

further immediately succeeding days which are holidays, and the next succeeding day which is not a holiday;

(e) save as otherwise provided in this Part of this Act regard shall be had to the like principles as immediately before the commencement of this Part of this Act were applicable to the computation of periods of prescription for the purposes of the Prescription Act 1617.

(2) In this section "holiday" means a day of any of the following descriptions, namely, a Saturday, a Sunday and a day which, in Scotland, is a bank holiday under the Banking and Financial Dealings Act 1971.

By section 5(1) "deed" includes a judicial decree, and by section 1(3), in the computation of a prescriptive period where the deed in question is a decree of adjudication for debt, any period before the expiry of the legal shall be disregarded. Under the previous law it was settled that decree of adjudication of heritage for debt and sasine thereon, followed after 10 years by a decree of declarator of expiry of the legal, constituted an unassailable title to the heritage, because the declarator had finally ended the debtor's right of redemption.

Equally it has been held that decree of adjudication of heritage for debt and sasine thereon, recorded, followed by possession for the long negative prescriptive period from the date of expiry of the legal, together with declarator of expiry thereof, was a good prescriptive title, the debtor's right to redeem being extinguished by the negative prescription.[67]

Both these cases remain possible bases for prescription today; section 1(3) states the *terminus a quo* of the prescriptive period as being "the expiry of the legal"; there is no requirement of obtaining declarator of the expiry, but if declarator of expiry of the legal be obtained (after 10 years) prescriptive possession for 10 more years renders the title unassailable, whereas if declarator be not obtained after the lapse of the 10 years of the legal, possession for 20 more years may be required to extinguish by the long negative prescription the debtor's equitable right to redeem.

Under the law in force between 1874 and 1973 a decree of adjudication with infeftment thereon, duly recorded, even though followed by a decree of declarator of expiry of the legal was not an "*ex facie* valid irredeemable title," such as could be validated by 20 years' possession, and 40 years possession was still necessary.[68] This rule disappears with the principle that only irredeemable titles gave a foundation for prescription.

During the running of the prescriptive period possession both evidences the possessor's claim to proprietary right and is an important element in interpreting that claim. "But when possession, consistent with and ascribed to infeftment on a habile title, has once reached the prescriptive term, its effect is wholly altered. It is no longer evidence of the construction of a written title, but operates as in itself the constitution of a right of property, and thenceforth the construction of the written title is of no consequence at all, excepting so far as habile as a groundwork for prescription."[69]

---

[67] *Johnston v. Balfour* (1745) Mor. 10789; *Caitcheon v. Ramsey* (1791) Mor. 10810; *Robertson v. Duke of Athol* (1803) Hume 463, (1815) 3 Dow 108, 1 Ross L.C. 208.

[68] *Hinton v. Connell's Tr.* (1883)10 R. 1110.

[69] *Auld v. Hay* (1880) 7 R. 663 at p. 669, *per* L.J.-C. Moncreiff, citing *Forbes v. Livingston* (1827) 6 S. 167.

"openly, peaceably"

Possession must be exercised openly, not secretly.[70] Thus no amount of salmon-fishing by dead of night will amount to possession of the fishings. In a case of coal-working[71] it was observed: "But it was not necessary to prove either that the officers of the Crown had been apprised of the workings, or that they in fact knew of them. Apart from this, the evidence shews that the workings under the sea were in no sense clandestine; that they were well known in the district; that they had been the subject of public scientific discussion, and that they were inspected and reported on in the usual way by the Government Inspector of Mines."

Possession must be exercised peaceably, and possession maintained by force, even if for 10 years, would not suffice for prescription. The word "peaceably" is carried over from the Act of 1617. If an occupier's possession were secured initially by forcible eviction, or, though initially lawful, were maintained only by forcible ejection of a competing claimant, it is not enjoyed "peaceably."

It has never been a requisite that possession be begun or continued *in bona fide*.[72]

"and without any judicial interruption"

In the 1617 Act the phrase was "without any lawful interruption." Interruption is any "step taken by the owner of a right or debt against the possessor or debtor for preserving it from prescription".[73] Under the former Acts interruption of the continuity of a period of possession invalidated the period which had already run and required it to recommence. Interruption might be effected (1) extra-judicially, by "any act by which a proprietor of … an heritable… subject uses or asserts his right against the possessor,"[74] as by adverse possession, known as natural interruption, or by making a notarial protest against the possession, known as civil interruption,[75] by preparing an Instrument of Interruption which, to be available to or against singular successors had to be extended and recorded in the General Register of Sasines,[76] or (2) judicially, by citing the possessor in an action challenging the right, though a citation, unless it became a process, had to be renewed every seven years[77] and, if it were to be effective against a singular successor of the possessor, required to be recorded in the General Register of Sasines, or by actually calling the action and proceeding with it or by presenting or concurring in a petition for sequestration or liquidation. An action brought into court was effective as an interruption for 40 years.[78]

The effect of section 1(1)(*a*) of the 1973 Act appears to be that extra-judicial interruption is only effective if it contravenes the word "peaceably";

---

[70] *cf* Ersk., II, 1, 23.
[71] *Wemyss' Trs. v. Lord Advocate* (1896) 24 R. 216 at p. 229, *per* L.P. Robertson.
[72] Stair II, 12, 6, 11 and 19; Mackenzie, III, 7, 5; Ersk. III, 7, 15; Napier on *Prescription*, p. 51.
[73] Ersk., III, 7, 38.
[74] Ersk., III, 7, 39.
[75] Ersk., III, 7, 40; Bell, *Prin.*, § 2007.
[76] Land Registers (Scotland) Act 1868, s. 15.
[77] Prescription Act 1669.
[78] Ersk., III, 7, 43; Bell, *Prin.*, § 2007; *Wallace v. Earl of Eglintoun* (1830) 8 S. 1018.

thus a possessor who violently resists a claimant cannot acquire a title by any number of years' possession because he does not hold "peaceably."

Apart from that case 10 years' possession "without any *judicial* interruption" fortifies title and it would appear that extra-judicial interruption by notarial protest is now ineffective. Judicial interruption continues to have the effect of cancelling the effect of any period of possession which has run.

The 1973 Act provides:

Judicial interruption of periods of possession for purposes of sections 1, 2 and 3

4.—(1) In sections 1, 2 and 3 of this Act references to a judicial interruption, in relation to possession, are references to the making in appropriate proceedings, by any person having a proper interest to do so, of a claim which challenges the possession in question.

(2) In this section "appropriate proceedings" means—
  (a) any proceedings in a court of competent jurisdiction in Scotland or elsewhere, except proceedings in the Court of Session initiated by a summons which is not subsequently called;[79]
  (b) any arbitration in Scotland;
  (c) any arbitration in a country other than Scotland, being an arbitration an award in which would be enforceable in Scotland.

(3) The date of a judicial interruption shall be taken to be—
  (a) where the claim has been made in an arbitration and the nature of the claim has been stated in a preliminary notice relating to that arbitration, the date when the preliminary notice was served;
  (b) in any other case, the date when the claim was made.

(4) In the foregoing subsection "preliminary notice" in relation to an arbitration means a notice served by one party to the arbitration on the other party or parties requiring him or them to appoint an arbiter or to agree to the appointment of an arbiter, or, where the arbitration agreement or any relevant enactment provides that the reference shall be to a person therein named or designated, a notice requiring him or them to submit the dispute to the person so named or designated.

The claim which challenges the possession in question, to have effect as an interruption, must be made "by any person having a proper interest to do so," that is, be made by a person having both title and interest to make the kind of claim he makes. Whether a particular party has or has not title and interest to make the claim is an issue of law and may be a difficult one in particular circumstances.

A "claim which challenges the possession in question" can be of various kinds, *e.g.* an action of ejection of the possessor as one possessing without title, a declarator that the possessor had no title or that the party interrupting has a better title, or a reduction of the possessor's title.[80]

"Appropriate proceedings" includes proceedings initiated elsewhere than in Scotland. In England the Court of Chancery and, now, the Chancery Division, will assert jurisdiction *in personam* over a defendant even in relation to a dispute concerning land outwith the English jurisdiction.[81] Such an action could accordingly be "appropriate proceedings" for the purposes of section 4.

---

[79] A summons has been held to have been "subsequently called" though outwith the prescriptive period: *Barclay v. Chief Constable, Northern Constabulary,* 1986 S.L.T. 562.

[80] *e.g. Simpson v. Melville* (1899) 6 S.L.T. 355.

[81] *Penn v. Lord Baltimore* (1750) 1 Ves.Sen. 444; *Ewing v. Orr Ewing* (1883) 9 App. Cas. 34 at p. 40; *Orr Ewing's Trs. v. Orr Ewing* (1885) 13 R. (H.L.) 1 at pp. 3 and 8; *West & Partners v. Dick* [1969] 2 Ch. 424.

An arbitration furth of Scotland also counts as "appropriate proceedings" if the award in it is enforceable in Scotland. At common law an award under a foreign arbitration may be enforced in Scotland only by bringing an action for decree conform in the Court of Session.[82] Under the Arbitration Act 1950, Pt II, the Administration of Justice Act 1920, Pt II, and the Foreign Judgments (Reciprocal Enforcement) Act 1933, Pt I, amended by the Civil Jurisdiction and Judgments Act 1982, certain foreign arbitration awards are statutorily enforceable in Scotland.

Proceedings in the Court of Session were formerly held to effect interruption if the summons had merely been served,[83] but section 4(2)(*a*) now excepts this case and requires the summons to have been called for it to effect interruption. Citation alone will not now effect interruption. The "date when the claim was made" is accordingly the date of calling. But the section does not require any further step than calling to be taken in the process.

Judicial interruption once made by calling an action is effective for 40 years.[84]

"and (b) the possession was founded on"

The provision that the possession must have been "founded on" a deed or decree sufficient in terms to constitute a title appears to restate the former principle that possession must be referable to an *ex facie* valid title.[85] It is clear that no amount or duration of possession without some written title as a foundation for that possession will suffice; "exclusive possession will not prove or establish a right unless it follows upon a habile title"[86]; "mere possession will not suffice to establish a right of property in the defender unless the possession is referable to charters and dispositions followed by sasine"[87]; thus a squatter, even if his possession were undisturbed for more than 10 years, could not acquire any title by prescription, not having any written title to found on.[88] Nor can possession of ground beyond the boundary defined by a bounding title be a basis for prescription.[89]

Furthermore the written title must be one which affords legal foundation for the particular possession; thus a claim to land beyond the boundary stated in the deed or excepted from the grant cannot be fortified by prescription because possession thereof cannot be said to be "founded on" that deed.[90] Possession, that is, cannot establish a right contradictory of or inconsistent with the grant.[91] But a right may be acquired by prescription if

---

[82] *cf O'Connor v. Erskine* (1906) 22 Sh. Ct. Rep. 58; *Stoddart v. Hotchkis* (1916) 33 Sh. Ct. Rep. 60; *Strachan v. Strachan* (1951) 67 Sh. Ct. Rep. 51.

[83] *e.g. Simpson v. Melville* (1899) 6 S.L.T. 355.

[84] Ersk. III, 7, 43; Bell *Prin.* § 2007; Napier on *Prescription* p. 662; *Duke of Buccleuch v. Edinburgh Mags.* (1843) 5 D. 847.

[85] *Officers of State v. Earl of Haddington* (1830) 8 S. 867 at p. 874; *Milne's Trs. v. Lord Advocate* (1873) 11 M. 966; *Edmondstone v. Jeffray* (1886) 13 R. 1038; *Houstoun v. Barr,* 1911 S.C. 134; *Duke of Argyll v. Campbell,* 1912 S.C. 458.

[86] *Caledonian Ry. v. Jamieson* (1899) 2 F. 100 at p. 106, *per* Lord Trayner.

[87] *North British Ry. v. Hutton* (1896) 23 R. 522 at p. 525, *per* Lord McLaren.

[88] *cf. Johnston v. Fairfowl* (1901) 8 S.L.T. 480.

[89] *Nisbet v. Hogg,* 1950 S.L.T. 289.

[90] *North British Ry. v. Hutton, supra.* But incorporeal rights may be acquired by prescription beyond the limits of a bounding charter: *Earl of Zetland v. Tennent's Trs.* (1873) 11 M. 469.

[91] *Officers of State, supra*; see also *Ross v. Milne, Cruden & Co.* (1843) 5 D. 648; *Thain v. Thain* (1891) 18 R. 1196; *Ellice's Trs. v. Caledonian Canal Commrs.* (1904) 6 F. 325.

possessed for the statutory period as part and pertinent of a subject expressly conveyed, even against an express grant of the subject to another on which infeftment had followed.[92] The onus of proving that the interest claimed has been possessed not only along with but as part and pertinent of lands lies on the party asserting the right.[93] If there is a reason for possession inconsistent with the idea of possession as part and pertinent the possession will not fortify a claim to the interest claimed.[94]

It is competent to look at prior writs to ascertain the character of the claimant's possession,[95] or whether the granter of a conveyance of lands which purported to convey the teinds had a right to his teinds.[96]

It is not competent to refer to titles prior to but not connected by a proper progress with the title or series of titles which form the basis of the prescription for the purpose of explaining away, altering or qualifying the investiture secured by prescription[97]

If competing claimants produce titles equally good bases for prescription, the right will be determined by the evidence of possession.[97a] Similarly possession for the prescriptive period may explain a grant and define its extent.[98] Thus infeftment on a barony title followed by possession of salmon fishings for the prescriptive period will give a good title to the salmon fishings even against the Crown.[99]

Again, a cornice and sign-board above a shop, though extending above the centre-line of the joists of the first floor, having been there for 40 years, were held to have been possessed as part and pertinent of the shop and secured by prescription.[1] Again the rights of the feuars in a town square in the central garden were held to be measured by the past possession and administration thereof.[2]

A claimant fails to prove possession habile to fortify a claim to a particular interest in land, *e.g.* ownership, if he can prove only possession equally referable to another right, *e.g.* tenancy. In *Houstoun v. Barr*,[3] H, owner of a feu, claimed a strip of ground which was used as an access to a field owned by his superior, B, founding on possession for the prescriptive period. During the whole of that time H or his authors had leased the field from B or his authors. It was held that H had failed to prove the necessary possession, as all the acts of possession founded on were at least as referable to his right of tenancy as to his ownership of the

---

[92] *Perth Mags. v. Earl of Wemyss* (1829) 8 S. 82; *Earl of Fife's Trs. v. Cumming* (1830) 8 S. 326. Contrast *Troup v. Aberdeen Heritable Securities Co.*, 1916 S.C. 918.

[93] *Lord Advocate v. Hunt* (1867) 5 M. (H.L.) 1; *Scott v. Napier* (1869) 7 M. (H.L.) 35; *Duke of Argyll v. Campbell*, 1912 S.C. 458.

[94] *Duke of Argyll v. Campbell, supra*, at p. 477.

[95] *Duke of Argyll v. Campbell, supra*, at p. 458.

[96] *Mackintosh v. Lord Abinger* (1877) 4 R. 1069.

[97] *Meacher v. Blair-Oliphant*, 1913 S.C. 417; *cf. Troup v. Aberdeen Heritable Securities Co.*, 1916 S.C. 918.

[97a] *Carnegie v. MacTier* (1844) 6 D. 1381.

[98] *Braid v. Douglas* (1800) Mor. Property Appx. 2; *Ramsey v. Duke of Roxburghe* (1848)10 D. 661; *Fraser v. Grant* (1866) 4 M. 596; *Stuart v. McBarnet* (1868) 6 M. (H.L.) 123.

[99] *McDougall v. Lord Advocate* (1875) 2 R.(H.L.) 49; *Lord Advocate v. McCulloch* (1874) 2 R. 27.

[1] *McArly v. French's Trs.* (1883)10 R. 574.

[2] *Watson's Hospital v. Cormack* (1883)11 R. 320.

[3] 1911 S.C. 134.

feu. In *Duke of Argyll v. Campbell*[4] it was held by examination of prior
writs that a vassal's possession of a castle was not as proprietor but as
keeper for the superior and accordingly he could not found on his
possession as fortifying a claim to ownership. In *Robertson's Trustees v.
Bruce*[5] it was held that prescriptive possession of what was truly a
servitude of access by a staircase and not a right of property therein could
not turn a right of access into a right of property. In *Fothringham v.
Passmore*[6] it was observed that the possession of salmon fishings claimed
was inconsistent with the title founded on in that it was partial, possession
on three days per week only.

Prescriptive possession may also be held to determine the extent of an
estate where there is ambiguity or lack of specification in the title. In *Auld
v. Hay*[7] a description of lands could be construed to embrace the whole
lands, or part of them only, and uninterrupted and exclusive possession of
the whole followed, and it was held that prescription operated to protect
the possessor against claimants to the whole or any part of the lands. "The
terms of the grant may be ambiguous, or indefinite, or general, so that it
may remain doubtful whether the particular subject is or is not conveyed,
or, if conveyed, what is the extent of it. But if the instrument be conceived
in terms consistent with and susceptible of a construction which would
embrace such a conveyance, that is enough, and forty years' possession
following on it will constitute the right to the extent possessed."[8]

"and followed (i) the recording of"

By section 15(1) "recording" means recording in the General Register
of Sasines. It has long been settled that a sasine must be recorded to be a
good basis for prescription.[9] As the possession must have followed the
recording of the deed founded on, it follows that an unrecorded title provides
no foundation for prescriptive possession, and that no possession prior to
recording counts towards the 10-year period. The date of recording is the
earliest possible *terminus a quo* for the prescriptive period. Under the former
law it was held that the prescriptive period commenced at midnight on the
date of infeftment.[10]

In *Sempill v. Leith Hay*[11] an arbiter's award that certain lands should be
free of thirlage, subject to making an annual payment, was not registered
in the Register of Sasines and it was held that even 70 years' payments had
had no prescriptive effect against the lands.

"a deed"

A "deed" includes all the kinds of written instruments by which a title to
an interest in land may be created, such as a feu-charter, disposition, or

---

[4] 1912 S.C. 458.
[5] (1905) 7 F. 580.
[6] 1984 S.C. (H.L.) 96 at p. 99.
[7] (1880) 7 R. 663.
[8] *ibid.* 668, *per* L.J.-C. Moncreiff.
[9] *Crawford v. McMichen* (1729) 2 Ross L.C. 112; *Kibbles v. Stevenson* (1830) 9 S. 233.
[10] *Simpson v. Melville* (1899) 6 S.L.T. 355; *Simpson v. Marshall* (1900) 2 F. 447.
[11] (1903) 5 F. 868.

trust deed and notice of title. It includes a Crown charter,[12] a charter of a royal burgh,[13] and a statute conveying a title,[14] but not a mere resolution of a body to grant a title,[15] nor a land plan prepared by the claimants themselves.[16]

The 1973 Act enacts:

Further provisions supplementary to sections 1, 2 and 3

5.—(1) In sections 1, 2 and 3 of this Act "deed" includes a judicial decree; and for the purposes of the said sections any of the following, namely an instrument of sasine, a notarial instrument and a notice of title, which narrates or declares that a person has a title to an interest in land shall be treated as a deed sufficient to constitute that title in favour of that person.

(2) Where a deed has been at any time *ex facie* invalid by reason of an informality of execution within the meaning of section 39 of the Conveyancing (Scotland) Act 1874, but the appropriate court has subsequently declared, in pursuance of that section, that it was subscribed by the granter or maker and the witnesses, the deed shall be deemed for the purposes of the said sections 1, 2 and 3 not to be, and not at anytime to have been, *ex facie* invalid by reason of any such informality of execution.[17]

The kinds of judicial decrees equivalent to and comprehended within the category of "deed" will include a decree of adjudication in an action of ranking and sale,[18] a decree of adjudication for debt, and a decree of service of one person as heir of another.[19]

As regards section 5(1) formerly no one of these kinds of deeds was a sufficient basis for prescription by itself without production of the warrant on which it proceeded, *e.g.* the precept of sasine, deed of gift, will or other grant which warranted the expeding of the instrument of sasine, notarial instrument or notice of title. The instrument of sasine, notarial instrument or notice of title is now sufficient by itself but it may be necessary to go back to earlier deeds to explain the capacity in which a person has right to the interest in land carried by the sasine or other deed.[20]

In the case of a decree of adjudication for debt, the decree is valid as a "deed" as a foundation for prescriptive possession but is a redeemable title only and, by section 1(3), in the computation of the prescriptive period any period before the expiry of the legal is to be disregarded. The legal, *i.e.* the period within which the debtor may redeem the lands and during which the creditor's right therein under the decree remains redeemable, is 10 years. Thereafter the creditor may obtain decree of declarator of expiry of the legal and 10 years' possession will give him an indefeasible title; or he may take no action to obtain such declarator in which case the debtor's right to redeem will be cut off by the running of the long negative prescription.[21]

---

[12] *Walker v. Miln* (1871) 9 M. 823.
[13] *Macpherson v. Mackenzie* (1881) 8 R. 706.
[14] *Aitken's Trs. v. Rawyards Colliery Co.* (1894) 22 R. 201.
[15] *Bain v. Grant* (1884) 22 S.L.R. 132.
[16] *Caledonian Ry. v. Jamieson* (1899) 2 F. 100.
[17] Section 5(2) is repealed with effect from August 1, 1995, by the Requirements of Writing (Scotland) Act 1995, s. 14(2) and Sched. 5.
[18] *Hilson v. Scott* (1895) 23 R. 241.
[19] *Duke of Argyll v. Campbell,* 1912 S.C. 458.
[20] *ibid.*
[21] See further G.L. Gretton, "Prescription and the Foreclosure of Adjudications", 1983 J.R. 177.

As regards section 5(2)[22] if a deed has suffered from an "informality of execution" but that defect has been cured by declarator under the 1874 Act, s. 39, it is now deemed not to be, and never to have been, *ex facie* invalid.

"Informality of execution" curable under the 1874 Act, s. 39, was held to cover: absence of a testing clause[23]; a deed on more than one sheet subscribed on the last page only[24]; lack of the designations of the subscribing witnesses[25]; signature of a will on the last page only[26]; a codicil written partly at the end of a probative will and partly on a separate sheet and signed on the latter only[27]; a settlement not probative but validly attested by the law of New Zealand[28]; a discrepancy between the name in the testing clause and the signature of a witness.[29]

Section 39 does not, however, cover fatal defects. This category has been held to include cases where the signature was neither adhibited nor acknowledged in the presence of one of the attesting witnesses[30]; where the signatures were adhibited before the granter subscribed and the witnesses neither saw him sign nor heard him acknowledge his subscription[31]; where one witness subscribed after the lapse of some time and after the granter's death.[32]

Petition under section 39 has been dismissed as unnecessary where there was a discrepancy between the signature of the granter and the name of the granter in the body of the deed and the testing clause.[33]

Section 39 was held not to apply to notarial execution.[34]

If, however, the deed is *ex facie* invalid for other reasons than mere "informality of execution" cured by declarator, it is invalid and is not a sufficient basis for possession. "Prescription does not cure *ex facie* nullities, but only excludes grounds of challenge not disclosed on the face of the title."[35] In *Fleeming v. Howden*[36] superiorities were sold, the disposition conveying the lands themselves with all right, title and interest vested in the disponers. It was held that this deed did not convey the minerals, which had previously been created a separate tenement, and opinions were expressed that if the disposition had conveyed the minerals the purchaser would not have acquired right thereto by prescription, the nullity of the conveyance, as a conveyance of anything but the superiority, appearing *ex facie* of the deed.

Divergent opinions have been expressed on whether a disposition, null *ab initio* for want of execution, but supported by a deed of ratification by

---

[22] Repealed, with effect from August 1, 1995, by the Requirements of Writing (Scotland) Act 1995, s. 14(2) and Sched. 5.

[23] *Addison* (1875) 2 R. 457.

[24] *McLaren v. Menzies* (1876) 3 R. 1151.

[25] *Thomson's Trs. v. Easson* (1878) 6 R. 141. *cf. Garrett* (1883) 20 S.L.R. 756; *Nisbet* (1897) 24 R. 411.

[26] *Inglis' Trs. v. Inglis* (1901) 4 F. 365.

[27] *Brown* (1883) 11 R. 400.

[28] *Browne* (1882) 20 S.L.R. 76.

[29] *Richardson's Trs.* (1891) 18 R. 1131.

[30] *Forrests v. Low's Trs.*, 1907 S.C. 1240.

[31] *Smyth v. Smyth* (1876) 3 R. 573.

[32] *Walker v. Whitwell*, 1916 S.C. (H.L.) 75.

[33] *Grieve's Trs. v. Japp's Trs.*, 1917 1 S.L.T. 70.

[34] *Kissack v. Webster's Trs.* (1894) 2 S.L.T. 172.

[35] *Glen v. Scales' Tr.* (1881) 9 R. 317 at p. 325, *per* Lord Craighill.

[36] (1868) 6 M. 782.

the apparent heir of the granter of the disposition, was a sufficient title to found prescription.[37]

"which is sufficient in respect of its terms to constitute in favour of that person a title"

It is a question of its terms and their interpretation whether a deed is "sufficient in respect of its terms to constitute... a title." "The prescriptive title must be habile to sustain prescriptive possession, by which I understand intrinsically valid and *per se* sufficient to support the possession which is attributed to it."[38] The deed must be such in its terms as would have warranted sasine thereon at common law, and such as now is accepted for recording in the Register of Sasines or the Land Register. It must also bear to constitute a title in the grantee. It is not permissible to refer to titles prior to but not connected by a proper progress with the title forming the basis for the prescription for the purpose of altering, explaining away or qualifying the investiture secured by prescription.[39]

In *Buchanan and Geils v. Lord Advocate*[40] a title to property bounded by the River Clyde and to "the shore ground thereof" was held to be sufficient in its terms, as explained by possession, to constitute a title to the foreshore of the river.

In *Simpson v. Marshall*[41] a testator directed his trustees to convey heritage to his daughter in liferent and her issue in fee. After one of her children had died, they conveyed the fee to the remaining children *nominatim*, and they completed title by notarial instrument which set out the testator's directions as its warrant. Opinions were expressed that the children had a habile title to found prescription as the disconformity between the warrant and the infeftment did not appear *ex facie* of the title. This decision seems confirmed by section 5(1) which makes an instrument of sasine, a notarial instrument or a notice of title a deed sufficient to constitute a title without production of the warrant.

In *Mead v. Melville*[42] a title to the basement floor of a building including two cellars in the front area but not containing a clause of parts and pertinents was held habile to prescribe a right to a third cellar.

In *Borthwick-Norton v. Gavin Paul & Sons*[43] trustees sold land to a farmer reserving the minerals and later conveyed to a company the reserved substances. The company extracted sand from the farmer's land, paying him compensation until his successor challenged the company's right to do so. It was held that the company had failed to establish that sand was included in the reserved minerals, and that it had not established a right to the sand by prescription, either on the ground that their possession was not for the prescriptive period or on the ground that their title was not habile to carry sand, sand not being within the grant.

---

[37] *Glen v. Scales' Tr.* (1881) 9 R. 317.
[38] *Duke of Argyll v. Campbell*, 1912 S.C. 458 at p. 484, *per* Lord Johnston.
[39] *Duke of Montrose v. Bontine* (1840) 2 D. 1186; *Meacher v. Blair-Oliphant*, 1913 S.C. 417.
[40] (1882) 9 R. 1218.
[41] (1900) 2 F. 447.
[42] 1915 1 S.L.T. 107.
[43] 1947 S.C. 659.

"a title to that interest in the particular land"

It is a question of interpretation to what legal interest, and in what land, a deed creates a title in the grantee of the deed.[44] Thus there may be doubt whether a deed creates title to an interest of a proprietor, or of a liferenter, or of a tenant.[45] Where there is a bounding charter no words can create any interest in land beyond the boundary,[46] though they may create an interest in an incorporeal right extending beyond the boundary, such as a right of fishing.[47]

A title to salmon fishings, apart from express grant, requires a title and sasine to which the possession can be referred, either a grant with the words *cum piscationibus* or a general grant of a barony title; in each case the possession serves to define the extent of what is comprehended in the general words of grant.[48]

If a particular interest in particular land has by law or by reservation been made a separate tenement the disponee does not acquire title thereto by prescription.[49]

"or in land of a description habile to include the particular land"

This phrase means "in land (including, by section 15(1), heritable property of any description) capable of including the particular land or other heritable right being acquired." "By habile I understand to be meant a title which, though it does not in terms bear to convey, is conceived in terms capable of being construed as conveying the subject in question. It may be general, indefinite or even ambiguous, so that it remains doubtful whether the particular subject is conveyed, or what is the extent of the subject conveyed. But if the title is couched in terms susceptible of a construction which will embrace the subject in question that is enough. Prescription intervenes and does the rest. More shortly put, the party pleading prescription need not produce a title which *ex facie* comprehends, but only one which may comprehend (*per* Lord Justice-Clerk Moncreiff, in *Auld v. Hay*). The door is then open for prescriptive possession. Where the title is thus habile, inquiry into more ancient writs is excluded."[50] "A habile title does not mean a charter followed by sasine, which bears to convey the property in dispute, but one which is conceived in terms capable of being so construed. The terms of the grant may be ambiguous, or indefinite, or general, so that it may remain doubtful whether the particular subject is or is not conveyed, or if conveyed, what is the extent of it."[51]

Accordingly an unqualified disposition of land is "habile to include" the buildings thereon, the subjacent minerals and the right of trout-fishing in streams flowing through the land, but is not "habile to include" salmon fishings, because a right of salmon fishing is a distinct interest in land

---

[44] *cf. Hilson v. Scott* (1895) 23 R. 241; *Wallace v. St. Andrews University Court* (1904) 6 F. 1093.

[45] *cf. Aitken's Trs. v. Rawyards Colliery Co. Ltd.* (1894) 22 R. 201.

[46] *St. Monance Mags. v. Mackie* (1845) 7 D. 582; *Reid v. McColl* (1879) 7 R. 84; *North British Ry. v. Hutton* (1896) 23 R. 522; *Lord Advocate v. Wemyss* (1899) 2 F. (H.L.) 1; *Brown v. North British Ry.* (1906) 8 F. 534.

[47] *Earl of Zetland v. Tennent's Trs.* (1873) 11 M. 469.

[48] *Lord Advocate v. McCulloch* (1874) 2 R. 27.

[49] *Fleeming v. Howden* (1868) 6 M. 782; *Millar v. Marquess of Lansdowne,* 1910 S.C. 618.

[50] *Duke of Argyll v. Campbell,* 1912 S.C. 458 at p. 490, *per* Lord Johnston.

[51] *Auld v. Hay* (1880) 7 R. 663 at p. 668, *per* L.J.-C. Moncreiff.

which is not carried *sub silentio* or by a clause conveying "parts and pertinents."[52] A charter of a royal burgh is a habile title on which to prescribe a right to exact harbour and shore dues.[53]

Thus in *Cooper's Trustees v. Stark's Trustees*[54] a conveyance of buildings "with the whole parts, pendicles, privileges and pertinents" followed by possession of a saloon built to the rear, was a title habile to include the saloon. In *Brown v. North British Railway*[55] it was held that measurements of land were taxative and that there was no title on which to prescribe a title to the lands in dispute. In *Troup v. Aberdeen Heritable Securities Co.*[56] it was held that a disposition of land was not a bounding title but was habile as a foundation for prescription, and prescriptive possession had followed thereon. In *Marquess of Ailsa v. Monteforte*[57] it was held that a landlord had a right of property in the foreshore; though his titles did not expressly include the foreshore they were habile to do so on proof of prescriptive possession, and this was established. In *Borthwick-Norton v. Gavin Paul & Sons*[58] it was held that sand was not within the grant and accordingly that the title was not a habile one on which to acquire by prescription a right to sand. In *Suttie v. Baird*[59] an unclear description of land conveyed by a feu disposition was sufficiently precise to be habile to convey a strip of ground in dispute.

or (ii) registration of that interest in favour of that person in the Land Register of Scotland, subject to an exclusion of indemnity under section 12(2) of the Land Registration (Scotland) Act 1979

This amendment, introduced by the 1979 Act, is intended to continue the benefit of positive prescription in the only case where that may still be valuable under a system of registered titles to land, namely where the registration of title has been made subject to an exclusion of indemnity. On the circumstances in which an interest in land becomes registrable in the Land Register see the Land Registration (Scotland) Act 1979, s. 2; on the legal effect of registration see the 1979 Act, s. 3.

"then, as from the expiration of the said period"

The "said period" is the continuous period of 10 years from the date of recording of the deed constituting the title, or from the cessation of any judicial interruption, which is probably the date of absolvitor in, or final dismissal of, any action brought to challenge the possessor's title. The "said period" expires on the day having the same number in the month of the same name 10 years after the recording, or conclusion of interrupting action.

Subsection (3) deals with the special case where the deed constituting the title is a decree of adjudication for debt and provides that in that case

---

[52] On "parts and pertinents," see *Young v. North British Ry.* (1887)14 R. (H.L.) 53 at p. 56; *Cooper's Trs. v. Stark's Trs.* (1898) 1 F. 1160.
[53] *Macpherson v. Mackenzie* (1881) 8 R. 706.
[54] (1898) 1 F. 1160.
[55] (1906) 8 F. 534.
[56] 1916 S.C. 918.
[57] 1937 S.C. 805.
[58] 1947 S.C. 659 at pp. 696 and 699. See also *Nisbet v. Hogg*, 1950 S.L.T. 289.
[59] 1992 S.L.T. 133.

any period before the expiry of the legal shall be disregarded; the prescriptive period runs from the date of final decree in a declarator of expiry of the legal. At common law a decree of adjudication of lands for debt followed by sasine was a basis for prescription, though without declarator of expiry of the legal, but such a title was not ex facie irredeemable, so that 40 years' possession after expiry of the legal was necessary to operate prescription.[60]

By subsection (4) there is retained the rule stated in the Conveyancing and Feudal Reform (Scotland) Act 1970, s. 8(1), that in relation to claims against the Crown to ownership of any foreshore or any salmon-fishings, the prescriptive period remains 20 years. In relation, however, to the acquisition by a purchaser of such an interest against a seller, not being the Crown, the period will be 10 years.

"the validity of the title so far as relating to the said interest in the particular land"

The effect of the completion of the running of the prescriptive period is that the title is validated "so far as relating to the said interest in the particular land" only. Thus if the title bears to be title to the *dominium utile* it is validated so far as relates to the vassal's interest but this does not validate or otherwise affect title to any other interest in the particular land, such as the interest of the superior or the holder of a right in security.

"shall be exempt from challenge"

These words state the effect of the running of the 10-year prescriptive period. The effect is that the validity of the title cannot thereafter be challenged and is accordingly fortified and validated beyond question. As under the previous law, all inquiry into the origin and transmission of the title is excluded.[61] "Prescription is a good defence against objections to the titles, grounded either on nullities in those titles which are not required to be produced; or on latent nullities or extrinsic objections ... but it is no defence against intrinsic nullities."[62] "The effect of forty years' possession on a habile title is not, in any accurate sense, to construe the title. Its effect is to establish right. It is of no consequence what the true construction of the title may be, as long as it is susceptible of a construction consistent with the prescriptive possession, and when that has run, it is the possession, not the words of the charter, which establishes the right."[63] It matters not that the title was bad in origin: "It is the great purpose of prescription to support bad titles. Good titles stand in no need of prescription,"[64] "It is the policy of the law of prescription to exclude all question as to the right and title of the maker of a deed on which peaceable possession has endured for forty years."[65] "All inquiry into the validity of the prior title is excluded, even although the prior title is narrated in *gremio* of the titles on which

---

[60] *Robertson v. Duke of Atholl* (1808) Hume 463; (1815) 3 Dow 108; *Hinton v. Connell's Trs.* (1883) 10 R. 1110.
[61] *Millers v. Dickson* (1766) Mor. 10937; *Forbes v. Livingstone* (1828) 1 W. & S. 657. *cf. Ramsay v. Spence,* 1909 S.C. 1441.
[62] Bell, *Prin.,* § 2015.
[63] *Auld v. Hay* (1880) 7 R. 663 at p. 668, *per* L.J.-C. Moncreiff.
[64] *Scott v. Bruce Stewart* (1779) Mor. 13519; 3 Ross L.C. 334.
[65] *Glen v. Scales' Tr.* (1881) 9 R. 317 at p. 325, *per* Lord Young.

possession is pleaded... The positive prescription operates by excluding all inquiry, beyond the prescriptive period, into the previous titles and rights to the lands...."[66]

After the period of prescription has run it is incompetent to investigate prior titles, the origin of the possession or other factors.[67]

"(1A) Subsection (1) above shall not apply where—(a) possession was founded on the recording of a deed which is invalid ex facie*"*

There are only two exceptions under the section to the rule that prescriptive possession fortifies title. "Prescription does not cure *ex facie* nullities, but only excludes grounds of challenge not disclosed on the face of the title."[68] A deed is invalid *ex facie* if it lacks any of the essentials of that kind of deed, *e.g.* if it contains no words of conveyance, or does not adequately identify the grantee, or does not indicate what kind of interest is being conveyed, or is *ex facie* not validly executed.

It is very questionable whether the omission or inaccuracy of less fundamental clauses, such as the clause of assignation of writs or the clause of warrandice, would render a deed "invalid." It is submitted that the deed would not be "invalid," but only defective.

By section 5(2) a deed is not deemed *ex facie* invalid if the invalidity was only by reason of an informality of execution within the meaning of the Conveyancing (Scotland) Act 1874, s. 39, and the defect has been cured by declarator of court that it was subscribed by the granter or maker and witnesses.

The invalidity must, moreover, be *ex facie* of the deed, that is, such that a competent conveyancer, on a careful reading of the deed and without knowledge of background circumstances, would notice the defect. Invalidity not appearing *ex facie* of the deed, such as the fact that it has been granted *a non domino*, or by a trustee not having power of sale, does not vitiate. Such defects are only discoverable by inquiry into facts other than the deed. In *Abbey v. Atholl Properties Ltd.,*[69] the purchaser of lands from the defenders contended that an alleged nullity attaching to a deed of 1907, whereby the late Duke of Atholl conveyed the estate to the present Duke by a disposition which declared that the estate was freed from the restrictions contained in a deed of entail of 1898 under which the late Duke had held the estate, was an *ex facie* nullity; it was held that as the late Duke in the disposition of 1907 clearly professed his possession of a power to dispone in fee simple there was no *ex facie* nullity in the deed.

Another way of approaching the question whether a deed is invalid *ex facie* or not is considering the question whether a deed is intrinsically null or not. If it is intrinsically null it does not afford a foundation for the operation of prescription. A deed is intrinsically null if it suffers on the face of it from an incurable defect in its essentials. Intrinsic defects deprive a deed of *ex facie* validity. If the defect is intrinsic the deed is null *ab initio* and the

---

[66] *Fraser v. Lord Lovat* (1898) 25 R. 603 at p. 616, *per* L.P. Robertson.
[67] *Auld v. Hay* (1880) 7 R. 663; *Cooper's Trs. v. Stark's Trs.* (1898) 1 F. 1160.
[68] *Glen v. Scales' Trs.* (1881) 9 R. 317 at p. 325, *per* Lord Craighill.
[69] 1936 S.N. 97.

nullity can be declared at any time. If, however, the defect in the deed is not intrinsic but extrinsic the deed is a good title on which to prescribe. "The test as to whether a nullity is intrinsic or extrinsic would seem to be this—if the nullity can be conclusively established from an examination of the deed itself, it is intrinsic; if, on the other hand, it is necessary to go *dehors* the deed to ascertain whether or not there is a fundamental nullity, the flaw is extrinsic. Examples of nullities which are intrinsic are met with where a deed has not been signed either by a party or by an instrumentary witness or where essential matter has been written on an erasure—*Shepherd*, 6 D. 464, affd. 6 Bell's App. 173. See also Stair II, xii, 25; Ersk. III, vii. 9. Examples of nullities which were held to be extrinsic are to be found in the following cases:—*Scott*, M. 13519; *Ainslie*, 1 Ross's L.C. (Land Rights) 196; *Forbes*, 6 S. 167; *Cubbison*, 16 S. 112; *Thomson*, 2 D. 564; *Graham*, 7 D. 183; *Fraser*, 25 R. 603."[70] In *Cooper Scott v. Gill Scott*[71] a truster instructed his trustees to entail land on a series of heirs. They executed a deed of entail narrating the destination directed but in the dispositive clause interposing a substitute heir not mentioned in the trust deed; the true substitute sued the substitute called by the dispositive clause for declarator that he was entitled to the estate; it was held that the entail was not intrinsically null by reason of the discrepancy and, 40 years' possession having been had under the entail, that the substitute called by the dispositive clause of the entail was entitled to keep the estate.

"or was forged"

Forgery of the deed has always been recognised as an invalidity which prevents it being a basis for prescription. "Falsehood" was expressly excepted from the grounds of challenge of titles excluded by the Prescription Act 1617 and falsehood was construed as forgery.[72] Forgery is the creation of a deed which falsely pretends to be genuine; it might be by substitution of a false page in a genuine deed or, probably usually, by creation of a deed which falsely bears to have been authenticated by a particular person, such as a disposition bearing to have been signed by the heritable proprietor but truly not signed by him, or a deed notarially executed but without the authority of the person for whom it was executed,[73] or an unauthorised alteration to an authenticated document.

"or (b) possession was founded on registration in respect of an interest in land in the Land Register of Scotland proceeding on a forged deed and the person appearing from the Register to be entitled to the interest was aware of the forgery at the time of registration in his favour."

The force of positive prescription in rendering a title unchallengeable is not to avail the person in right of the deed if the registration of his interest proceeded on a deed known by the person entitled to the interest at the time his title was registered to have been a forgery.

---

[70] *Cooper Scott v. Gill Scott,* 1924 S.C. 309 at p. 344, *per* Lord Anderson.
[71] *Cooper Scott v. Gill Scott, supra.*
[72] *Duke of Buccleuch v. Cunynghame* (1826) 5 S. 57.
[73] *Hume on Crimes,* I, 143; Alison, *Criminal Law,* I, 377–378.

ACQUISITION OF TITLE BY PRESCRIPTION AGAINST CROWN

By section 24 the 1973 Act binds the Crown.

By section 1(4) section 1 may be pled in any question involving an interest in any foreshore or in any salmon fishings against the Crown as owner of the regalia, and a subject may acquire rights in foreshore or salmon fishings in the same way as he might acquire other rights against subjects, but in this special case the prescriptive period is 20 years.

It has been held that a Crown title which did not expressly extend the vassal's right beyond high-water mark might be shown, by such long continued possession as could only be ascribed to a right of property, to include the foreshore,[74] that a riparian proprietor on a barony title who proved prescriptive possession of the foreshore had a right of property therein,[75] that a proprietor with a title from a subject superior to property "bounded by the sea" could, by proving prescriptive possession, acquire property in the seashore against the Crown,[76] that proprietors of lands bounded by the river Clyde and of the "shore ground thereof" who proved prescriptive possession had title to the foreshore,[77] and that a proprietor was not entitled to declarator of property in the foreshore by possession for the prescriptive period of the sea-greens or strips of pasture covered by occasional tides.[78]

FORTIFICATION BY PRESCRIPTION OF
INTERESTS IN LAND HELD ON LEASE, ALLODIALLY, OR OTHERWISE

The 1973 Act enacts:

Interests in land: special cases

2.—(1) If in the case of an interest in particular land, being an interest to which this section applies,—

    (a) the interest has been possessed by any person, or by any person and his successors, for a continuous period of twenty years openly, peaceably and without any judicial interruption, and

    (b) the possession was founded on, and followed the execution of, a deed (whether recorded or not) which is sufficient in respect of its terms to constitute in favour of that person a title to that interest in the particular land, or in land of a description habile to include the particular land,

then, as from the expiration of the said period, the validity of the title so far as relating to the said interest in the particular land shall be exempt from challenge except on the ground that the deed is invalid *ex facie* or was forged.

    (2) This section applies—

    (a) to the interest in land of the lessee under a lease;

    (b) to any interest in allodial land;

    (c) to any other interest in land the title to which is of a kind which, under the law in force immediately before the commencement of this Part of this Act was sufficient to form a foundation for positive prescription without the deed constituting the title having been recorded.

    (3) This section is without prejudice to the operation of section 1 of this Act.

---

[74] *Agnew v. Lord Advocate* (1873)11 M. 309.
[75] *Lord Advocate and Clyde Trs. v. Lord Blantyre* (1889) 6 R. (H.L.) 72.
[76] *Young v. North British Ry.* (1887) 14 R. (H.L.) 53.
[77] *Buchanan and Geils v. Lord Advocate* (1882) 9 R. 1218.
[78] *Aitken's Trs. v. Caledonian Ry.* (1904) 6 F. 465. See also *Keiller v. Dundee Mags.* (1886) 14 R. 191.

GENERAL NOTE ON SECTION 2

Section 2 deals with three special cases of interests in particular land. It applies:

(*a*) to the interest in land of the lessee under a lease;

(*b*) to any interest in allodial land;

(*c*) to any other interest in land the title to which was hitherto sufficient to be a foundation for positive prescription though the deed was unrecorded.

In any of these cases the effect of possession for 20 years continuously, openly, peaceably and without judicial interruption, founded on, and following the execution of a deed sufficient to constitute a title to that interest in the particular land, is that the validity of the title is exempt from challenge except on the ground that the deed is invalid *ex facie* or was forged.

By section 2(3) sections 1 and 2 are mutually consistent, neither prejudicing the operation of the other.

VERBAL COMMENTARY ON SECTION 2

Subsection (1) is verbally identical with subsection (1) of section 1, save that in branch (*a*) the period is twenty years, not ten years, and in branch (*b*) the possession must have "followed the execution of a deed (whether recorded or not)"; under section 2(1) the deed need not have been recorded, whereas under section 1(1) the deed must have been recorded. Reference is accordingly made to the verbal commentary on the phrases where they occurred in the context of section 1.

Subsection (2) states the cases to which this section applies.

Case (*a*) covers the interest in land of the long-leaseholder[79] or long-subleaseholder, of land, whether his title is recorded, as it may be if the land does not exceed 50 acres and is let for 20 years or more, under the Registration of Leases Act 1857,[80] or is not recorded.[81] The definition in section 15(1) of "lease" does not specify any duration of lease but as the lessee's interest is fortified only by 20 years' possession, the section can have no application to any lease shorter than 20 years. The title thus fortified is the title of leaseholder or sub-leaseholder.

Though the Prescription Act 1617 was in terms applicable only to feudal titles completed by infeftment, it was in practice extended by analogy to long leases,[82] and this provision continues that practice.

Hitherto the prescriptive period in the case of both recorded and unrecorded titles to leasehold property has probably been 40 years. It is now set at 20 years.

Case (*b*) deals with interests in allodial land. Allodial land is land held in absolute ownership and not of any superior under feudal tenure. "By the usage of Scotland no lands are allodial except, first, those of the king's

---

[79] *e.g. Mure v. Heritors of Dunlop* (1746) Mor. 10820; *Maule v. Maule* (1829) 1 Sh.App. 41; *Carlyle v. Baxter* (1869) 6 S.L.R. 425.

[80] See amendments to this Act in Land Tenure Reform (Scotland) Act 1974, Sched. 6, para. 3.

[81] *e.g. Rodger v. Crawfords* (1867) 6 M. 24.

[82] Bell, *Prin.*, §§ 2008 and 2013.

own property; secondly, the superiorities which the sovereign, as the fountain of feudal rights reserves to himself in the property-lands of his subjects; and, thirdly, churches, church-yards, manses and glebes, the right of which is fully perfected by the designation of the presbytery without any grant by the crown."[83] Udal land in Orkney and Shetland is of the same character, but some udal land has been feudalised and is held by feudal titles.[84]

Hitherto it is understood that some titles to allodial land have been, but others have not been, recorded in the Register of Sasines. This provision will enable both kinds of titles to be fortified by prescription in the same way as titles to feudal property. The prescriptive period has hitherto probably been 40 years but is now set at 20 years.

Akin to allodial land is land acquired under compulsory purchase powers, where the authorising legislation may extinguish the feudal relation which existed between the superior and the vassal of the lands acquired.[85]

Case (c) deals with any other interest in land the title to which under the previous law was a sufficient foundation for prescription without the deed constituting the title having been recorded. By reason of the definition of "interest in land" in section 15(1) this case does not deal with a servitude. This case would cover the former rule that prescription applied to teinds, which were effectually carried by a merely personal title where they had not been feudalised,[86] that of the interest in land of a widow entitled to terce or a widower to courtesy, in the case of the other spouse's death intestate prior to June 10, 1964, when these rights were abolished by the Succession (Scotland) Act 1964, s. 10, that of an adjudger or creditor in possession as creditor for expenses laid out on repairing a building, under a jedge and warrant granted by the Dean of Guild court,[87] that of a creditor in a future or contingent debt who has obtained decree of adjudication of lands in security, and whose right remains perpetually redeemable, there being no legal period after which the debtor's right to redeem can be foreclosed, that of a creditor in an agricultural charge[88] or a floating charge not recorded in the Register of Sasines,[89] that of the creditor (whether an owner or a local authority) in a charging order for an annuity to repay the cost of works executed on a house or building, though such a charging order must be recorded in the Register of Sasines or Land Register.[90]

The Land Registration (Scotland) Act 1979, s. 3 makes registration of an interest in land a means of creating a real right or obligation, without prejudice to any other means, save that (subs. (3)) lessees under a long lease, proprietors under udal tenure (which is a kind of allodial holding), and kindly tenants may obtain real rights in their interests only by

---

[83] Ersk., II, 3, 8. *cf.* Bell, *Prin.,* § 667. But most churches and manses are now vested in the General Trustees of the Church of Scotland: Church of Scotland (Property and Endowments) Act 1925, s. 28. Churchyards and glebes are usually still allodial.

[84] Ersk., II, 3, 18.

[85] *Elgin Mags. v. Highland Ry.* (1884) 11 R. 950; *Inverness Mags. v. Highland Ry.* (1893) 20 R. 551; *Duke of Argyll v. L.M.S. Ry.,* 1931 S.C. 309; see also *Campbell's Trs. v. L.N.E. Ry.,* 1930 S.C. 182. See also *Young's Trs. v. Grainger* (1904) 7 F. 232.

[86] *Gordon v. Kennedy* (1758) Mor. 10825; *Irvine v. Burnet* (1764) Mor. 10830.

[87] Bell, *Comm.,* I, 784; *Peterkin v. Harvey* (1902) 9 S.L.T. 434. These are now in desuetude.

[88] Agricultural Credits (Scotland) Act 1929, ss. 5–9.

[89] Companies Act 1985, s. 462.

[90] Housing (Scotland) Act 1987, Sched. 9, para. 3.

registration. Accordingly once land registration is introduced in an area prescription will not suffice to give such landholders real rights.

The 1979 Act, s. 28, includes a definition of "overriding interests," which comprises interests which may be real interests in land though not required to be recorded in the Register of Sasines or registered in the Land Register. These include the interests of lessees under leases which are not long leases, of crofters, cottars, small landholders or statutory small tenants, proprietors of the dominant tenement in a servitude, the holder of a floating charge and various other persons.

ACQUISITION BY PRESCRIPTION OF POSITIVE SERVITUDES AND PUBLIC RIGHTS OF WAY

Section 3 of the 1973 Act enacts:

Positive servitudes and public rights of way

3.—(1) If in the case of a positive servitude over land—
  (*a*) the servitude has been possessed for a continuous period of twenty years openly, peaceably and without any judicial interruption, and
  (*b*) the possession was founded on, and followed the execution of, a deed which is sufficient in respect of its terms (whether expressly or by implication) to constitute the servitude,
then, as from the expiration of the said period, the validity of the servitude as so constituted shall be exempt from challenge except on the ground that the deed is invalid *ex facie* or was forged.

(2) If a positive servitude over land has been possessed for a continuous period of twenty years openly, peaceably and without judicial interruption, then, as from the expiration of that period, the existence of the servitude as so possessed shall be exempt from challenge.

(3) If a public right of way over land has been possessed by the public for a continuous period of twenty years openly, peaceably and without judicial interruption, then, as from the expiration of that period, the existence of the right of way as so possessed shall be exempt from challenge.

(4) References in subsections (1) and (2) of this section to possession of a servitude are references to possession of the servitude by any person in possession of the relative dominant tenement.

(5) This section is without prejudice to the operation of section 7 of this Act.

GENERAL NOTE ON SECTION 3

Section 3 deals with (1) positive servitudes over land founded on written constitution, (2) positive servitudes over land founded only on actual possession, and (3) public rights of way over land founded on possession by the public, and provides that in each case 20 years' possession renders the servitude or right of way exempt from challenge. Hitherto the period has been 40 years. The section has no application to negative servitudes, which can be acquired only by express grants.[91]

Positive servitudes may be created by express grant, by implied grant where such grant is necessary for the reasonable use of the dominant tenement, or by grant presumed from possession for the period of the positive prescription.[92]

---

[91] *Cowan v. Stewart* (1872) 10 M. 735; *Dundas v. Blair* (1886) 13 R. 759; *Inglis v. Clark* (1901) 4 F. 288.
[92] Bell, *Prin.*, §§ 992–993.

Section 3(1) deals with the first and second of these modes of constitution, section 3(2) with the third. Questions may arise of the power of particular persons to grant servitude rights.[93] It may be doubtful whether a deed grants a full right of property or merely a servitude right,[94] or whether a right granted is a revocable personal right of the grantee or a real right of servitude affecting the tenement of land valid against singular successors.[95]

Section 3 (5) declares that the section is without prejudice to the operation of section 7 which creates the long negative prescription of 20 years, which, where it applies, has the effect of extinguishing entirely obligations of any kind, except such as are imprescriptible.

VERBAL COMMENTARY ON SECTION 3
SECTION 3(1)—POSITIVE SERVITUDE CREATED BY GRANT, EXPRESS OR IMPLIED

"If in the case of a positive servitude over land"

A servitude is a conventional right by virtue of which the owner of one tenement of land possesses certain privileges, as such, as against the owner, as such, of a neighbouring tenement. Such rights are inseparable from the dominant tenement. They comprise positive servitudes, by which the owner of the dominant tenement may exercise some privilege over the servient tenement, and negative servitudes, by which the owner of the dominant tenement may require the owner of the servient to submit to a restriction of his liberties.[96] The Act deals only with positive servitudes.

The category of positive servitudes is not fixed or closed but it certainly includes such rights as servitude of way, of watering, of aqueduct, of pasturage, of fuel, feal and divot, of support, and eavesdrop.[97] It has been held not to include the right of grazing one cow on a common grazing.[98]

"(a) the servitude has been possessed"

By section 3(4) references to "possession" are references to possession of the servitude by any person in possession of the relative dominant tenement. By section 15(1) possession includes civil possession, *i.e.* by a tenant or employee.[99] A positive servitude can be said to be "possessed" if the occupier of the dominant tenement actually exercises the right which he has by right of servitude over the neighbouring tenement. Thus a servitude of way is possessed by going along the way, a servitude of fuel, feal and divot by actually cutting peat and turf and removing it. The possession

---

[93] *e.g. Bowman Ballantine* (1883) 10 R. 1061; *Macgregor v. Balfour* (1899) 2 F. 345.

[94] *Baird v. Feuars of Kilsyth* (1878) 6 R. 116; *Robertson's Trs. v. Bruce* (1905) 7 F. 580.

[95] *Murray v. Peddie* (1880) 7 R. 804; *Rome v. Hope Johnstone* (1884) 11 R. 653; *Winans v. Lord Tweedmouth* (1888)15 R. 540; *North British Ry. v. Park Yard Co.* (1898) 25 R. (H.L.) 47; *Kinross-shire C.C. v. Archibald* (1899) 7 S.L.T. 305; *Allan v. MacLachlan* (1900) 7 S.L.T. 427; *McTavish's Trs. v. Anderson* (1900) 8 S.L.T. 80; *Metcalfe v. Purdon* (1902) 4 F. 507.

[96] Bell, *Prin.*, §§ 979 *et seq.* A negative servitude is incapable of possession and cannot be acquired by prescription but only by express grant or agreement: Ersk., II, 9, 35; Bell, *Prin.*, § 994; Rankine, *Landownership* (4th ed.), 426; *Anderson v. Robertson,* 1958 S.C. 367 at p. 376.

[97] Stair, II, 7, 5 *et seq.*; Ersk., II, 9, 1 *et seq.*; Bell, *Prin.*, §§ 991 *et seq.*

[98] *Fearnan Partnership v. Grindlay,* 1992 S.L.T. 460; 1990 S.L.T. 704.

[99] *cf. Drummond v. Milligan* (1890) 17 R. 316.

must be exercised sufficiently often to make it plain that the right is being claimed and exercised.

In instructing a right of servitude the owner of the alleged dominant tenement is entitled to found on the exercise of the right by any one who has been, in fact, in possession of the praedium.[1]

If there is no evidence of "possession" this is a fact relevant to the counter-plea that, by section 7, the servitude has been extinguished by 20 years' disuse.

"for a continuous period of twenty years"

For the period of possession or exercise of the servitude right to be "continuous" it need not have been exercised every day or every week, but periodically and reasonably regularly, the number of occasions of exercise required to amount to "continuous" possession being a matter for the court. Particular importance attaches to instances of exercise shortly after the creation of the servitude right and to instances of exercise shortly before the expiry of the prescriptive period.

"openly, peaceably and without any judicial interruption"

For a servitude to be possessed openly the right must have been exercised in daylight and at normal hours, not stealthily or by dead of night.

For it to be possessed peaceably the right must have been exercised without threats, force, or show of force. Possession which involves forcing gates or breaking down fences is not peaceable possession.[2]

As regards "judicial interruption," see p. 22.

"and (b) the possession was founded on, and followed the execution of, a deed"

The possession or exercise of an alleged servitude must be "founded on" a deed, and must therefore be such as can reasonably be contended to have been granted by the deed invoked. Possession of a right of way cannot be "founded on" a grant of a right of pasturage.

The granter must have had power to grant a servitude right; a power to sell includes a power to create a servitude.[3]

The possession must also have followed the execution of the deed founded on, so that no possession or use prior to the date of execution can be relied on. The deed need not have been recorded,[4] though it may have been; in either case the terminus a quo of the prescriptive period is the date of execution.

If possession and use are established the nature and extent of the possession and use will determine the nature and extent of the servitude right; thus if use of a servitude road by carts is proved the decree will be

---

[1] *Drummond v. Milligan* (1890) 17 R. 316; *Maitland v. Lees* (1899) 6 S.L.T. 296.
[2] *cf. Strathclyde (Hyndland) Housing Society Ltd v. Cowie,* 1983 S.L.T. (Sh. Ct.) 61; *Cowie v. Strathclyde R.C.,* 1985 S.L.T. 333.
[3] *Bowman Ballantine* (1883) 10 R. 1061.
[4] *e.g. North British Ry. v. Park Yard Co.* (1898) 25 R. (H.L.) 47.

that the pursuer had a right to the road for the passage of carts[5]; if use of a close or passage from the High Street, at its narrowest point more than six feet wide, from time immemorial, be established, the party in right of the right of access is entitled to have it undiminished in width.[6]

But prescriptive possession cannot convert a servitude right into a right of property.[7]

"a deed which is sufficient in respect of its terms (whether expressly or by implication) to constitute the servitude"

Whether a particular deed is sufficient in respect of its terms to constitute a particular positive servitude over land consistent with the kind of right possessed by the party in right of the dominant tenement is a question of interpretation.[8] It may evidence a merely personal obligation. It has been held that the terms of a feu contract might be explained by the subsequent actings of parties to it.[9]

The sufficiency of the terms to constitute a servitude may appear expressly, as where the deed in terms grants or reserves a servitude right, or by implication, as where the terms of the deed together with the whole circumstances of the case indicate that it was intended to grant or reserve a servitude, as where a proprietor dispones land separated from the only public road by land retained by him, or dispones the land separating land retained by him from the only public road, in which cases he impliedly grants in the first case and impliedly reserves in the second a servitude right of way for access over the land adjacent to the public road if such be necessary.[10]

It has been held that an effectual servitude of passage has been constituted though the position and width of the stipulated access were not defined in the deed.[11]

By section 5(1) "deed" includes a judicial decree.

"then, as from the expiration of the said period, the validity of the servitude as so constituted shall be exempt from challenge"

The said period is 20 years and the expiration falls at midnight on the same date and month as the deed granting the servitude right was executed, 20 years later. By section 14(1) time occurring before the commencement of this Part of the Act is reckonable in like manner as time occurring thereafter, provided it is less than the total prescriptive period.

The effect of the complete running of the prescriptive period is that the validity of the servitude, as constituted by that deed, is exempt from challenge. But the servitude is not exempt from challenge if claimed or being exercised in a way other than or going beyond that constituted by

---

[5] *Malcolm v. Lloyd* (1886) 13 R. 512.

[6] *Grigor v. McLean* (1896) 24 R. 86; *cf Boyd v. Hamilton*, 1907 S.C. 912.

[7] *Robertson's Trs. v. Bruce* (1905) 7 F. 580 at p. 588.

[8] *North British Ry. v. Park Yard Co.* (1898) 25 R. (H.L.) 47.

[9] *Boyd v. Hamilton*, 1907 S.C. 912.

[10] *cf. Walton Bros. v. Glasgow Mags.* (1876) 3 R. 1130; *Union Heritable Securities Co. v. Mathie* (1886) 13 R. 670. But see *Gow's Trs. v. Mealls* (1875) 2 R. 729; *McLaren v. Glasgow Union Ry.* (1878) 5 R. 1042; *Campbell v. Halkett* (1890) 27 S.L.R. 1000; *Cullens v. Cambusbarron Co-operative Society.* (1895) 23 R. 209; *Shearer v. Peddie* (1899) 1 F. 1201; *Menzies v. Marquis of Breadalbane* (1901) 4 F. 59.

[11] *Cooper & McLeod v. Edinburgh Improvement Trs.* (1876) 3 R. 1106.

that deed. Thus if a servitude of way for pedestrians is granted by deed the owner of the dominant tenement cannot have a claimed servitude of way for vehicles rendered unchallengeable by 20 years' possession, because that is not the servitude "as so constituted." Moreover the words "as so constituted" mean that the servitude right once constituted is not to be modified or diminished; thus an access may not be diminished in breadth.[12]

"except on the ground that the deed is invalid ex facie *or was forged"*

This repeats the exceptions contained in sections 1(1) and 2(1). For comment, see pp. 33–35.

SECTION 3(2)—POSITIVE SERVITUDE ACQUIRED BY PRESCRIPTIVE USE

"If a positive servitude over land has been possessed…"

This subsection deals with the constitution of a positive servitude, though not granted expressly or impliedly by deed, by open, peaceable and uninterrupted possession thereof for 20 years.[13]

For verbal comments, see p. 40.

A claim fails where the evidence indicates that the use of the land was by tolerance rather than as a matter of right. Thus vehicular access over a track past a farm steading to beats for salmon fishing did not go to establish a servitude of way where the defenders had exercised control of the track by a padlocked gate, though allowing the pursuers keys of the padlock.[14]

In respect of "possession" there is "a practical distinction between the prescriptive possession which establishes a new and adverse right to the possessor, and the prescriptive possession which the law admits, for the purpose of construing or explaining, in a question with its author, the limits of an antecedent grant or conveyance. In the first case the rule obtains *tantum prescriptum quantum possessum.* In the second, it appears to me that a much more liberal effect has been given to partial acts of possession as evidencing proprietary possession of the whole, in cases where the subject of controversy has been in itself a distinct and definite tenement."[15] Where accordingly, as under the present subsection, the issue is of establishing a servitude right, evidence of possession, if adequate to constitute the right at all, also evidences and limits the nature and extent of the right, the right is no other and no more than is evidenced by the acts of possession proved. Thus to use a channel *in alieno solo* to carry away waste water is one thing, to use it to carry away closet sewage is quite another thing.[16]

---

[12] *Grigor v. MacLean* (1896) 24 R. 86. *cf. Mackenzie v. Carrick* (1868) 7 M. 419; *Bennett v. Playfair* (1877) 4 R. 321; *Shiel v. Young* (1895) 3 S.L.T. 171.

[13] *cf.* Bell, *Prin.,* § 993.

[14] *Middletweed v. Murray,* 1989 S.L.T. 11, approved in *Drury v. McGarvie,* 1993 S.L.T. 987.

[15] *Lord Advocate v. Wemyss* (1899) 2 F.(H.L.) 1 at p. 9, *per* Lord Watson, applied in *Kerr v. Brown,* 1939 S.C. 140, 147.

[16] *Kerr, supra,* 148.

"for a continuous period of twenty years"

It is not necessary to prove user for every year, and the further back the inquiry goes the less evidence there is likely to be.[17] But if the use is regular and uninterrupted, a jury, or a judge sitting as a jury, may presume that the possession has been continuous.[18]

In one case, decided when the prescriptive period was 40 years, it was held that though proof of user for 38 years did not warrant the presumption that the user had existed for longer, it did warrant the court in more readily inferring from user prior to the 38 years the existence of a user continuous with the later user which had been satisfactorily established.[18]

Accordingly if for the early part of the prescriptive period possession cannot be proved, it may be presumed if there is reasonable evidence of possession prior to the prescriptive period even though not continuous therewith, provided always that the gap is "not so formidable, either from length of time or from conspicuousness of successful interruption, as to affect your judgment of the quality of the earlier evidence."[19] The requisites of continuous and uninterrupted user desiderated in older cases are one and the same, viewed from different angles, and continuous user is one of which there has been no effective interruption.[20]

"openly, peaceably and without judicial interruption"

"It remains for the Court to say if it is satisfied that there has been continuous possession for the required period, not by stealth, nor by violence, nor by leave asked and given, but of right, which is to be inferred from simple user *nec clam nec vi nec precario*."[21]

When a mountain path which formed a short cut from one part of an estate to another through a projecting part of adjoining property was used from 1841 as a means of access during the deerstalking season, and it was not proved that this use of the path had come to the knowledge of the proprietor of the adjoining estate save on two occasions, in 1857 and 1882, and on both occasions it was challenged by him, it was held that the proved use of the path was not sufficient to establish a servitude right.[22] The use had not been "openly" and possibly not "peaceably" asserted. "In order to found a prescriptive right of servitude according to Scots law, acts of possession must be overt, in the sense that they must in themselves be of such a character or be done in such circumstances as to indicate unequivocally to the proprietor of the servient tenement the fact that a right is asserted, and the nature of the right. The proprietor who seeks to establish the right cannot in my opinion avail himself of any acts of possession *in alieno solo*, unless he is able to shew that they either were known, or ought

---

[17] *McGregor v. Crieff Co-operative Society*, 1915 S.C. (H.L.) 93 at p. 98. See also *Harvie v. Rodgers* (1828) 3 W. & S. 251; *Young v. Cuthbertson* (1854) 1 Macq. 455; *Douglas v. Hozier* (1878) 16 S.L.R. 14; *Mann v. Brodie* (1884) 12 R. (H.L.) 52.

[18] *McGregor, supra*, 102.

[19] *McGregor, supra*, 103.

[20] *Stevenson v. Donaldson*, 1935 S.C. 551 at p. 554.

[21] *McGregor, supra*, 98.

[22] *McInroy v. Duke of Atholl* (1891)18 R. (H.L.) 46.

to have been known to its owner or to the persons to whom he intrusted the charge of his property."[23]

The essence of interruption is an act or acts done by the servient owner that amount to an assertion of exclusive right, that is, acts that are a challenge to the prescriber's assertion of servitude. Thus acts done by the tenant of the servient owner against whom the user is being asserted, the effect of which is to interfere temporarily with the possession of the prescriber, do not prove interruption, unless the acts are done with the knowledge and consent of the servient owner in circumstances which show that they are a challenge of the prescriber's assertion of right.[24]

If there has been non-judicial interruption by actual attempt to stop the possession of the right asserted, as by putting a gate across an alleged access, the assertion of the right in face thereof cannot be described as "peaceable."

As to judicial interruption, see p. 22.

"then, as from the expiration of that period"

This states the date from which the running of time is effective to render the servitude unchallengeable. By section 14(1) time occurring before the commencement of this Part of the Act is reckonable in like manner as time occurring thereafter, provided it is less than the total prescriptive period.

"the existence of the servitude as so possessed shall be exempt from challenge"

The effect of the running of the full 20-year prescriptive period is that the servitude right is thereafter established and exempt from challenge. The right thus secured is "the servitude as so possessed," that is, as possessed for 20 years, and no other or greater right than that exercised is secured by prescription. This seems to indicate that prescriptive use defines not only the *existence* of the right but the *extent* of the right, and this is in accordance with older authorities. A more extensive right includes a less extensive use.[25] But prescriptive use does not limit the purposes to be served by the traffic. Hence if a servitude right, such as of access by carts, has been acquired by prescription the purposes for which it has been used, such as agricultural or market garden purposes, do not limit the use to these purposes, save in cases where there is some special feature attaching to the terminus to which the way leads, such as to a mill, a kirk or a peat moss.[25]

SECTION 3(3)—PUBLIC RIGHT OF WAY ACQUIRED BY PRESCRIPTIVE USE

"If a public right of way"

A public right of way is a path, track or road, across land owned by a private person and not held in trust for the public, regularly used by members of the general public as a matter of right, as a way from one determinate point to another.[26] It is a right of passage only, not of property.[27] The

---

[23] *McInroy v. Duke of Atholl* (1891) 18 R. (H.L.) 46 at p. 48, *per* Lord Watson, followed in *Kerr v. Brown,* 1939 S.C. 140.
[24] *Stevenson v. Donaldson,* 1936 S.C. 551 at p. 554.
[25] *Carstairs v. Spence,* 1924 S.C. 380 at p. 385.
[26] On its nature see Stair, II, 7, 10; *Galbreath v. Armour* (1845) 4 Bell 374.
[27] *Sutherland v. Thomson* (1876) 3 R. 485.

constitution of a public right of way does not depend on implied grant but on the fact of user by the public as a matter of right for the requisite period.[28] To be a public right of way there must be a distinct path, track or road, and it must have been used as a matter of public right, not by tolerance only.[29] A public right of way cannot be acquired by user over lands held by a railway company for railway purposes[30] though it can be acquired over land held by a statutory body for statutory purposes if it is not inconsistent with those purposes.[31]

A path or road alleged to be a public right of way must lead from one determinate public place, "a place to which the public resort for some definite and intelligible purpose,"[32] to another.[33] The places must be capable of simple definition, such as a harbour,[34] a public road.[35] A rock on the seashore frequented by members of the public cannot be a terminus of an alleged right of way.[36] It may comprise in whole or in part the line of an artificial structure, such as an elevated walkway.[37]

"A right of footpath cannot emerge in law from a mere practice of sauntering.... In order to make use the foundation of a right of way, it must be use along a definite line, in the assertion of a definite right. The privilege of wandering upon the face of an unenclosed hill, though it be for half a century, will not confer a right of way. But if there has been for the prescriptive period a walking along a definite line from one public place to another, in the assertion of a right to use that line, that may make the foundation of a right of way...."[38]

In determining whether a public right of way exists something depends on the nature of the road, and the kind of uses allowed to be made of it. It would be more difficult to suppose that a man was tolerating people driving carts and carriages upon his private road, than to suppose that he was allowing them to walk on it.[39] But the mere fact that a landowner has made a road on his private property for his own private purposes does not prevent a public right from being established.

"has been possessed by the public"

The constitution of a public right of way does not depend on implied grant but on the fact of user by the public as a matter of right for the requisite period.[40] The use is not, as in the case of a servitude of way, by the owner of a dominant tenement, but by members of the public.

---

[28] *Mann v. Brodie* (1885) 12 R. (H.L.) 52 at p. 57; *Kinross-shire C.C. v. Archibald* (1899) 7 S.L.T. 305.
[29] *Mackintosh v. Moir* (1871) 9 M. 574.
[30] *Edinburgh Mags. v. North British Ry.* (1904) 6 F. 620.
[31] *Kinross-shire C. C., supra.*
[32] *Duncan v. Lees* (1871) 9 M. 855.
[33] *Rodgers v. Harvie* (1826) 4 Murr. 25; 5 S. 917; 7 S. 287; 8 S. 611; *Burt v. Barclay* (1861) 24 D. 218; *Winans v. Lord Tweedmouth* (1888) 15 R. 540; *Rhins District Committee. v. Cuninghame,* 1917 2 S.L.T. 169; *Norrie v. Kirriemuir Mags.,* 1945 S.C. 302.
[34] *Moncreiffe v. Perth Harbour Trs.* (1842) 5 D. 298; *Duncan v. Lees* (1871) 9 M. 855.
[35] *Jenkins v. Murray* (1866) 4 M. 1046.
[36] *Duncan v. Lees* (1870) 9 M. 274.
[37] *Cumbernauld and Kilsyth D.C. v. Dollar Land (Cumbernauld),* 1992 S.L.T. 1035.
[38] *Mackintosh v. Moir* (1871) 9 M. 574 at pp. 578–579, *per* Lord Ardmillan.
[39] *Jenkins v. Murray* (1866) 4 M. 1046 at p. 1054, *per* Lord Deas.
[40] *Kinross-shire C.C. v. Archibald* (1899) 7 S.L.T. 305.

A right of way is "possessed by the public" if various members of the general public have actually passed along it and used it with fair regularity. "Public user is a fact which must be inferred from overt acts of possession, and defective evidence of user cannot be strengthened by proof of the motives which induced individuals to abstain from acts of that kind."[41] "The question is rather whether, having regard to the sparseness or density of the population, the user over the prescriptive period was in degree and quality such as might have been expected if the road had been an undisputed right of way. "[42] The test of use is objective and is whether the volume and character of use showed that the persons using it acted as if free to use the route without permission and without interference so as to alert the proprietor, conscious of the use, to the fact that it was inconsistent with his right to exclusive possession.[43]

"The user must be of the whole road, as a means of passage from the one terminus to the other, and must not be such user as can be reasonably ascribed either to private servitude rights or to the licence of the proprietor. Then, as regards the amount of user, that must just be such as might have been reasonably expected if the road in dispute had been an undoubted public highway. "[44]

Use by employees or friends of the proprietor, or persons visiting or seeking to do business with him, is not use or possession by the public; it is by the implied licence or even implied invitation of the proprietor. Thus use of the drive leading up to a hotel is not possession by the public. Nor is it possessed "by the public" if the only use is consistent with a servitude right of way enjoyed by the inhabitants of a dominant tenement of land.

The use by the public must have been as a matter of legal right, not by tolerance by the proprietors,[45] still less use in defiance of notices, fences or obstructions, or use asserted by pulling down gates or fences.[46] The notice "Trespassers Will Be Prosecuted" may be a vain threat but at least evidences non-toleration of any liberty of passage. Use of a way or track by the tolerance of the landowner can never ripen into right of way by prescription, because it is use by tolerance not in assertion of a right, and a landowner can always defeat a claim of public right of way by frankly permitting use by the public sometimes.

Public use may begin by the toleration of the landowner and later become a public right of way by prescription but in this case it is essential to establish when tolerance ceased and assertion of right began. In such a case there is no room for application of the principle of immemorial possession.

It is sufficient to prove use by the general public for a particular purpose and for it alone, provided it be definite and intelligible,[47] save that the purpose may not be for wandering about, picnicking, recreation or games.

---

[41] *Mann v. Brodie* (1885) 12 R. (H.L.) 52 at p. 58, *per* Lord Watson.
[42] *Marquis of Bute v. McKirdy & McMillan,* 1937 S.C. 93 at p. 119, *per* L.P. Normand.
[43] *Cumbernauld and Kilsyth D.C. v. Dollar Land (Cumbernauld),* 1991 S.L.T. 806; 1992 S.L.T. 1035; 1993 S.L.T. 1318 (H.L.).
[44] *Mann v. Brodie* (1885) 12 R. (H.L.) 52 at p. 58, *per* Lord Watson.
[45] *Napier's Trs. v. Morrison* (1851) 13 D. 1404; *Winans v. Lord Tweedmouth* (1888) 15 R. 540; *Macpherson v. Scottish Rights of Way Society* (1888) 15 R. (H.L.) 68.
[46] *Harvey v. Lindsey* (1853) 15 D. 768.
[47] *Geils v. Thompson* (1872) 10 M. 327.

The right is one of *way* or passage, not of occupation as if it were a public park.[48]

The public right need not be exercised from end to end of the way, but may be over any portion of it.[49]

In deciding the sufficiency of public possession factors which may be taken into account include whether the way alleged is a short-cut or is no shorter than by public road,[50] whether it is a through road or a *cul-de-sac*,[51] whether the track is crossed by fences and whether these have stiles or gates.[52]

Public user has been held not established where it was proved that frequently a door in the passage in question had been locked,[53] or it was admitted that the use by the public had always been restricted to about four days in the week.[54]

"for a continuous period of twenty years"

The prescriptive period is now 20 years only.[55] It runs from the first adequately proven instance of use by members of the public as of right.

The period of 20 years need not have been immediately preceding the action in which the right is in issue but a substantial period of exclusion of the public immediately preceding the action may rebut any presumption that user prior to the earliest proven user as of right had been of the same character.[56]

Evidence of use for a period shorter than the full prescriptive period will not suffice to establish the right, unless the use raises a presumption of prior use of the same character for the requisite period, and this presumption does not arise where the road over which the right was alleged had been private and the public use had commenced in tolerance.[57] Where a substitute or deviation road is provided in lieu of a previous public right of way, the full prescriptive period need not be proved to create a right in the substituted road if it is proved that there has been such use of the new road by the public as amounts to acquiescence by them in the shutting up of the old road and acceptance of the new one.[58]

"openly, peaceably and without judicial interruption"

The use made by the general public must be made openly, in daylight and at various ordinary times of the day. Possession by dead of night, or only on occasions when users were not likely to be observed or warned off is not "open." "Peaceably" involves that use of the alleged right of way is not made by force or show of force or by threats.

---

[48] *Dyce v. Hay* (1852) 1 Macq. 305; *Harvey v. Lindsey* (1853) 15 D. 768; *Burt v. Barclay* (1861) 24 D. 218.
[49] *McRobert v. Reid*, 1914 S.C. 633.
[50] *Rodgers v. Harvie* (1826) 4 Murr. 25; *Jenkins v. Murray* (1866) 4 M. 1046.
[51] *Cuthbertson v. Young* (1853) 1 Macq. 455.
[52] *Hay v. Morton's Trs.* (1861) 24 D. 116; *Sutherland v. Thomson* (1876) 3 R. 485.
[53] *Wallace v. Dundee Police Commissioners* (1875) 2 R. 565.
[54] *Ayr Burgh Council v. British Transport Commission*, 1955 S.L.T. 219.
[55] *cf. Richardson v. Cromarty Petroleum Co.*, 1982 S.L.T. 237.
[56] *Mann v. Brodie* (1885) 12 R. (H.L.) 52.
[57] *Edinburgh Mags. v. North British Ry.* (1904) 6 F. 620; *Mann v. Brodie, supra.*
[58] *Hozier v. Hawthorne* (1884) 11 R. 766; *Cadell v. Stevenson* (1900) 8 S.L.T. 8; *Kinloch's Trs. v. Young*, 1911 S.C. (H.L.) 1.

Non-judicial interruption, as by ploughing part of the ground traversed or erecting a fence across it is not sufficient to interrupt the prescriptive period if use can be and still is made of the way, but if the fence or other obstruction be such that it has to be overcome forcibly, possession is not being made of the right of way "peaceably."

It has been held that there is no material difference between the common law test of "use as of right" and this statutory test.[59]

On what is "judicial interruption," see p. 22.

"then, as from the expiration of that period"

The period is 20 years which runs from the time when members of the general public are proved first to have exercised and possessed the right of way. The period need not have been up to a date immediately prior to the action in which the right of way is asserted, provided that nothing after the expiry of the prescriptive period has raised a doubt about the existence of the right of way or amounted to its abandonment.[60]

By section 14(1)(*a*) time occurring before and time occurring after the commencement of Part I of the 1973 Act[61] are both reckonable towards the prescriptive period but any time reckoned under this paragraph shall be less than the prescriptive period, *i.e.* at least one day of the prescriptive period must be after the commencement of Part I.

Thus proven use 1957–1977 will establish a right of way, notwithstanding no evidence of use after 1977.

"the existence of the right of way as so possessed shall be exempt from challenge"

The effect of the running of 20 years complete is that the public right of way is established by prescription and exempt from challenge thereafter. "The effect of prescription… is not to constitute the right of the possessor, but to fortify it against all future challenge."[62] What is established is the right of way "as so possessed," that is as proved to have been possessed and used by members of the general public and not any diversion from or variant of the right of way proved, subject always to the principle that a substituted way will be deemed the same way as that superseded.[63]

EFFECT OF MINORITY OR LEGAL DISABILITY ON POSITIVE PRESCRIPTION

The Prescription Act 1617 provided that in the course of the 40 years prescription the years of minority should not be counted.[64]

By section 14(1)(*b*) of the 1973 Act any time during which any person against whom any provision of Part I of the 1973 Act is pled was under

---

[59] *Strathclyde (Hyndland) Housing Society v. Cowie,* 1983 S.L.T. (Sh. Ct.) 61.

[60] *cf. Mann v. Brodie* (1885) 12 R. (H.L.) 52 (public use 1820–1846; public excluded 1846–1883).

[61] July 25, 1976.

[62] *Mann v. Brodie* (1885) 12 R. (H.L.) 52 at p. 57, *per* Lord Watson.

[63] *Hozier v. Hawthorne* (1884) 11 R. 766; *Cadell v. Stevenson* (1900) 8 S.L.T. 8; *Kinloch's Trs. v. Young,* 1911 S.C. (H.L.) 1.

[64] Stair, II, 12, 18; Mack., II, 12, 15; Ersk., III, 7, 35; *Blair v. Sheddan* (1754) Mor. 11156; *Mackay and Fullerton v. Dalrymple* (1798) Mor. 11171.

legal disability (defined by section 15(1) as "legal disability by reason of nonage or unsoundness of mind") shall be reckoned as if the person were free from that disability. No extension of the prescriptive period falls to be made because the defender in the claim was under legal disability as defined.

CROWN RIGHTS

By section 24 thereof the 1973 Act binds the Crown. Rights may certainly be acquired against the Crown by prescription.[65] Under the previous law prescription might run in favour of the Crown[66] and there is no reason to suppose that this has been changed by the 1973 Act.

LAND REGISTRATION

Registration of an interest in the Land Register of Scotland will supersede the recording of a deed in the Register of Sasines but is without prejudice to any other means of creating or affecting real rights or obligations. But lessees under long leases, proprietors under udal tenure and kindly tenants will obtain real rights only by registration.[67]

DECENNALIS ET TRIENNALIS POSSESSIO

An old Scottish common law rule akin to a positive prescription is the *decennalis et triennalis possessio* which gives a clergyman a presumptive though temporary right to subjects included in his benefice if there has been 13 years' actual or constructive possession of them.[68] Substantially continuous possession down to the raising of the action is required. As possession for 10 years confers an absolute title this presumption would appear to have utility only if there is no title on which positive prescription can operate. It is not affected by the 1973 Act.

---

[65] *e.g. Wemyss' Trs. v. Lord Advocate* (1896) 24 R. 216.
[66] *Cheape v. Lord Advocate* (1871) 9 M. 377.
[67] Land Registration (Scotland) Act 1979, s. 3.
[68] Stair, II, 1, 25; II, 8, 29; Ersk., III, 7, 33.

CHAPTER 3

SHORT NEGATIVE PRESCRIPTION

IT has been pointed out that various older statutes established various prescriptions which operated after shorter periods than that of the long negative prescription of 40, reduced in 1924 to 20, years. Of these older prescriptions, the triennial, quinquennial, sexennial and vicennial prescriptions did not extinguish the obligations to which they severally applied but merely, after the lapse of their respective periods, reversed the onus of proof and required that proof to be given by writ or oath only. The septennial prescription of cautionary obligations, however, wholly extinguished the cautioner's liability.

Not the least of the difficulties caused by the older statutes, particularly those regulating the triennial and quinquennial prescriptions, were the problems of interpreting the phrases which determined the application of those statutes, which gave rise to a large volume of case-law, and the anomalies produced by decisions that certain kinds of transactions were within and others outwith the scope of one or other of the short prescriptions.

THE MODERN LAW

The 1973 Act repealed,[1] with effect from July 25, 1976,[2] the triennial,[3] quinquennial,[4] sexennial,[5] and vicennial[6] prescriptions. Transitional provision is made for cases affected by any one of these provisions prior to that date by section 16(3); it provides:

(3)[7] Where by virtue of any Act repealed by this section the subsistence of an obligation in force at the date of the commencement of this Part of this Act was immediately before that date, by reason of the passage of time, provable only by the writ or oath of the debtor the subsistence of the obligation shall (notwithstanding anything in sections 16(1) and 17(2)(a) of the Interpretation Act 1978, which relates to the effect of repeals) as from that date be provable as if the said repealed Act had not passed.

The effect of this provision is that where on July 25, 1976, an obligation had been affected by one of these prescription statutes and was provable only by the writ or oath of the debtor it is thereafter to be provable *prout de jure*. How long the obligation continues to subsist depends on sections 6 and 7 of the 1973 Act.

The 1973 Act also repealed the septennial prescription of cautionary obligations[8] with effect from July 25, 1976.

---

[1] 1973 Act, s. 16(2).
[2] 1973 Act, s. 25(2)(b).
[3] Prescription Act 1579, c. 21.
[4] Prescription Act 1669, c. 14.
[5] Bills of Exchange (Scotland) Act 1772.
[6] Prescription Act 1669, c. 14.
[7] As amended by the Interpretation Act 1978, s. 25(2).
[8] Cautioners Act 1695, c. 7.

The New Short Negative Prescription

In place of the provisions of the Acts which regulated the triennial, quinquennial, sexennial and vicennial prescriptions, and the septennial prescription of cautionary obligations, the 1973 Act, by section 6, substituted a new negative prescription of five years. Section 6 enacts, in substance, that if an "obligation" of defined kinds has subsisted for five years continuously and in that time the creditor has neither made a claim for payment nor has the debtor acknowledged the debt, it is then extinguished. It has to be noted (a) that the new provision is a uniform one of five years in place of the various periods under the repealed Acts; (b) that the new provision does not merely alter the onus and mode of proof, but extinguishes the obligation entirely; and (c) that it applies not to the particular categories of obligations affected by one or other of the repealed provisions, but to much broader categories of obligations defined in Schedule 1.

"Obligations," "Rights" and Their Correlatives

The word "obligation" is properly used of a legal relationship creating *juris vinculum*, a legal bond, between two parties which imports mutual rights and duties; a legal relationship productive of obligation may be created by contract, commission of a delict, circumstances inferring liability to make restitution or recompense and in other ways. But the term "obligation" is also used as a synonym for "duty," for the side of the legal relationship on which the party is obliged, or bound, or under a duty, to do or pay.

By section 15(2), in Part I of the Act, "unless the context otherwise requires, any reference to an obligation or to a right includes a reference to the right or, as the case may be, to the obligation (if any) correlative thereto." This definition appears to refer to the analysis of the concept of a "right" developed by Hohfeld[9] in which he brought out that the word "right" and its related terms, privilege, power and immunity, all connoting legal advantages, have correlatives, usually designated duty, no-right, liability and disability, all connoting legal disadvantages. The correlative relationship imports that the presence of any one concept in one person to a legal relationship implies the presence of the correlative concept in the other person to the legal relationship. Thus in the buyer-seller relationship the right to delivery has as its correlative the duty to deliver; in the wrongdoer-victim relationship the duty to make reparation has as its correlative the right to obtain reparation. In the teacher-pupil relationship the power of the teacher to impose detention has as its correlative the liability of the pupil to suffer detention, and so on.

The questions which may arise in a case of an obligation affected by the short negative prescription are:
1. whether the claim is one to which section 6 is applicable (Schedule 1);
2. if so, from what date does the prescriptive period run (Schedule 2 and section 11);

---

[9] "Fundamental Legal Conceptions" (1913) 23 Yale L.J. 16; (1917) 26 Yale L.J. 710, reprinted in book form, edited by W. W. Cook, in 1923.

3. whether the prescriptive period has run continuously (section 14);
4. whether both of the conditions for the extinction of the obligation (section 6(1) (*a*) and (*b*), and sections 9 and 10) have been satisfied;
5. whether any periods have to be excluded from computation of the prescriptive period (section 6(3) and (5).

A positive answer to either of questions (4) or (5) implies a negative answer to question (3), and conversely.

Section 6 enacts:

Extinction of obligations by prescriptive periods of five years

6.—(1) If, after the appropriate date, an obligation to which this section applies has subsisted for a continuous period of five years—

(*a*)   without any relevant claim having been made in relation to the obligation, and

(*b*)   without the subsistence of the obligation having been relevantly acknowledged,

then as from the expiration of that period the obligation shall be extinguished:

Provided that in its application to an obligation under a bill of exchange or a promissory note this subsection shall have effect as if paragraph (*b*) thereof were omitted.

(2) Schedule 1 to this Act shall have effect for defining the obligations to which this section applies.

(3) In subsection (1) above the reference to the appropriate date, in relation to an obligation of any kind specified in Schedule 2 to this Act is a reference to the date specified in that Schedule in relation to obligations of that kind, and in relation to an obligation of any other kind is a reference to the date when the obligation became enforceable.

(4) In the computation of a prescriptive period in relation to any obligation for the purposes of this section—

(*a*)   any period during which by reason of—

(i) fraud on the part of the debtor or any person acting on his behalf, or

(ii) error induced by words or conduct of the debtor or any person acting on his behalf,

the creditor was induced to refrain from making a relevant claim in relation to the obligation, and

(*b*)   any period during which the original creditor (while he is the creditor) was under legal disability,

shall not be reckoned as, or as part of, the prescriptive period:

Provided that any period such as is mentioned in paragraph (*a*) of this subsection shall not include any time occurring after the creditor could with reasonable diligence have discovered the fraud or error, as the case may be, referred to in that paragraph.

(5) Any period such as is mentioned in paragraph (*a*) or (*b*) of subsection (4) of this section shall not be regarded as separating the time immediately before it from the time immediately after it.

Interpretation

Section 15, assigning meanings to certain terms used in Part I of the 1973 Act, applies to section 6. For section 15, see pp. 14–15.

VERBAL COMMENTARY ON SECTION 6

Obligations to which short negative prescription applies

"If... an obligation to which this section applies"

By section 6(2), Schedule 1 to the Act has effect to define the obligations to which the section applies.

Schedule 1 provides:

Section 6 SCHEDULE 1

Obligations Affected by Prescriptive Periods of Five Years Under Section 6

1. Subject to paragraph 2 below, section 6 of this Act applies—
   (*a*) to any obligation to pay a sum of money due in respect of a particular period—
   (i) by way of interest;
   (ii) by way of an instalment of an annuity;
   (iii) by way of feuduty or other periodical payment under a feu grant;
   (iv) by way of ground annual or other periodical payment under a contract of ground annual;
   (v) by way of rent or other periodical payment under a lease;
   (vi) by way of a periodical payment in respect of the occupancy or use of land, not being an obligation falling within any other provision of this sub-paragraph;
   (vii) by way of a periodical payment under a land obligation, not being an obligation falling within any other provision of this sub-paragraph;
   (*b*) to any obligation based on redress of unjustified enrichment, including without prejudice to that generality any obligation of restitution, repetition or recompense;
   (*c*) to any obligation arising from *negotiorum gestio*;
   (*d*) to any obligation arising from liability (whether arising from any enactment or from any rule of law) to make reparation;
   (*e*) to any obligation under a bill of exchange or a promissory note;
   (*f*) to any obligation of accounting, other than accounting for trust funds;
   (*g*) to any obligation arising from, or by reason of any breach of, a contract or promise, not being an obligation falling within any other provision of this paragraph.

2. Notwithstanding anything in the foregoing paragraph, section 6 of this Act does not apply—
   (*a*) to any obligation to recognise or obtemper a decree of court, an arbitration award or an order of a tribunal or authority exercising jurisdiction under any enactment;
   (*b*) to any obligation arising from the issue of a bank note;
   (*c*)[10] to any obligation constituted or evidenced by a probative writ, not being a cautionary obligation nor being an obligation falling within paragraph 1(*a*) of this Schedule;
   (*d*) to any obligation under a contract of partnership or of agency, not being an obligation remaining, or becoming, prestable on or after the termination of the relationship between the parties under the contract;
   (*e*) except as provided in paragraph 1(*a*) of this Schedule, to any obligation relating to land (including an obligation to recognise a servitude);
   (*f*) to any obligation to satisfy any claim to terce, courtesy, legitim, *jus relicti* or *jus relictae*, or to any prior right of a surviving spouse under section 8 or 9 of the Succession (Scotland) Act 1964;
   (*g*) to any obligation to make reparation in respect of personal injuries within the meaning of Part II of this Act or in respect of the death of any person as a result of such injuries;
   (*gg*)[11] to any obligation to make reparation or otherwise make good in respect of defamation within the meaning of section 18A of this Act;
   (*ggg*)[12] to any obligation arising from liability under section 2 of the Consumer Protection Act 1987 (to make reparation for damage caused wholly or partly by a defect in a product);

---

[10] Repealed with effect from August 1, 1995 by Requirements of Writing (Scotland) Act 1995, s. 14(2) and Sched. 5.

[11] Added with effect from December 30, 1985, by the Law Reform (Miscellaneous Provisions) (Scotland) Act 1985, s. 12(5).

[12] Added with effect from March 1, 1988, by the Consumer Protection Act 1987, Sched. 1, para. 12.

(*h*) to any obligation specified in Schedule 3 to this Act as an imprescriptible obligation.

3.[12a]—(1) Subject to sub-paragraph (2) below, where by virtue of a probative writ two or more persons (in this paragraph referred to as "the co-obligants") are bound jointly and severally by an obligation to pay money to another party the obligation shall, as respects the liability of each of the co-obligants, be regarded for the purposes of sub-paragraph (*c*) of the last foregoing paragraph as if it were a cautionary obligation.

(2) Nothing in the foregoing sub-paragraph shall affect any such obligation as respects the liability of any of the co-obligants with respect to whom the creditor establishes—

(*a*) that that co-obligant is truly a principal debtor, or

(*b*) if that co-obligant is not truly a principal debtor, that the original creditor was not aware of that fact at the time when the writ was delivered to him.

4.[13] In this Schedule—

(*a*) "land obligation" has the same meaning as it has for the purposes of the Conveyancing and Feudal Reform (Scotland) Act 1970;

(*b*) "probative writ" means a writ which is authenticated by attestation or in any such other manner as, in relation to writs of the particular class in question, may be provided by or under any enactment as having an effect equivalent to attestation.

VERBAL COMMENTARY ON SCHEDULE 1

Schedule 1 accordingly defines the kinds of obligations to which the five-year prescription does (para. 1) and does not (para. 2) apply.

Obligations affected by short negative prescription

By paragraph 1, section 6 applies—

(*a*) To any obligation to pay sums of money due in respect of particular periods by way of (i) interest; (ii) instalment of an annuity; (iii) feu-duty; (iv) ground annual; (v) rent; (vi) other periodical payment for the occupancy or use of land; or (vii) periodical payment under a land obligation within the meaning of the Conveyancing and Feudal Reform (Scotland) Act 1970. It does not extinguish the continuing relationship in any such case nor the continuing obligation to make payments as they become due but only the obligation to make payments for particular years, half-years, or other periods of payment. Thus if interest is allowed to fall into arrears the relationship of creditor and debtor is unaffected, as is the obligation to repay the capital and the interest, but as time goes on the obligation to pay each half-year's payment of interest is extinguished as soon as five years have elapsed from the time it was due. Thus if no interest is paid for seven years the earliest four half-yearly sums of interest must be treated as extinguished by prescription, but all later half-yearly sums are unaffected by prescription and remain exigible. Interest does not include interest on unpaid tax.[14] An obligation to pay wages due by the week prescribes week by week.[15]

(*b*) and (*c*) To any obligation based on redress of unjustified enrichment, including the obligations of restitution, repetition,[16] recompense and arising

---

[12a] Repealed with effect from August 1, 1995 by Requinements of Writing (Scotland) Act 1995, s. 14(2) and Sched. 5.

[13] *ibid.*

[14] *Lord Advocate v. Butt*, 1993 S.L.T. 10.

[15] *Reid v. Beaton*, 1995 S.C.L.R. 382.

[16] *cf. Campbell's Trs. v. Sinclair* (1878) 5 R. (H.L.) 119; *Edinburgh Magistrates v. Heriot's Trust* (1900) 7 S.L.T. 371.

from *negotiorum gestio*.[17] An obligation to make recompense was held to have become enforceable when the defenders were first enriched by making up and selling goods sold to them.[18] Section 6 does not expressly apply to the obligations to pay general average contribution or reward for salvage services. Historically, both of these obligations to pay are founded on the general maritime law, not the Roman law which is the basis of the general law of unjust enrichment, yet both fall within the general principle of obligations "based on redress of unjustified enrichment," and it is submitted that both obligations fall under paragraph 1(*b*).

(*d*) To any obligation arising from liability under statute or at common law to make reparation. "Reparation" involves damages for a wrongful act.[19] An action to have a local authority reinstate a shop has been held not to be one for "reparation" and accordingly not affected by prescription.[20] Nor is the obligation to pay statutory compensation under planning legislation a claim for "reparation".[21] This subparagraph accordingly covers most obligations arising *ex delicto* founded on breach of common law or statutory duty. By paragraph 2(*g*) there is excluded from the application of section 6 an obligation to make reparation for personal injuries or death, probably because such are subject to the limitation of time for suing contained in Part II of the Act.[22] But under this subparagraph section 6 applies to obligations to make reparation for all other kinds of breaches of duty, *e.g.* property damage, damage to self-esteem or reputation, and damage to economic interests.[23] This subparagraph will apply to, *inter alia*, actions of spuilzie formerly regulated by the Prescription (Ejections) Act 1579. It will also apply to obligations, such as under the Resale Prices Act 1976, s. 25, the Sex Discrimination Act 1975, s. 66, the Race Relations Act 1976, s. 57, and certain other statutes, which are statutorily made actionable as breaches of statutory duty. In view of subparagraph (*g*) below, liability to make reparation under this head does not extend to reparation for breach of contract.

(*e*) to any obligation under a bill of exchange or a promissory note, though by paragraph 2(*b*) section 6 does not apply to bank notes. Under this subparagraph the five-year extinctive prescription replaces the former sexennial prescription of bills of exchange under the Bills of Exchange (Scotland) Act 1772, ss. 37, 39 and 40.

(*f*) to any obligation of accounting, *e.g.* the duty of an agent to account to his principal, of a cashier to account to his employer but not the obligation of a taxpayer to account to the Inland Revenue.[24] This category will cover cases formerly falling under the decennial prescription of actions of accounting between pupils and minors and their tutors and curators, introduced by the Prescription Act 1696, c. 9. The obligation of accounting

---

[17] On these see generally Walker, *Principles of Scottish Private Law* (4th ed.), Chaps. 4.26–27.

[18] *N.V. Devos Gebroeder v. Sunderland Sportswear,* 1989 S.L.T. 382.

[19] *Hobday v. Kirkpatrick's Trs.,* 1985 S.L.T. 197 where held that objections to trust accounts were not directed to reparation but to restoring alienations to the estate.

[20] *Miller v. City of Glasgow D.C.,* 1989 S.L.T. 44.

[21] *Holt v. City of Dundee District Council,* 1990 S.L.T. (Lands Tr.) 30.

[22] Chap. 6, *infra.*

[23] *e.g. Dunlop v. McGowans,* 1980 S.C. (H.L.) 73.

[24] *Lord Advocate v. Hepburn,* 1990 S.L.T. 530; *Lord Advocate v. Butt,* 1991 S.L.T. 248.

for trust funds is, however, expressly excepted; most such cases are, by Schedule 3(*e*), imprescriptible.

(*g*) to any obligation arising from a contract or promise, *e.g.* to pay or do something,[25] or arising by reason of any breach of a contract or promise, *e.g.* to implement it, or to pay damages for breach of it, which in either case is not an obligation falling within any other provision of paragraph 1.[26] This subparagraph covers an obligation to refer a dispute or difference under a building contract to the contract engineer.[27] It applies to, *inter alia,* cautionary obligations, even where, as is normal, such an obligation is constituted by probative writing, (and accordingly under this subparagraph the five-year extinctive prescription replaces the former septennial prescription of cautionary obligations under the Cautioners Act 1695).[28] A probative performance bond has been held to be a cautionary obligation and not enforceable until an architect's certificate had been issued.[29]

This provision relates only to obligations constituted or evidenced by actings or oral expressions of will or improbative writings (including writings in *re mercatoria*). If, however, the obligation, whether it needs to be so constituted or evidenced or not, is constituted or evidenced by a probative writ (as defined in para. 4(*b*) of the Schedule) then, so long as it is not a cautionary obligation nor an obligation falling within paragraph 1(*a*) of the Schedule, section 6 does not, by reason of paragraph 2(*c*), apply and the obligation will not be extinguished by section 6 but only under the long negative prescription (s. 7).

Where sums are due under contract for services provided partly outwith and partly within the five years, the former are *prima facie* extinguished by prescription, unless it was made plain to the defender, from invoices tendered or otherwise, that the services were rendered on a continuing account, and not as distinct services on separate occasions.[30]

Paragraph 1 and section 6 relate primarily to issues of private right, but not exclusively so.[31]

Obligations not affected by short negative prescription

By paragraph 2, section 6 does not apply—

(*a*) to any obligation to recognise or obtemper a decree of court, arbitration award or order of a tribunal or authority exercising a statutory jurisdiction.

This subparagraph does not include orders of a domestic tribunal exercising a contractual jurisdiction, *e.g.* a club committee or a trade union disciplinary committee, or other non-statutory jurisdiction. Such orders might fall under paragraph 1(*g*), above, as being "obligations arising from ... a contract."

---

[25] *e.g.* an undertaking to create a real burden: *Pearson v. Malachi* (1892) 20 R. 167; the undertaking of a bank to pay money lodged on current account: *Macdonald v. North of Scotland Bank*, 1942 S.C. 369; a contractual right to acquire a real right to heritable subjects: *Macdonald v. Scott's Exrs.*, 1981 S.C. 75; a written undertaking to convey heritage without price, not implemented for 25 years: *Skinner v. Skinner*, 1953 S.L.T. (Notes) 83.

[26] *Riddick v. Shaughnessy, Quigley & McColl*, 1981 S.L.T. (Notes) 89.

[27] *Milne (Douglas) v. Borders R. C.*, 1990 S.L.T. 558.

[28] *Royal Bank v. Brown*, 1982 S.C. 89 at p. 92.

[29] *City of Glasgow D.C. v. Excess Insurance Co.*, 1986 S.L.T. 585; *City of Glasgow D.C. v. Excess Insurance Co.*, *(No. 2)* 1990 S.L.T. 225.

[30] *Robertson v. Murray International Metals*, 1988 S.L.T. 747.

[31] *Lord Advocate v. Hepburn*, 1990 S.L.T. 530; *Lord Advocate v. Butt*, 1991 S.L.T. 248.

(*b*) to any obligation arising from the issue of a bank note. This excepts a bank's undertaking to pay on bank notes from the five-year extinctive prescription. Accordingly the date of a bank note is irrelevant for prescription.

(*c*) to any obligation constituted or evidenced by a probative writ, (defined in para. 4(*b*)), not being a cautionary obligation (which is affected by para. 1(*g*)[32]) nor being an obligation falling within paragraph 1(a). Subject to these exceptions obligations either constituted or evidenced by a probative writ are not extinguished by the five-year prescription under section 6 but only by the long negative prescription established by section 7 and provided the conditions of that section are satisfied. But an obligation to make reparation for breach of a term of a probative lease is not itself an obligation constituted or evidenced by a probative writing, nor was an obligation to do something on land itself an obligation relating to land.[33] By paragraph 3 of the Schedule, where by virtue of a probative writ two or more persons— "co-obligants" —are bound jointly and severally by an obligation to pay money to another party the obligation is, as respects the liability of each of them, to be regarded for the purposes of subparagraph (*c*) as if it were a cautionary obligation, but this does not affect any such obligation as respects the liability of any of the co-obligants with respect to whom the creditor establishes (a) that he is truly a principal debtor, or (b) if he is not truly a principal debtor, that the original creditor was not aware of that fact when the writ was delivered to him. This relates to the case of improper cautionry, where principal debtor and cautioner(s) are bound jointly and severally, *ex facie* all as co-obligants.

(*d*) to any obligation under a contract of partnership or of agency, not being one remaining, or becoming, prestable on or after the termination of the partnership or agency relationship. It is thought that this is confined to obligations between partners, or between principal and agent, and not one between partner or agent and a third party.

(*e*) to any obligation relating to land, including an obligation to recognise a servitude, but not the obligations to pay sums of money due in respect of particular periods listed in paragraph 1(*a*). This subparagraph would apply to obligations to build or not to build under feu charters, and obligations therein restrictive of construction or use, but not to an obligation to make subjects good at the end of a lease,[34] nor to the obligation to deliver a valid disposition of land in implement of missives.[35]

(*f*) to any obligation to satisfy a claim to terce, courtesy, legitim, *jus relicti or jus relictae* or to any prior right of a surviving spouse under the Succession (Scotland) Act 1964, ss. 8 or 9 (as amended in amounts under the Succession (Scotland) Act 1973). Hitherto claims to legal rights have not been cut off until the lapse of the long negative prescription, and by reason of this subparagraph this principle is unaffected. These claims are all of the nature of debts due by the deceased's estate and, but for express

---

[32] *Royal Bank v. Brown*, 1982 S.C. 89 at p. 92; *Smithy's Place v. Blackadder and McMonagle*, 1991 S.L.T. 790
[33] *Lord Advocate v. Shipbreaking Industries*, 1991 S.L.T. 838.
[34] *ibid.*
[35] *Barratt Scotland v. Keith*, 1993 S.C.L.R. 120.

mention here, might have been held to be extinguished by the five-year prescription under paragraph 1(*f*).

The obligations to pay shares of dead's part, legacies or shares of residue are not mentioned and claims to them will not be excluded by negative prescription. They can be held to be of the nature of trust funds, and liability to account for trust funds is imprescriptible, under Schedule 3(*e*)(iii). The definition of trustee in section 15(1) is wide enough to cover all executors; it includes a "trustee within the meaning of the Trusts (Scotland) Act 1921" which by s. 2 thereof includes *ex-officio* trustees, executors nominate, tutors, curators and judicial factors. (The definition of "judicial factor" for the purposes of s. 2 is amended by the Trusts (Scotland) Act 1961, s. 3.)

(*g*) to any obligation to make reparation for personal injuries, or death; these are affected by the limitation period of three years, with possible extension, under sections 17 to 22, not by the five-year prescription.

(*gg*) The Law Reform (Miscellaneous Provisions) (Scotland) Act 1985, s. 12 inserted a new section 18A in the 1973 Act creating a limitation period of three years for actions for defamation. Accordingly an obligation to make reparation for defamation is affected by the limitation period of three years, with possible extension, not by the five-year prescription.

(*ggg*) The Consumer Protection Act 1987 creates a ten-year prescription for obligations arising from liability under that Act to make reparation for damage caused by a defect in a product. Such an obligation is accordingly excluded from the application of sections 6 and 7 of the 1973 Act.

(*h*) to any obligation specified in Schedule 3 as "imprescriptible", *i. e.* one not capable of being extinguished by prescription or any lapse of time.[36]

Inclusion under one of these heads of paragraph 2 does not mean that such an obligation is *never* affected by prescription, but merely that it is not affected by the five-year prescription created by section 6. Section 7, which creates the long negative prescription, by subsection (2), applies to an obligation of any kind (including an obligation to which section 6 applies), but not to an obligation specified in Schedule 3 as being imprescriptible. In general, therefore, apart from imprescriptible obligations, obligations mentioned in paragraph 2 as not extinguished by the short negative prescription under section 6 are extinguished by the long negative prescription under section 7.

Starting date for short negative prescriptive period

"If, after the appropriate date,"

The "appropriate date" is the starting date for the running of the prescriptive period of five years established by this section for the kinds of obligations to which it applies, and has to be determined differently in different cases.

By subsection (3) the reference in subsection (1) to the "appropriate date" (a) in relation to an obligation of any kind specified in Schedule 2 to the Act, is a reference to the date specified in that Schedule in relation to

---

[36] For commentary on "imprescriptible obligations" see p. 77.

obligations of that kind, and (b) in relation to an obligation of any other kind is a reference to the date when the obligation became enforceable.

(a) "appropriate date" for obligations specified in Schedule 2

Schedule 2 provides:

Section 6 SCHEDULE 2

APPROPRIATE DATES FOR CERTAIN OBLIGATIONS FOR PURPOSES OF SECTION 6

1.—(1) This paragraph applies to any obligation, not being part of a banking transaction, to pay money in respect of—

(*a*) goods supplied on sale or hire, or

(*b*) services rendered,

in a series of transactions between the same parties (whether under a single contract or under several contracts) and charged on continuing account.

(2) In the foregoing sub-paragraph—

(*a*) any reference to the supply of goods on sale includes a reference to the supply of goods under a hire-purchase agreement, a credit-sale agreement or a conditional sale agreement as defined (in each case) by section 1 of the Hire-Purchase (Scotland) Act 1965;[37] and

(*b*) any reference to services rendered does not include the work of keeping the account in question.

(3) Where there is a series of transactions between a partnership and another party, the series shall be regarded for the purposes of this paragraph as terminated (without prejudice to any other mode of termination) if the partnership or any partner therein becomes bankrupt; but, subject to that, if the partnership (in the further provisions of this sub-paragraph referred to as "the old partnership") is dissolved and is replaced by a single new partnership having among its partners any person who was a partner in the old partnership, then, for the purposes of this paragraph, the new partnership shall be regarded as if it were identical with the old partnership.

(4) The appropriate date in relation to an obligation to which this paragraph applies is the date on which payment for the goods last supplied, or, as the case may be, the services last rendered, became due.

2.—(1) This paragraph applies to any obligation to repay the whole, or any part of, a sum of money lent to, or deposited with, the debtor under a contract of loan or, as the case may be, deposit.

(2) The appropriate date in relation to an obligation to which this paragraph applies is—

(*a*) if the contract contains a stipulation which makes provision with respect to the date on or before which repayment of the sum or, as the case may be, the part thereof is to be made, the date on or before which, in terms of that stipulation, the sum or part thereof is to be repaid, and

(*b*) if the contract contains no such stipulation, but a written demand for repayment of the sum, or, as the case may be, the part thereof, is made by or on behalf of the creditor to the debtor, the date when such demand is made or first made.

3.—(1) This paragraph applies to any obligation under a contract of partnership or of agency, being an obligation remaining, or becoming, prestable on or after the termination of the relationship between the parties under the contract.

(2) The appropriate date in relation to an obligation to which this paragraph applies is—

(*a*) if the contract contains a stipulation which makes provision with respect to the date on or before which performance of the obligation is to be due, the

---

[37] This Act was repealed by the Consumer Credit Act 1974, Sched. 5, which by s. 189 defines the three kinds of agreements. The definitions in the 1974 Act are probably to be deemed substituted under the Interpretation Act 1978, s. 17(2)(*a*).

date on or before which, in terms of that stipulation, the obligation is to be performed; and
(b) in any other case the date when the said relationship terminated.
4.—(1) This paragraph applies to any obligation—
(a) to pay an instalment of a sum of money payable by instalments, or
(b) to execute any instalment of work due to be executed by instalments, not being an obligation to which any of the foregoing paragraphs applies.
(2) The appropriate date in relation to an obligation to which this paragraph applies is the date on which the last of the instalments is due to be paid or, as the case may be, to be executed.

Schedule 2 accordingly states "appropriate dates" from which prescriptive periods may run for four classes of obligations, dealt with in the four several paragraphs of the Schedule.

Class 1: obligations, not being part of a banking transaction, to pay money for (a) goods supplied on sale (including hire-purchase, credit-sale or conditional sale) or hire or (b) services rendered, apart from the work of keeping the account in question, in a series of transactions between the same parties and charged on continuing account.

This class of obligation does not deal with single transactions, but covers a running account, *e.g.* with a supplier, under which various sales or supplies are made and charged to an account, or various items of services rendered.[38] The starting date for the prescriptive period is not the date of the last sale or services but the date on which payment therefor became due, which cannot be earlier than the date on which the account therefor is rendered and may indeed be later, such as the end of the month or quarter in which the account is rendered. It seems implied by the reference to "continuing account" that while the starting date is determined by the last sale or service the sum due may be in respect of earlier transactions also. Thus an account may be rendered in April and payable by April 30, for goods sold and services rendered on several occasions between January 1 and March 31. This paragraph does not cover liability for wages due week by week.[39]

Sub-paragraph (3) deals with the special case where one party to the series of transactions is a partnership.

In this class of obligation the "appropriate date" is the date on which payment for the goods last supplied or the services last rendered became due.

Class 2: obligations to repay the whole or part of money lent to or deposited with a debtor under a contract of loan or deposit.

In this class of obligation the "appropriate date" is either (a) the date, if stipulated, on or before which the money is to be repaid, or (b) failing such stipulated date, the date when a written demand for repayment is made.

This class of obligation is important as it would appear to cover loans of money to or by banks, building societies and the like, and by money-lenders. In *Royal Bank of Scotland v. Brown*[40] the bank sued the representatives of

---

[38] *Robertson v. Murray International Metals*, 1988 S.L.T. 747; *R. Peter & Co. v. The Pancake Place*, 1993 S.L.T. 322.
[39] *Reid v. Beaton*, 1995 S.C.L.R. 382.
[40] 1982 S.C. 89.

two guarantors of the debts of a company now in liquidation. The guarantee provided for payment "on demand". The defenders contended that the appropriate date was the date when the obligation became enforceable which was, at latest, the date when the bank had claimed in the liquidation. The bank claimed that the appropriate date was the date when payment was demanded from the guarantors. It was held that the words "on demand" made the obligation enforceable only when payment was demanded from the guarantors. In *Bank of Scotland v. Laverock*[41] a letter to the judicial factor on a person's business, detailing claims against the business, was held not to be a "demand"; a claim asserted a right, a demand requested payment. The word "debtor" in paragraph 2 of Schedule 2 may not mean the same as "debtor" in paragraph 2(1).[41]

Class 3: obligations under contracts of partnership or agency.

The appropriate date is (a) the date on or before which, in terms of any stipulation in the contract, the obligation is to be performed, or (b) the date when the relationship of partnership or agency terminated.

Class 4: obligations to pay an instalment of money, or to do an instalment of work to be done in instalments, not falling within any of the three previous classes.

The "appropriate date" in this class of case is the date on which the last instalment is due to be paid or executed.

Particularly in the case of work to be done in instalments, *e.g.* laying out a garden over a season, the dates for performance of the instalments may not be clearly fixed and there may be difficulty in proving when the last instalment was due to be executed.

(b) "appropriate date" for obligations of any kind other than those specified in Schedule 2

Obligations of kinds within section 6 but other than those specified in Schedule 2 would include, *e.g.* obligations to pay money in a lump sum for a single transaction of sale or hire, service or employment, obligations to repay a loan, and obligations to pay money due as legal rights, prior rights, share of intestate estate or due as a legacy. In such cases the "appropriate date" is (s. 6(3)) "the date when the obligation became enforceable." In the case of sale this is prima facie the time of delivery, delivery of the goods and payment of the price being concurrent conditions[42]; in the case of money lent it is the date agreed for repayment, or the time when demand is made for repayment; in the case of money due from the estate of a deceased the executor cannot be compelled to pay until six months after the death, and the obligation is not enforceable till then, and not even then if there is reasonable doubt as to the solvency of the estate.[43] In the case of a cautionary

---

[41] 1992 S.L.T. 73.
[42] Sale of Goods Act 1979, s. 28.
[43] *Taylor & Ferguson v. Glass's Trs.*, 1912 S.C. 165.

obligation it is enforceable when demand is made on the cautioners[44] or on the day of the principal debtor's default.[45] A principal debtor's obligation to repay a cautioner becomes enforceable when the cautioner makes payment.[46] Time began to run when a supplier supplied goods which were found to be faulty and a contractual claim to indemnity from a third party arose at the same time; in the circumstances it had prescribed.[47]

Section 11 makes express provision as to the date when certain kinds of obligations to make reparation become enforceable.

Section 11 enacts:

Obligations to make reparation

11.—(1) Subject to subsections (2) and (3) below, any obligation (whether arising from any enactment, or from any rule of law or from, or by reason of any breach of, a contract or promise) to make reparation for loss, injury or damage caused by an act, neglect or default shall be regarded for the purposes of section 6 of this Act as having become enforceable on the date when the loss, injury or damage occurred.

(2) Where as a result of a continuing act, neglect or default loss, injury or damage has occurred before the cessation of the act, neglect or default the loss, injury or damage shall be deemed for the purposes of subsection (1) above to have occurred on the date when the act, neglect or default ceased.

(3) In relation to a case where on the date referred to in subsection (1) above (or, as the case may be, that subsection as modified by subsection (2) above) the creditor was not aware, and could not with reasonable diligence have been aware that loss, injury or damage caused as aforesaid[48] had occurred, the said subsection (1) shall have effect as if for the reference therein to that date there were substituted a reference to the date when the creditor first became, or could with reasonable diligence have become, so aware.

(4)[49]Subsections (1) and (2) above (with the omission of any reference therein to subsection (3) above shall have effect for the purposes of section 7 of this Act as they have effect for the purposes of section 6 of this Act.

It is noteworthy that section 11 covers obligations to make reparation whether arising from any enactment, *i.e.* from breach of a statutory duty, or from any rule of law, *i.e.* from breach of a common law duty not to cause harm, or from or by reason of any breach of, a contract or promise, *i.e.* from voluntary undertaking or contractual duty to pay or perform, or from duty to pay damages for breach of a contract or promise. This echoes Schedule 1, paragraph 1(*d*) and (*g*) and applies the word "reparation" to the whole. It does not deal with events which are independent of any act, neglect or default by the defender.[50] The wording is broad enough to cover obligations to make reparation in damages for personal injuries or death, but such an obligation is, by Schedule 1, paragraph 2(*g*), one to which section 6 is inapplicable; it is covered by section 7. Other obligations to pay damages, *e.g.* for property damage, are, however, covered by section 6.

---

[44] *Royal Bank v. Brown*, 1982 S.C. 82 at p. 89.

[45] *City of Glasgow D.C. v. Excess Insurance Co.*, 1986 S.L.T. 585.

[46] *Smithy's Place v. Blackadder and McMonagle*, 1991 S.L.T. 790.

[47] *Scott Lithgow v. Secretary of State for Defence*, 1989 S.L.T. 236 (H.L.).

[48] This has been held to require not only that damage had been caused by the act, but that it gave rise to an obligation to make reparation: *Dunfermline D. C. v. Blyth & Blyth Associates*, 1985 S.L.T. 345.

[49] As amended by the Prescription and Limitation (Scotland) Act 1984, Sched. 2.

[50] *McPhail v. Cunninghame D.C.*, 1983 S.C. 246.

An "act, neglect or default" does not give rise to a claim for reparation until some loss, injury or damage has resulted from it.[51] An "act, neglect or default" covers positive doing, neglecting or not-doing, and failure to do when one should have done, which probably covers all the modes in which conduct which ultimately turns out to be harmful can be done.[52] This potentially harmful conduct must have been a substantial causal factor in the incurring of the loss, injury or damage in issue. "The phrase 'loss, injury or damage' is a phrase of style commonly used to comprehend the various types of loss which may be sustained as a result of breach of a legal duty or obligation. It covers all kind of *damnum*. As soon as any form of loss, injury or damage occurs following a breach of legal duty or obligation (the *injuria*) the concurrence takes place. There can be only one point of concurrence and this is it. There may be further loss, injury and/or damage which arises consequential upon and the natural and probable result of that breach, but these do not constitute separate breaches so as to give rise to the right to raise separate actions therefor. "[53] There must be a concurrence of *injuria* (act, neglect or default) and *damnum* (loss, injury or damage), caused thereby, before a claim becomes enforceable and, accordingly, before time starts to run.[54] It matters not that the *damnum* cannot then be accurately quantified. A wife had not suffered any loss until something occurred to prevent a transaction which solicitors had been instructed some years earlier to effect (to transfer her husband's reversionary interest in his house to her) from being brought to completion. This happened when he was sequestrated in 1983 and the trustee claimed the interest. In the circumstances her claim had not prescribed.[55] A beneficiary under a will had not suffered loss before another party had acquired a right to her share of the property bequeathed because she had not taken steps to vindicate her claim to the share.[56] Section 11(1) gives no warrant for splitting loss, injury and damage; the obligation to make reparation is single and indivisible.[57]

The obligation to make reparation, *i.e.* to pay compensation, is to be regarded as having become enforceable on the date when the loss, injury or damage occurred. When contractors were refused planning permission and work done had to be demolished, the service of the notice caused loss, injury and damage and prescription ran from that date.[58] Loss was held to occur when defenders, as depositaries, parted with possession of goods wrongfully delivered to another.[59] Time began to run against contractors when their suppliers' materials were found to be defective.[60] "'Enforceable' means that there has been created a legal right which can be enforced through

---

[51] *Watson v. Fram Reinforced Concrete Co. and Winget Ltd.*, 1960 S.C.(H.L.) 92.

[52] See *Brownlie v. Mags. of Barrhead*, 1923 S.C. 915; *Watson, supra*, at pp. 111 and 115.

[53] *Dunlop v. McGowans*, 1979 S.C. 22 at p. 33, *per* L.J.-C. Wheatley.

[54] *Dunlop v. McGowans, supra*, at p. 30, *per* L.J.-C. Wheatley, at p. 40 *per* Lord Kissen; and in H.L. 1980 S.C.(H.L.) 73 at p. 80, *per* Lord Keith.

[55] *Duncan v. Aitken, Malone & McKay*, 1989 S.C.L.R. 1 (Sh.Ct.).

[56] *Fergus v. MacLennan*, 1991 S.L.T. 391.

[57] *Dunlop v. McGowans, supra*.

[58] *George Porteous (Arts) v. Dollar Rae*, 1979 S.L.T. (Sh.Ct.) 51.

[59] *East Hook Purchasing Corporation v. Ben Nevis Distillery Ltd.*, 1985 S.L.T. 442.

[60] *Scott Lithgow v. Secretary of State for Defence*, 1989 S.L.T. 236 (H.L.)

the processes of the law. That means a point has to be reached when there is a concurrence of *injuria* and *damnum.* "[61]

This date may be other, and later, than the date when breach of contract or breach of other legal duty took place.[62] Thus, if breach of contract is made by non-delivery or defective delivery, at most nominal loss, injury or damage is suffered prior to the time when the goods which should have been delivered are actually needed for use. If delict is done by negligent misrepresentation, loss, injury or damage is not suffered until the misrepresentation is relied on and detriment occurs.[63] In relation to partnership debts or obligations the period runs from the date when the debt or obligation is constituted against the partnership by decree.[64] It may be difficult to set a precise date as that by which loss, injury or damage had been suffered. In *Porteous v. Dollar Rae Ltd.* [65] it was held to have been suffered when the local planning authority served an enforcement notice requiring demolition of a building for which the defenders had failed to get planning permission. In *Lawrence v. M'Intosh & Hamilton*[66] an action was brought against a deceased person's solicitor for alleged failure to obey his instructions, so that his estate passed on intestacy to his wife and not to the pursuer. It was held that the appropriate date was the date when the obligation had become enforceable, which was the date of the deceased's death.

In *Duncan v. Aitken, Malone & Mackay,*[67] a wife claimed from solicitors for loss resulting from their having failed in 1963 to transfer her husband's reversionary interest in his house to her; he was sequestrated in 1983 and she lost that interest. It was held that she had not suffered any loss until something occurred which prevented the transfer being effected. In *Beard v. Beveridge, Herd & Sandilands*[68] landlords claimed damages from solicitors who had been instructed to draw a lease of shop premises for 42 years from 1966, with a rent review after 21 years. The rent review clause was in 1987 held void for uncertainty and the landlords claimed for the loss resulting from not having the rent increased for the second 21 years. It was held that the *injuria* took place before the defective lease was executed and the landlords could have sued at once though damages would then have had to be estimated. Accordingly the action had prescribed. This seems questionable; it could not have been certain in 1966 that any loss would ever be sustained, as the general level of shop rents might have fallen. Also, there was no *injuria* until the relevant clause was declared void.

In *Renfrew Golf Club v. Ravenstone Securities Ltd.,*[69] where greens on a new golf course were affected by flooding by reason of defects in design

---

[61] *Dunlop v. McGowans,* 1979 S.C. 22 at p. 31, *per* L.J.-C. Wheatley.
[62] *e.g. Davie v. New Merton Board Mills* [1959] A.C. 604; *Watson v. Fram Reinforced Concrete Co. and Winget Ltd.,* 1960 S.C. (H.L.) 92.
[63] *e.g. Esso Petroleum Co. v. Mardon* [1976] Q.B. 801.
[64] *Highland Engineering Ltd. v. Anderson,* 1979 S.L.T. 122.
[65] 1979 S.L.T.(Sh.Ct.) 51.
[66] 1981 S.L.T.(Sh.Ct.) 73.
[67] 1989 S.C.L.R. 1.
[68] 1990 S.L.T. 609.
[69] 1984 S.C. 22, following *Pirelli v. Faber* [1983] 1 All E.R. 65 (H.L.), where it was held that the crucial time was when physical damage to a building occurred, though it was not then discoverable. By reason of s. 11(3) of the 1973 Act the actual decision in *Pirelli* would have been otherwise in Scots law.

and construction, it was held that defects in design or workmanship would not give rise to *damnum* until actual damage was sustained.

Sellers of cloth were held in breach of contract with the buyers by supplying cloth some of which was defective, and, being debarred from claiming under the contract by reason of their breach, claimed for recompense. It was held that the obligation on the buyers to make recompense began to subsist when they had been enriched by making up and selling the usable parts of the cloth and further that the obligation to make payment and the obligation to pay recompense were quite separate so that the claim for payment under the contract did not interrupt the prescriptive period in the claim for recompense.[70]

Section 11(2) deals with a continuing act, neglect or default, such as the failure of a supplier of machinery to have made provision for lubrication of a moving part, whereby loss, injury or damage has occurred, *e.g.* by the part seizing up or becoming deformed; or the failure of a builder to provide adequately against permeation of water; or the failure of a supplier to open a ventilator in a hopper storing animal feed.[71] In such a case the loss, injury or damage is to be deemed to have occurred on the date when the act, neglect or default ceased and the wrong is actionable for five years from that date.

Section 11(3) allows an extension of time, where the creditor in the obligation to make reparation was not aware and could not with reasonable diligence have become aware that loss, injury or damage had occurred, to the date when the creditor first became aware, or could with reasonable diligence have become aware, that loss, injury or damage had occurred. It follows that owners of property must show reasonable diligence in inspecting for defects and cannot complain if a defect which could and should have been noticed is not noticed and time accordingly expires. It may be extremely difficult to establish when a person did, or should have, become aware that injury had been suffered. This principle of awareness might be relevant in a case of progressive damage not discovered till sometime after it had started.[72]

It was later held that section 11(3) looked for awareness of the fact of loss having occurred and also that it was a loss caused by negligence, but it did not defer the start of the running of the prescriptive period when the creditor in the obligation knew of the loss and that it was caused by negligence, but did not know the identity of the party on whom the obligation had been incumbent.[73]

In a case where defects in a building were discovered long after it had been built it was held that the builders' "act, neglect or default" was not a breach of the general duty to construct in accordance with the contract but was constituted by specific failures in design and construction, that minor defects discovered earlier did not constitute *injuria* in relation to different and major defects which emerged later, and the *damnum* later discovered

---

[70] *N.V. Devos Gebroeder v. Sunderland Sportswear,* 1990 S.L.T. 473.
[71] Example founded on *Parsons v. Uttley Ingham & Co.* [1978] 1 All E.R. 525.
[72] *e.g. Watt v. Jamieson,* 1954 S.C. 56 (progressive damage to building).
[73] *Greater Glasgow Health Board v. Baxter, Clark & Paul,* 1992 S.L.T. 35.

earlier and that the pursuers were not aware of the loss, injury or damage before the discovery of the later, major, defects.[74]

"If... an obligation ... has subsisted for a continuous period of five years"

The starting date of the prescriptive period is the "appropriate date" when under subsection (3) the obligation to which section 6 applies became enforceable, *i.e.* exigible by action. Thereafter the earliest time at which it may be extinguished by prescription is after the lapse of a continuous period of five years from that date, and that provided that the two conditions in the following phrases are both satisfied, *viz.* absence of "relevant claim" by the creditor and of "relevant acknowledgment" by the debtor. An obligation to pay the price of heritage against a disposition was held to become enforceable only when the disposition was tendered, though the missives had been entered into eight years earlier.[75]

The conditions for extinction by the lapse of time

"(a) without any relevant claim having been made in relation to the obligation,"

The two conditions set out in paragraphs (*a*) and (*b*) in substance restate the ways enumerated by Erskine[76] as those in which the course of the negative prescription is effectually interrupted, *viz.* written acknowledgment by the debtor, citation or action at the suit of the creditor, diligence used on the debt, and partial payment.

The principle is that either relevant claim by the creditor or relevant acknowledgment by the debtor during the currency of the prescriptive period interrupts it and it must commence again from the date of the interruption. If a period of prescription is interrupted that counters the plea of prescription not only in the original forum but in any other court having jurisdiction.[77] A continuing state, such as an action being in dependence, can effect interruption.[78]

"Relevant claim" is defined by section 9(1) as follows:

Definition of "relevant claim" for purposes of sections 6, 7, 8 and 8A

9.[79]—(1) In sections 6, 7, and 8A of this Act the expression "relevant claim," in relation to an obligation, means a claim made by or on behalf of the creditor for implement or part-implement of the obligation, being a claim made—

(*a*) in appropriate proceedings or;

(*b*) the presentation of, or the concurring in, a petition for sequestration or by the submission of a claim under section 22 or 48 of the Bankruptcy (Scotland) Act 1985;

---

[74] *Sinclair v. McDougall Estates*, 1994 S.L.T. 76.

[75] *Muir and Black v. Nee*, 1981 S.L.T.(Sh.Ct.) 68.

[76] III, 7, 39, approved in *Yuill's Trs. v. Maclachlan's Trs.*, 1939 S.C.(H.L.) 40 at p. 51, *per* Lord Macmillan.

[77] *B.R. Board v. Strathclyde R.C.*, 1981 S.C. 90; *Kinnaird v. Donaldson*, 1992 S.C.L.R. 694.

[78] *Hood v. Dunbarton C.C.*, 1983 S.L.T. 238.

[79] As amended by the Prescription and Limitation (Scotland) Act 1984, Sched. 1, para. 3, and, with effect from April 1, 1986, the Bankruptcy (Scotland) Act 1985, Sched. 7, para. 11, and, with effect from December 29, 1986, the Prescription (Scotland) Act 1987, s. 1. December 29, 1986, was the date when the Insolvency Act 1986, and the Insolvency (Scotland) Rules came into force.

(c) by a creditor to the trustee acting under a trust deed as defined in section 5(2)(c) of the Bankruptcy (Scotland) Act 1985; or

(d) by the presentation of, or the concurring in, a petition for the winding up of a company or by the submission of a claim in a liquidation in accordance with rules made under section 411 of the Insolvency Act 1986,

and for the purposes of the said sections 6, 7 and 8A the execution by or on behalf of the creditor in an obligation of any form of diligence directed to the enforcement of the obligation shall be deemed to be a relevant claim in relation to the obligation.

(2) [Refers only to section 8.]

(3) Where a claim which, in accordance with the foregoing provisions of this section, is a relevant claim for the purposes of sections 6, 7, 8 or 8A of this Act is made in an arbitration, and the nature of the claim has been stated in a preliminary notice relating to that arbitration, the date when the notice was served shall be taken for those purposes to be the date of the making of the claim.

(4) In this section the expression "appropriate proceedings" and, in relation to an arbitration, the expression "preliminary notice" have the same meanings as in section 4 of this Act.

A "relevant claim" must have been one made against the debtor in the obligation, not against another party even though based on the same obligation.[80] To draw a cheque on a current account with a banker is a claim for implement.[81]

A *"claim made by or on behalf of the creditor for implement or part-implement of the obligation"* clearly includes actions for payment, for specific implement, and for damages, and such special forms of claim as actions for sequestration for rent or of maills and duties. Service of a summons or initial writ specifying the obligation sought to be enforced will suffice; it matters not that the grounds of the obligation are inadequately pleaded and require amendment.[82] An initial writ warranted but not served, followed by registration of letters of inhibition on the dependence of the action, was held a "relevant claim" which interrupted prescription on the date of registration.[83] An action later abandoned is a "relevant claim" for the purposes of a later action.[84] It is probable that an action later dismissed as irrelevant could still be a "relevant claim"; the point is: did it indicate an intention to press the claim rather than let it be extinguished? A claim of damages for breach of contract was held another aspect of the contractual obligation to make payment and accordingly a "relevant claim".[85] The obligations to make payment under contract and to make recompense have however been held quite separate and a claim for payment did not affect interruption of a claim for recompense.[86] And a claim based on delict does not constitute a "relevant claim" which will save from prescription a claim based on breach of contract, since the former was founded on reparation for loss and the latter on breach of an agreement.[87] Whether a claim under one clause of a contract was a "relevant claim" in respect of obligations

---

[80] *Kirkcaldy D.C. v. Household Manufacturing Co.*, 1987 S.L.T. 617.
[81] *Macdonald v. North of Scotland Bank*, 1942 S.C. 369.
[82] *B.R. Board, supra; Kinnaird, supra.*
[83] *Hogg v. Prentice*, 1994 S.C.L.R. 426 (Sh. Ct.).
[84] *Hood v. Dunbarton, supra*. See also *G.A. Estates v. Caviapen Trs.*, 1993 S.L.T. 1051.
[85] *Ductform Ventilation (Fife) v. Andrews-Weatherfoil*, 1995 S.L.T. 88.
[86] *N.V. Devos Gebroeder v. Sunderland Sportswear*, 1989 S.L.T. 382; 1990 S.L.T. 473.
[87] *Middleton v. Douglass*, 1991 S.L.T. 726. See also *Wylie v. Avon Insurance Co.*, 1988 S.C.L.R. 570.

under another clause depended on whether they were separate obligations.[87a] A letter requesting arbitration was held not to be a relevant claim when the nature of the claim was not stated.[87b] A fundamentally null action cannot be a "relevant claim", nor effect interruption.[88]

An action which has been commenced in time can be amended after the prescriptive period has expired even though the amendment effected substantial elaboration of the grounds of action.[89] But timeous commencement of an action based on one ground of obligation cannot save from the operation of prescription a claim based on a different obligation and later substituted by amendment.[90]

For discussion of "appropriate proceedings," see p. 23. The important point is that informal claim, as by letter, will not suffice. It must be a claim in a court of competent jurisdiction, and not merely a summons served but not called,[91] or a claim in an arbitration in Scotland,[92] or in an arbitration elsewhere the award in which would be enforceable in Scotland.

The *"presentation of or concurring in a petition for sequestration, or by the submission of a claim under section 22 or 48 of the Bankruptcy (Scotland) Act 1985"* are respectively the request that a debtor be sequestrated, the submission of a claim, with voucher constituting *prima facie* evidence of the debt, for voting purposes at the statutory meeting, and the submission of a claim to the permanent trustee for his adjudication as to the creditor's entitlement to vote and to draw a dividend.

A claim by the creditor to the trustee under a trust-deed within the 1985 Act, the presentation of a petition for winding-up under the Insolvency Act 1986, and the submission of a claim in a liquidation under that Act are all similarly clear indications of intention not to let a claim lapse by prescription.

Intimation that one is a creditor to the person acting in relation to a company voluntary arrangement,[93] or to the person acting as administrator of a company,[94] or to the receiver of a company,[95] are not mentioned and do not count as "relevant claims".

"Any form of diligence directed to the enforcement of the obligation" would include arrestment or inhibition or adjudication in security, sequestration in security of rent, and summary diligence on a bill or bond. Diligence in execution such as poinding can be said to be "directed to the enforcement of the obligation" but must be preceded by an earlier stage, such as obtaining decree, which itself would be a "relevant claim."

For discussion of "preliminary notice," see p. 23.

[87a] *G.A. Estates v. Caviapen Trs (No. 2)*, 1993 S.L.T. 1045.

[87b] *Milne (Douglas) v. Borders R. C.*, 1990 S.L.T. 558.

[88] *Shanks v. Central R.C.*, 1987 S.L.T. 410; 1988 S.L.T. 212.

[89] *Macleod v. Sinclair*, 1981 S.L.T. (Notes) 38. See *Stewart v. Highlands and Islands Development Board*, 1991 S.L.T. 787.

[90] *Lawrence v. J.D. McIntosh & Hamilton*, 1981 S.L.T. (Sh. Ct.) 73, followed in *N.V. Devos Gebroeder, supra.*

[91] A summons has been held to have been "subsequently called" though called only after the five year period had elapsed: *Barclay v. Chief Constable, Northern Constabulary*, 1986 S.L.T. 562.

[92] *John O'Connor (Plant Hire) v. Kier Construction*, 1990 S.C.L.R. 761. See also *R. Peter & Co. v. The Pancake Place*, 1993 S.L.T. 322.

[93] Insolvency Act 1986, ss. 1–7.

[94] *ibid.*, ss. 8–27.

[95] *ibid.*, ss. 50–72.

"and (b) without the subsistence of the obligation having been relevantly acknowledged"

By the proviso to section 6(1), in the application of the section to an obligation under a bill of exchange or a promissory note, paragraph (*b*) is to be omitted and it is sufficient if paragraph (*a*) is satisfied, *i.e.* if no relevant claim had been made during the five years.

By section 10 "relevant acknowledgment" is defined for the purposes of sections 6, 7 and 8A as follows:

Relevant acknowledgment for purposes of sections, 6, 7 and 8A

10.[96]—(1) The subsistence of an obligation shall be regarded for the purposes of sections 6, 7 and 8A of this Act as having been relevantly acknowledged if, and only if, either of the following conditions is satisfied, namely—

(*a*) that there has been such performance by or on behalf of the debtor towards implement of the obligation as clearly indicates that the obligation still subsists;

(*b*) that there has been made by or on behalf of the debtor to the creditor or his agent an unequivocal written admission[97] clearly acknowledging that the obligation still subsists.

(2) Subject to subsection (3) below, where two or more persons are bound jointly by an obligation so that each is liable for the whole, and the subsistence of the obligation has been relevantly acknowledged by or on behalf of one of those persons then—

(*a*) if the acknowledgment is made in the manner specified in paragraph (*a*) of the foregoing subsection it shall have effect for the purposes of the said sections 6, 7 and 8A as respects the liability of each of those persons, and

(*b*) if it is made in the manner specified in paragraph (*b*) of that subsection it shall have effect for those purposes only as respects the liability of the person who makes it.

(3) Where the subsistence of an obligation affecting a trust estate has been relevantly acknowledged by or on behalf of one of two or more co-trustees in the manner specified in paragraph (*a*) or (*b*) of subsection (1) of this section, the acknowledgment shall have effect for the purposes of the said sections 6, 7 and 8A as respects the liability of the trust estate and any liability of each of the trustees.[98]

(4) In this section references to performance in relation to an obligation include, where the nature of the obligation so requires, references to refraining from doing something and to permitting or suffering something to be done or maintained.

The words *"if, and only if"* make clear that nothing other than satisfaction of one or other of the conditions (*a*) and (*b*) in subsection (1) will amount to relevant acknowledgment. The conditions (*a*) and (*b*) are alternatives and it suffices if either is satisfied.

(*a*) *"performance … towards implement"* would include payment of interest[99] and part-payment or other part-performance.[1] By subsection (4) performance includes, where appropriate, negative performance, refraining from doing something and permitting or suffering something to be done or maintained.

---

[96] As amended by the Prescription and Limitation (Scotland) Act 1984, Sched. 1, para. 4.

[97] *Lieberman v. Tait*, 1987 S.L.T. 585.

[98] See *Fortunato's J.F. v. Fortunato*, 1981 S.L.T. 277.

[99] *cf. Kermack v. Kermack* (1874) 2 R. 156 at p. 158.

[1] *cf. Garden v. Rigg* (1743) Mor. 11274; *Inverlochy Castle v. Lochaber Power Co.*, 1987 S.L.T. 466.

Whether there has or has not been "*such performance ... as clearly indicates that the obligation still subsists*" would appear to be a question of fact and of degree in each case. It must presumably be such a kind of act or abstention as can only reasonably be explained by reference to the particular obligation in question.[2] If a debtor owes money to a creditor both for rent and in respect of money borrowed four years ago, and makes a payment of the sum due as rent but not attributed to either debt, is the creditor entitled to attribute it to the loan so as to interrupt the prescription of that claim? Probably he is.[3]

(*b*) "*unequivocal written admission clearly acknowledging....*" The admission must be written; it need not be probative nor in any set form. It must be made "*by or on behalf of the debtor to the creditor or his agent*"; this excludes admissions by or to third parties. Whether a particular written admission is "unequivocal" or not or "clearly acknowledging" that the obligation still subsists is a question of interpretation in particular circumstances.[4]

Where there are distinct obligations between two parties, such as on an insurer to provide an accurate policy and to indemnify on a loss occurring, a relevant acknowledgement of one does not also acknowledge the other.[5]

Subsections (2) and (3) deal with joint and several obligations. Subsection (2) says in substance that if several persons are bound jointly and severally an acknowledgment by performance by one binds all, but an acknowledgment by written admission by one binds himself only. But by subsection (3) an acknowledgment of an obligation affecting a trust estate made in either mode by a trustee is effective as regards the liability of the trust estate and any liability of each trustee.

Effect of claim or acknowledgment

The effect of the making of a "relevant claim" or of the granting of a "relevant acknowledgment" is not expressly stated, but it seems implied that either has the effect of interrupting the prescriptive period, cancelling the time which has run and requiring it to start running again. It will commence to run again from the day after making of the relevant claim or the granting of the relevant acknowledgment. This was the effect of interruption prior to the 1973 Act.[6]

A claim preserved in being by the interruption of the prescriptive period may be preserved further by another interruption and so on indefinitely.

Effect of time running uninterrupted

"*then, as from the expiration of that period, the obligation shall be extinguished*"

An obligation of one of the kinds to which section 6 applies is wholly extinguished by the lapse of a continuous period of five years after the

---

[2] Passage approved in *Gibson v. Carson*, 1980 S.C. 356 at p. 360 *per* Lord Allanbridge.

[3] *cf.* Ersk., III, 4, 2; *Good v. Smith* (1779) Mor. 6816; *Bremner v. Mabon* (1837) 16 S. 213; *Watt v. Burnett's Trs.* (1839) 2 D. 132; *Wauchope v. North British Ry.* (1863) 2 M. 326; *Jackson v. Nicoll* (1870) 8 M. 403; *Buchanan v. Main* (1900) 3 F. 215.

[4] *cf. W. Briggs v. Swan's Exr.* (1854) 16 D. 385 at p. 394; *Greater Glasgow Health Board v. Baxter Clark & Paul*, 1992 S.L.T. 35.

[5] *Wylie v. Avon Insurance Co.*, 1988 S.C.L.R. 570.

[6] Ersk. III, 7, 41; Napier on *Prescription*, 704; Millar on *Prescription*, 107; *cf. Hogg v. Prentice*, 1994 S.C.L.R. 426 (Sh. Ct.)

"appropriate date," provided that neither relevant claim nor relevant acknowledgment has been made within that time to preserve the claim in existence. Tentative opinions have been expressed[7] that prescription does not run while an action is in court but recommences on the day it is dismissed or abandoned.

Periods to be disregarded

Subsections (4) and (5) of section 6 enact:

"(4) In the computation of a prescriptive period in relation to any obligation for the purposes of this section—

    (*a*) any period during which by reason of—

        (i) fraud on the part of the debtor or any person acting on his behalf, or

        (ii) error induced by words or conduct of the debtor or any person acting on his behalf,

he creditor was induced to refrain from making a relevant claim in relation to the obligation, and

    (*b*) any period during which the original creditor (while he is the creditor) was under legal disability,

shall not be reckoned as, or as part of, the prescriptive period:

Provided that any period such as is mentioned in paragraph (*a*) of this subsection shall not include any time occurring after the creditor could with reasonable diligence have discovered the fraud or error, as the case may be, referred to in that paragraph.

(5) Any period such as is mentioned in paragraph (*a*) or (*b*) of subsection (4) of this section shall not be regarded as separating the time immediately before it from the time immediately after it."

The effect of subsection (4) is to exclude from the reckoning any periods during which the creditor was induced to refrain from making a relevant claim by the debtor's fraud, or by error induced by him (so long as neither was discoverable by reasonable diligence) or the creditor was under legal disability.

"*Fraud*" is "a machination or contrivance to deceive".[8] It clearly includes any deliberately deceitful statement or conduct intended to mislead the creditor, but not a merely negligent or, still less, innocent misrepresentation. Under the corresponding provision in English law it has been held that bad building work, covered up by completion of the building and consequently not discoverable, was fraud which prevented the running of time[9]; and that failing to disclose to a purchaser that a building had been erected on a filled-in rubbish tip was also fraud.[10] "Fraud" means "unconscionable conduct".[11] It may be accordingly that "fraud" should be given a broad interpretation, covering any conduct calculated to mislead.[12] "Person acting on his behalf" may also require a broad interpretation. "Fraud" was held to cover the case where a deceased person had wrongfully removed money from a company of which he was controlling director in circumstances

---

[7] *G.A. Estates v. Caviapen Trs.*, 1993 S.L.T. 1051.

[8] Bell, *Prin.*, § 13.

[9] *Archer v. Moss* [1971] 1 All E.R. 747.

[10] *King v. Victor Parsons & Co.* [1973] 1 All E.R. 206.

[11] *Bartlett v. Barclays Bank Trust Co.* [1980] 1 All E.R. 139; see also *Beaman v. A.R.T.S. Ltd.* [1949] 1 All E.R. 465; *Kitchen v. R.A.F. Association* [1958] 2 All E.R. 241; *Clark v. Woor* [1965] 2 All E.R. 353.

[12] *cf. Cartledge v. Jopling* [1963] A.C. 758 at pp. 771–772; [1963] 1 All E.R. 341 at p. 343, *per* Lord Reid.

when it was unlikely that the loss would be detected for a long time. Proof was on balance of probabilities.[13]

"Error induced" means any mistaken understanding by the creditor of a material fact, brought about by the debtor's words or conduct. The error may have been produced by words or conduct intentional, negligent or even innocent.[14]

It is essential to prove that by reason of the fraud or induced error the creditor was induced to refrain from making a claim; it will not suffice if he refrained by indolence or choice.

By the proviso the extension of time for bringing an action does not include time after the creditor could with reasonable diligence have discovered the fraud or error. If he has grounds and opportunities for suspecting fraud or error he must exercise reasonable diligence to discover the truth, and may be precluded from relying on the extension of time if he has not done so.

"Legal disability" is defined by section 15(1) as meaning "legal disability by reason of nonage or unsoundness of mind." This replaces the common law plea of *non valens agere.*[15] At common law nonage included both pupillarity and minority [16] By the Age of Legal Capacity (Scotland) Act 1991, s. 1(2) references in statutes to "legal disability" or "incapacity by reason of nonage", so far as relating to events after the commencement of the 1991 Act (September 25, 1991) are to be construed as a reference to a person under 16 years. By sections 8 and 11(2) of the same Act, where any person referred to in the 1973 Act, ss. 6(4)(*b*), 17(3), 18(3) and 18A(2) as having been under disability by reason of nonage was of or over the age of 16 but under 18 immediately before September 25, 1991, any period prior to that date is not to be reckoned as or as part of the period of five years or three years specified respectively in sections 6, 17, 18 or 18A.

"Unsoundness of mind" is not a defined legal category; it pretty certainly covers patients detained as patients in mental hospitals and probably patients received into guardianship, both under the Mental Health (Scotland) Act 1984, and may even cover persons outside either of these categories, such as have been held at common law to be incapacitated.[17]

Subsection (4) has been said to appear to have been designed to cover the situation where a plea of personal bar might run.[18]

The proviso to subsection (4) makes clear that there is a duty to show reasonable diligence in investigating if there are grounds for suspecting fraud or error induced and that the prescriptive period will start to run from the time fraud or error should have been discovered, even if it was not.

The effect of subsection (5) is that a prescriptive period is not made discontinuous by a period of refraining from action induced by fraud or

---

[13] *Fisher & Donaldson v. Steven,* 1988 S.C.L.R. 337 (Sh.Ct.).
[14] See Walker, *Law of Contracts and Related Obligations in Scotland* (3rd ed.), §§ 14.50–94.
[15] Stair, II, 12, 27; More's Note to Stair, cclxvii; *Earl of Fife v. Duff* (1887) 15 R. 238; *Harvie v. Robertson* (1903) 5 F. 338 at pp. 340 and 343.
[16] *Fyfe v. Croudace,* 1986 S.L.T. 528; *Forbes v. House of Clydesdale,* 1988 S.L.T. 594.
[17] *e.g. Laidlaw v. Laidlaw* (1870) 8 M. 882; *Ballantyne v. Evans* (1886) 13 R. 652; *Sivewright v. Sivewright's Trs.,* 1920 S.C. (H.L.) 63.
[18] *Greater Glasgow Health Board v. Baxter Clark & Paul,* 1992 S.L.T. 35.

error or of legal disability, but that period of time is not counted, and the prescriptive period must be lengthened to that extent.

Computation of prescriptive periods

14.—(1) In the computation of a prescriptive period for the purposes of any provision of this Part[19] of this Act—

(a) time occurring before the commencement of this Part of this Act[20] shall be reckonable towards the prescriptive period in like manner as time occurring thereafter, but subject to the restriction that any time reckoned under this paragraph shall be less than the prescriptive period;

(b) any time during which any person against whom the provision is pled was under legal disability[21] shall (except so far as otherwise provided by section 6(4) of this Act) be reckoned as if the person were free from that disability;

(c) if the commencement of the prescriptive period would, apart from this paragraph, fall at a time in any day other than the beginning of the day, the period shall be deemed to have commenced at the beginning of the next following day;

(d) if the last day of the prescriptive period would, apart from this paragraph, be a holiday, the period shall, notwithstanding anything in the said provision, be extended to include any immediately succeeding day which is a holiday, any further immediately succeeding days which are holidays, and the next succeeding day which is not a holiday;

(e) save as otherwise provided in this Part of this Act regard shall be had to the like principles as immediately before the commencement of this Part of this Act were applicable to the computation of periods of prescription for the purposes of the Prescription Act 1617.

(2) In this section "holiday" means a day of any of the following descriptions, namely, a Saturday, a Sunday and a day which, in Scotland, is a bank holiday under the Banking and Financial Dealings Act 1971.

By subsection (1)(a) part of the prescriptive period may have run before July 25, 1976, but at least one day must be after it.[22] The effect of this subsection is not to revive rights which had prescribed prior to the passing of the 1973 Act. [23]

Subsection (1)(b) is qualified in its application to section 6 by section 6(4).

The "like principles" referred to in section 14(1)(e) as were previously applicable to the computation of periods of prescription for the purposes of the Prescription Act 1617 were:

(i) Negative prescription begins to run from the date at which the right of action against which it is pleaded has emerged;

(ii) It runs *de die in diem*, and therefore commences to run from the earliest moment of the next day to the last moment of the day of the same number in the same month five years later.

---

[19] Pt. I (ss. 1 to 15).
[20] July 25, 1976.
[21] Defined by s. 15(1) as meaning legal disability by reason of nonage or unsoundness of mind.
[22] See the explanation of s. 14 in *Dunlop v. McGowans,* 1979 S.C. 22 at p. 32, *per* L.J.-C. Wheatley, at p. 38, *per* Lord Kissen; 1980 S.C. (H.L.) 73 at p. 79, *per* Lord Russell, at p. 81, *per* Lord Keith.
[23] *Porteous's Exrs. v. Ferguson,* 1995 S.L.T. 649.

CHAPTER 4

LONG NEGATIVE PRESCRIPTION

THE theoretical basis of the long negative prescription is the "loss or forfeiture of a right, by the proprietor's neglecting to exercise or prosecute it during that whole period which the law hath declared to infer the loss of it."[1] "The doctrine of prescription ... infers, by operation of the law itself, from the mere lapse of time, a presumption of abandonment or of payment."[2]

The long negative prescription was established originally by the Prescription Acts 1469, 1474 and 1617 (second portion) which established the rule that obligations not enforced and certain rights in property not exercised for 40 years continuously were extinguished.[3] The period of 40 years was reduced to 20 years by the Conveyancing (Scotland) Act 1924, s. 17, amended by the Conveyancing (Scotland) Act 1938, s. 4, except in the cases of extinction of servitudes, public rights of way or other public right. This reduction applied both to heritable and to moveable rights.[4]

The Acts were given a liberal application and with limited exceptions applied to "all absolute rights and obligations whatever, mutual or unilateral, heritable or moveable, if not insisted on within the term."[5]

MODERN LAW

The Prescription Acts 1469, 1474 and 1617, were repealed,[6] with effect from July 25, 1976,[7] by the 1973 Act, and there was substituted a new long negative prescription of 20 years, the running of which extinguishes obligations and rights relating to property affected by it.

This new prescription is created by sections 7, 8 and 8A, dealing respectively with obligations of any kind (including obligations affected by the short (five-year) negative prescription created by section 6),[8] with any right to property, with certain exceptions, and with obligations to make contribution between wrongdoers.

In the context of section 7 an "obligation" means a bilateral relationship, a *juris vinculum* imposing mutual rights and duties in the parties.

In the context of section 8 a "right relating to property" means a claim to or over or in relation to any object, whether heritable or moveable, of proprietary right.

The questions which may arise for consideration in a case to which the long negative prescription may apply are:

---

[1] Ersk., III, 7, 8; *cf.* Hume, *Lect.*, III, 64; *Mill's Trs. v. Mill's Trs.*, 1965 S.C. 384 at pp. 392 and 394.
[2] Bell, *Prin.*, § 605. *cf.* Bell, *Comm.*, I, 352.
[3] Stair, II, 12, 12; Ersk., III, 7, 8.
[4] *Sutherland C. C. v. Macdonald*, 1935 S.C. 915; see also *Marr's Exx. v. Marr's Trs.*, 1936 S.C. 64.
[5] Bell, *Prin.*, § 603, approved in *Pettigrew v. Harton*, 1956 S.C. 67 at p. 74.
[6] 1973 Act, Sched. 5, Pt. I.
[7] *ibid.*, s. 25(2).
[8] On which see Chap. 3, *supra*.

1. *to what obligations, or rights in property, that Act applies; these are stated, for obligations, by section 7(2) and Schedule 3, and for property, by section 8(2) and Schedule 3;*
2. *the starting date for the long negative prescription, which is stated for obligations by sections 7(1) and 11, and for property by section 8(1);*
3. *whether the prescriptive period has run continuously for the prescriptive period;*
4. *whether in the case of an obligation both the conditions for extinguishing the obligation (sections 7(1), 9 and 10) have been satisfied, and in the case of a right of property, both the different conditions for extinguishing the right (sections 8(1) and 9) have been satisfied.*

EXTINCTION OF OBLIGATIONS

Section 7 enacts:

Extinction of obligations by prescriptive periods of twenty years

7.—(1) If, after the date when any obligation to which this section applies has become enforceable, the obligation has subsisted for a continuous period of twenty years—

(*a*) without any relevant claim having been made in relation to the obligation, and

(*b*) without the subsistence of the obligation having been relevantly acknowledged,

then as from the expiration of that period the obligation shall be extinguished:

Provided that in its application to an obligation under a bill of exchange or a promissory note this subsection shall have effect as if paragraph (*b*) thereof were omitted.

(2)[9] This section applies to an obligation of any kind (including an obligation to which section 6 of this Act applies), not being an obligation to which section 22A of this Act applies or an obligation specified in Schedule 3 to this Act as an imprescriptible obligation or an obligation to make reparation in respect of personal injuries within the meaning of Part II of this Act or in respect of the death of any person as a result of such injuries.

VERBAL COMMENTARY ON SECTION 7

"If, after the date when any obligation to which this section applies"

By subsection (2) this provision applies to an obligation of any kind (including an obligation to which section 6 of the Act applies, *i.e.* one listed in Schedule 1, paragraph 1),[10] which is not an obligation arising from section 22A, *i.e.* from liability under the Consumer Protection Act 1987 for a defect in a product,[11] nor an obligation specified in Schedule 3 to the Act as an imprescriptible obligation, *i.e.* one not affected by the running of time, however long, nor an obligation to make reparation for personal injuries or wrongful death. The source of the obligation is immaterial. It applies to obligations arising from promise or agreement, and to obligations

---

[9] As amended by the Prescription and Limitation (Scotland) Act 1984, Sched. 1, para. 2, as regards any obligation not extinguished before September 26, 1984: *ibid.*, s. 5(3), and by the Consumer Protection Act 1987, Sched. I, para. 8, in respect of the reference to s. 22A.

[10] p. 54, *supra.*

[11] On liability under s. 22A see Chap. 5, *infra.*

arising by force of law, both common law and statute. This section accordingly applies to obligations arising from or arising by reason of any breach of, a promise or contract, including obligations to make periodical payments of money, obligations based on unjustified enrichment or quasi-contractual obligation, obligations arising from liability at common law or resulting from breach of statutory duty to make reparation (except reparation for personal injuries or death), and all the kinds of obligations affected by section 6. It also applies to those kinds of obligations to which section 6 of the Act does not apply, *i.e.* those listed in Schedule 1, paragraph 2.[12]

The long negative prescription under the statute previously in force has been held to apply to, and to extinguish: a right to dam up water in a stream[13]; an obligation constituted by letter to create a real burden[14]; a claim for repayment of money paid in error[15]; a servitude of thirlage[16]; a right to follow moveables which belonged to an ancestor[17]; the claims of an ancestor's creditors to a preference over the debtor's creditors, having lost the right to follow moveables which had belonged to the ancestors[18]; the obligation to pay for the care of a person in hospital[19]; the obligation contained in a bond of corroboration, notwithstanding that the principal bond was subsisting[20]; the obligation of a bank to pay a sum standing at the credit of a current account[21]; the obligations constituted by a bond and disposition in security of heritage[22]; a claim for legitim, the starting date being the date of the parent's death[23]; a claim for *ius relictae*, the starting date being normally the date of the husband's death;[24] a claim by a legatee against an executor.[25]

All of these would now be covered by section 7 or section 8.

Section 7 has been held applicable to the obligation, arising from a contract of sale of a house, to grant a disposition of the house in return for full payment of the price.[26]

Exclusions: obligations arising from liability under the Consumer Protection Act 1987

The Consumer Protection Act 1987 imposed a new statutory liability for damage caused wholly or partly by a defect in a product and section 22A of the 1973 Act, inserted by the Consumer Protection Act 1987, Sched. I, para. 10, creates a new 10-year prescription of obligations arising from

---

[12] p. 56, *supra*.
[13] *Hunter and Aitkenhead v. Aitken* (1880) 7 R. 510.
[14] *Pearson v. Malachi* (1892) 20 R. 167.
[15] *Edinburgh Mags. v. Heriot's Trust* (1900) 7 S.L.T. 371.
[16] *Brown v. Carron Co.*, 1909 S.C. 452; *Brown v. Livingstone-Learmonth's Trs.* (1906) 14 S.L.T. 142.
[17] *Traill's Trs. v. Free Church*, 1915 S.C. 655.
[18] *ibid.*
[19] *Sutherland C.C. v. Macdonald*, 1935 S.C. 915.
[20] *Yuill's Trs. v. Maclachlan's Trs.*, 1939 S.C.(H.L.) 40.
[21] *Macdonald v. North of Scotland Bank*, 1942 S.C. 369.
[22] *Marr's Exx. v. Marr's Trs.*, 1936 S.C. 64.
[23] *Sanderson v. Lockhart-Mure*, 1946 S.C. 298.
[24] *Campbell's Trs. v. Campbell's Trs.*, 1950 S.C. 48; but see *Mill's Trs. v. Mill's Trs.*, 1965 S.C. 384, where intestacy supervened long after a testator's death and the starting date was the date when it supervened.
[25] *Jamieson v. Clark* (1872) 10 M. 399.
[26] *Gibson v. Carson*, 1980 S.C. 346. But see *Macdonald v. Scott*, 1981 S.L.T. 128.

liability under the 1987 Act.[27] Such liability is accordingly excluded from the ambit of applicability of section 7.

Exclusions: imprescriptible obligations

Sections 7 or 8 do not extinguish any obligation specified in Schedule 3 to the Act as being an imprescriptible obligation.

Schedule 3 provides:

Sections 7 & 8: Schedule 1   SCHEDULE 3

RIGHTS AND OBLIGATIONS WHICH ARE IMPRESCRIPTIBLE FOR THE PURPOSES OF SECTIONS 7 AND 8 AND SCHEDULE 1

The following are imprescriptible rights and obligations for the purposes of sections 7(2) and 8(2) of, and paragraph 2(*h*) of Schedule 1 to, this Act, namely—

(*a*) any real right of ownership in land;

(*b*) the right in land of the lessee under a recorded lease;

(*c*) any right exercisable as a *res merae facultatis*;

(*d*) any right to recover property *extra commercium*;

(*e*) any obligation of a trustee—

    (i) to produce accounts of the trustee's intromissions with any property of the trust;

    (ii) to make reparation or restitution in respect of any fraudulent breach of trust to which the trustee was a party or was privy;

    (iii) to make furthcoming to any person entitled thereto any trust property, or the proceeds of any such property, in the possession of the trustee, or to make good the value of any such property previously received by the trustee and appropriated to his own use;

(*f*) any obligation of a third party to make furthcoming to any person entitled thereto any trust property received by the third party otherwise than in good faith and in his possession;

(*g*) any right to recover stolen property from the person by whom it was stolen or from any person privy to the stealing thereof;

(*h*) any right to be served as heir to an ancestor or to take any steps necessary for making up or completing title to any interest in land.

Comments on rights and obligations excepted from liability to prescribe

(a) A "*real right of ownership in land*" is constituted by the recording of the deed vesting the title or ownership in the claimant in the General Register of Sasines, or registration in the Land Register of Scotland[28]; it is a *jus in rem*, availing against persons generally; it is distinct from the merely personal right to land constituted by a contract or other obligation to convey land, which is valid only against the person thereby bound.[29] A claim to heritable property founded on a writing purporting to bequeath the property to the claimant is a merely personal claim, not a right of property in land.[30]

---

[27] For examination of s. 22A see Chapter 5, *infra*.

[28] Land Registration (Scotland) Act 1979, s. 3(1)(*a*).

[29] On the distinction between a personal right under a disposition of heritage and the real right acquired by recording the disposition in the General Register of Sasines see *Gibson v. Hunter Home Designs Ltd. (in liquidation)*, 1976 S.C. 23 at p. 27.

[30] *Pettigrew v. Harton*, 1956 S.C. 67; *cf Paterson v. Wilson* (1859) 21 D. 322.

"Property rights are not lost merely *non utendo*."[31] "The authorities are clear that a right to heritage, not completed by infeftment and being therefore only a personal right, is not a right of property in land and is subject to the long negative prescription." The effect of this head is that a real right of ownership will never be affected by prescription, even if the holder never takes possession or exercises any of the incidental rights of ownership.

(b) The *"right in land of the lessee under a recorded lease*[32]*,"* i.e. one within the Registration of Leases Act 1857, as amended, and recorded in the General Register of Sasines, or the Land Register of Scotland[33] is a real right availing against the landlord and his successors, not merely a personal right against the landlord.[34]

(c) A *"right exercisable as a* res merae facultatis" is a proprietary right which may be exercised or neglected at the pleasure of the party to whom it belongs but which cannot be extinguished by non-use for any length of time, however long.[35] Rights of this kind include the rights to exact payments of feu-duty, rent, interest and similar periodical payments; the rights to particular terms' payments are extinguished by the short negative prescription, but the continuing right to exact payments as they fall due is not extinguished.[36] Other examples include the right to use a watercourse as a navigable canal,[37] the right to use a common stair,[38] the right reserved in the titles to open a door from a house into a common stair,[39] the right to put a wicket-gate across a right of way across one's lands,[40] a right to redeem a burden,[41] a reserved right to use a strip of ground as a road,[42] and to retain open or to close up a ditch on one's own land.[43] The category may include a servitude.[44] Statutory powers are probably in the same position; the persons vested with them can exercise them at any time.[45]

(d) Property *"extra commercium"* comprises rights which cannot be treated as subjects of commerce[46] and articles of property exempted from commerce on account of their destination to special uses.[47] The category has been held to include presbytery records.[48] It may include things lent for exhibition, or deposited for the use of scholars.

---

[31] *Pettigrew v. Harton,* 1956 S.C. 67 at p. 74, *per* Lord Patrick.

[32] *ibid.* citing *Paul v. Reid,* February 8, 1814, F.C.; Hume, *Lect.* IV, 535–536, and *Robertson v. Robertson* (Mor. 10694 there referred to).

[33] Land Registration (Scotland) Act 1979, s. 3(3)(*a*).

[34] 1857 Act, s. 2.

[35] Bell's *Dictionary, s.v. cf.* Ersk., III, 7, 10; Bell, *Prin.,* §§ 609, 999, 2017, note (p); Napier, *Prescription,* pp. 645–647; Millar, *Prescription,* pp. 86–87.

[36] Bell, *Prin.,* § 609; *Duke of Buccleuch v. Officers of State* (1770) M. 10751; see also *Warrand's Trs. v. Mackintosh* (1890) 17 R. (H.L.) 13 at p. 19.

[37] *Swan's Trs. v. Muirkirk Iron Co.* (1850) 12 D. 622.

[38] *Leck v. Chalmers* (1859) 21 D. 408.

[39] *Gellatly v. Arrol* (1863) 1 M. 592.

[40] *Sutherland v. Thomson* (1876) 3 R. 485.

[41] *Reid's Trs. v. Duchess of Sutherland* (1881) 8 R. 509.

[42] *Smith v. Stewart* (1884) 11 R. 921.

[43] *Anderson v. Robertson,* 1958 S.C. 367.

[44] *Smith, supra.*

[45] *Ayr Harbour Trs. v. Oswald* (1883) 10 R. (H.L.) 85 at p. 90; *Ellice's Trs. v. Caledonian Canal Commissioners* (1904) 6 F. 325.

[46] *Earl of Lauderdale v. Scrymgeour Wedderburn,* 1910 S.C. (H.L.) 35 at pp. 41–42.

[47] Ersk., II, 1, 7. *cf.* Stair, II, 12, 10; *Dumbarton Mags. v. Edinburgh University,* 1909 1 S.L.T. 51.

[48] *Edinburgh Presbytery v. Edinburgh University* (1890) 28 S.L.R. 567.

(e) *"Any obligation of a trustee..."* The word "trustee" is widely defined in section 15(1) and can include not only trustees *eo nomine* but public bodies acting in a trust capacity.[49] The definition includes trustees within the meaning of the Trusts (Scotland) Act 1921, s. 2, which includes trustees *ex officio*, executors nominate, tutors, curators and judicial factors, which last term is redefined by the Trusts (Scotland) Act 1961, s. 3.

(i) *"To produce accounts:"* prescription can never bar the claim of beneficiaries to an accounting from trustees or their representatives[50] though it may bar a claim for payment of a particular share or sum.

This obligation extends to funds held in trust, having been consigned as payable to debenture holders.[51] But a claim for a sum alleged to be due under a trust is a claim not of trust accounting but of debt and liable to negative prescription.[52]

(ii)*" To make reparation or restitution in respect of any fraudulent breach of trust to which the trustee was a party or was privy."* A fraudulent breach of trust certainly covers a breach done with intention to defraud, but it is questionable if it is confined to that; it may include a breach of trust, even negligent, which has the effect of defrauding a beneficiary of what he is rightly entitled to under the trust. "It is settled law... that no trustee can acquire by prescription a right to perpetuate a breach of trust ... no prescriptive possession would have enabled the trustee to have got rid of this trust obligation so long as he continued to hold the property... it is well-settled law that the negative prescription would not extinguish this claim by long possession alone unaided by anything like repudiation or discharge."[53] The trustee must however have been a party to, or privy to, the breach of trust. Similarly, it has been held that trustees cannot by prescription acquire a right to perpetuate a breach of trust.[54]

(iii) *"To make furthcoming to any person entitled thereto any trust property or the proceeds of any such property, in the possession of the trustee or to make good the value of any such property previously received by the trustee and appropriated to his own use."* Thus where trustees sold trust property to themselves as local authority it was held that the running of prescription did not protect them against a claim for restitution. "No trustee of such an endowment as this can by any course of time prescribe a right to perpetuate a breach of trust."[55] "It is I think, well settled law that, so long as a trust subject remains entire in the hands of a trustee, no lapse of time will bar a claim for it by the beneficiary."[56] "It is well settled ... that

---

[49] *Dundee Presbytery v. Dundee Mags.* (1858) 20 D. 849; (1861) 4 Macq. 223; 23 D. (H.L.) 14.

[50] *Barns v. Barns's Trs.* (1857) 19 D. 626; *Bertram Gardner & Co.'s Tr. v. K. & L.T.R.,* 1920 S.C. 555; *Cooper Scott v. Gill Scott,* 1924 S.C. 309; *Hastie's J.F. v. Morham's Exrs.,* 1951 S.C. 668.

[51] *United Collieries v. Lord Advocate,* 1950 S.C. 458.

[52] *Murray v. Mackenzie* (1897) 4 S.L.T. 231.

[53] *Thain v. Thain* (1891) 18 R. 1196 at p. 1201, *per* Lord Kinnear referring to *Aberdeen Mags. v. Aberdeen University* (1877) 4 R. (H.L.) 48.

[54] *Grant v. Henry* (1894) 21 R. 358.

[55] *Aberdeen University v. Aberdeen Mags.* (1876) 3 R. 1087 at p. 1094; affd. 4 R.(H.L.) 48.

[56] *United Collieries v. Lord Advocate,* 1950 S.C. 458 at p. 467, *per* Lord Mackintosh, citing *Aberdeen University v. Irvine* (1866) 4 M. 392 at p. 401, affd. 6 M. (H.L.) 29 at p. 37; *Cooper Scott v. Gill Scott,* 1924 S.C. 309; *Bertram, Gardner & Co.'s Tr. v. K. & L.T.R.,* 1920 S.C. 555 at p. 565. See also *Baird v. Baird's Trs.,* 1954 S.C. 290.

prescription cannot be pleaded against the right of a beneficiary ... to follow extant trust property (or its identifiable proceeds or surrogatum) into the hands of a trustee or of anyone acquiring from such a trustee, not being a *bona fide* purchaser for value without notice of the trust."[57]

(f) *"Any obligation of a third party to make furthcoming to any person entitled thereto any trust property received by the third party otherwise than in good faith and in his possession."* A third party who receives trust property in good faith, for value and without notice of breach of trust is entitled to keep it, but if he does not so take it, he is bound for all time to restore it to the trustee, so long as it is still in his possession.[58] If it is not in his possession he is bound to restore to the trust only any profit made by him by intromitting with the property, and any claim for restitution must be brought against the party in actual possession at the time.

(g) *"Any right to recover stolen property from the person by whom it was stolen or from any person privy to the stealing thereof."* Stolen property is by the manner of its taking impressed with a *vitium reale* which taints it so long as it is in the hands of the thief, or of any resetter or other person who is privy to the stealing; in the hands of any such person it remains for ever stolen property and is recoverable by the true owner.[59] An exception exists in the cases of negotiable instruments, bank notes and coin which pass by mere delivery to the effect of conferring a good title on every taker subsequent to the actual thief, provided he has taken in good faith, for value and without notice of the theft.

(h) *"Any right to be served as heir to an ancestor or to take any steps necessary for making up or completing a title to any interest in land."* Service as heir in heritage of a person deceased intestate can, since the Succession (Scotland) Act 1964 came into force, arise only in relation to deaths occurring before then. If an individual is truly the person entitled to any interest in land by a succession which opened before then his right to take the steps necessary to establish his relationship and complete title to the interest in land is never excluded by lapse of time. In *Bosville v. Lord Macdonald*[60] a grandson of a son of the third Lord Macdonald sued the sixth Lord Macdonald and sought to dispute the succession. It was held that service of another son of the third Lord Macdonald in 1832 did not bar the action as it would not exclude the pursuer from serving as heir- male to his great-grandfather. A retour or decree of service granted by a competent court (now only the Sheriff Court of Chancery) was reducible for 20 years but thereafter not challengeable.[61] In *Macdonald v. Scott's Exors.*[62] M acquired in 1952 a contractual right to demand a disposition from S of certain parts of a building. The question was whether this right was imprescriptible under head (h). It was held that the right which was

---

[57] *Hastie's J.F. v. Morham's Exrs.*, 1951 S.C. 668 at p. 676, *per* L.P. Cooper.

[58] *cf. Armour v. Glasgow Royal Infirmary*, 1909 S.C. 916.

[59] Stair, II, 12, 10; *Dalhanna Knitwear Ltd. v. Mohammed Ali*, 1967 S.L.T. (Sh.Ct.) 74. See also Stair, II, 12, 10; Ersk., III, 7, 14. It is not clear if this applies also to property held under a void title, *e.g. Morrisson v. Robertson*, 1908 S.C. 332.

[60] 1910 S.C. 597.

[61] Prescription Act 1617, Bell, *Prin.*, § 2024; see also *Sibbald's Heirs v. Harris*, 1947 S.C. 601. The repeal of the 1617 Act would seem to make modern services challengeable indefinitely. See also *Bain v. Bain*, 1994 G.W.D. 7. 410.

[62] 1981 S.C. 75.

imprescriptible was one related to an interest in land such as a personal right to land, and not a contractual right to require from a seller the acquisition of such a personal right. M's right to acquire a disposition had prescribed. *Macdonald* was not followed in *Porteous's Executors v. Ferguson*[63] where a right to be served as heir was held to have prescribed under the law in force before the 1973 Act came into force. An obligation to grant a disposition of land is not an imprescriptible obligation under this sub-head.[64]

On what is an "interest in land" see p. 15.

At common law the negative prescription did not bar a challenge of a right which could be upheld only by founding on a nullity, such as a forged deed,[65] or a deed entirely unauthenticated.[66] It is thought that this principle still applies; an alleged right based on a nullity has no existence.

Exclusions: obligations to make reparation for personal injuries or death

In the 1973 Act as originally passed the long negative prescription applied to cases of personal injury or death. The Scottish Law Commission feared that prescription might in some cases cut off a claim before an injured person had realised that he had been injured and had sued.[67] On its recommendation this exclusion provision was added by the 1984 Act. The limitation period of three years under section 17, which period may be extended, is now the only restriction on time for suing for personal injuries or death.

Starting date for long negative prescription

"If, after the date when any obligation ... has become enforceable"

These words define the starting date for the running of the long negative prescription. They echo the former rule that negative prescription could not be said to run until the demand of the creditor had become enforceable.[68] An obligation becomes enforceable when the creditor can exercise his right under the obligation or, if need be, take appropriate legal proceedings to vindicate his claim. It has been laid down that in ascertaining the *terminus a quo* the material date is not the date when the right in question vests or accrues, but the date when a claim was first enforceable by action.[69] In that case the widow of a man who died in 1930 enjoyed a liferent until her death in 1962. Her children predeceased, the last dying in 1951; her executors claimed *jus relictae* from the fee which by the children's deaths had fallen into intestacy. It was held that the long negative prescription applicable to her claim to *jus relictae* ran from 1951, and it had not prescribed. It was a potential claim from 1930, but an enforceable claim only from 1951. Similarly a contractual obligation becomes enforceable

---

[63] 1995 S.L.T. 649.

[64] *Stewart's Exrs. v. Stewart*, 1993 S.L.T. 440; altered on other points: 1994 S.L.T. 466.

[65] Ersk., III, 7, 12; *Graham v. Watt* (1843) 5 D. 1368 at p. 1369; affd. (1846) 5 Bell 172.

[66] *Kinloch v. Bell* (1867) 5 M. 360 at p. 370.

[67] *cf. Cartledge v. Jopling* [1963] 1 All E.R. 341, later overruled by statute.

[68] *Earl of Fife v. Duff* (1888) 15 R. 238 at p. 253; *cf.* Ersk., III, 7, 36; Napier on *Prescription*, 656; Millar on *Prescription*, 97; Gloag on *Contract*, 738; *Campbell's Trs. v. Campbell's Trs.*, 1950 S.C. 48 at p. 57; *Mill's Trs. v. Mill's Trs.*, 1965 S.C. 384 at p. 388.

[69] *Mill's Trs. v. Mill's Trs.*, 1965 S.C. 384. *cf. Sanderson v. Lockhart-Mure*, 1946 S.C. 298.

when the date for performance has arrived but performance has not been made and the creditor can sue for implement or for damages for non-performance, a delictual obligation not when breach of duty has taken place but only when harm has been done and the injured party can sue for reparation therefor.[70]

In relation to obligations to make reparation section 11 enacts:

Obligations to make reparation

11.—(1) Subject to subsections (2) and (3) below, any obligation (whether arising from any enactment, or from any rule of law or from, or by reason of any breach of, a contract or promise) to make reparation for loss, injury or damage caused by an act, neglect or default shall be regarded for the purposes of section 6 of this Act as having become enforceable on the date when the loss, injury or damage occurred.

(2) Where as a result of a continuing act, neglect or default loss, injury or damage has occurred before the cessation of the act, neglect or default the loss, injury or damage shall be deemed for the purposes of subsection (1) above to have occurred on the date when the act, neglect or default ceased.

(3)...

(4)[71] Subsections (1) and (2) above (with the omission of any reference therein to subsection (3) above) shall have effect for the purposes of section 7 of this Act as they have effect for the purposes of section 6 of this Act.

For verbal comments on section 11(1) and (2), see p. 62.

This section in its application to section 7 deals with the starting date for prescription of all obligations to make reparation, whatever their legal ground. The starting date is the date when loss, injury or damage resulting from the breach of duty occurred. Thus if a building is erected on inadequate foundations the starting date is the date when subsidence became apparent.

The omission of subsection (3) from section 11 in its application to cases covered by section 7 means that, for the purposes of the long negative prescription, it does not matter whether the creditor in the obligation was or was not aware, or could or could not with reasonable diligence have been aware, that loss, injury or damage had occurred. There is no reference to "discoverability" of the harm.

It has been observed that the effect of section 11(4) is to provide that the long negative prescription continues to run even while loss remained undiscovered.[72]

"the obligation has subsisted for a continuous period of 20 years"

These words state the period of the long negative prescription as 20 years, always provided that neither of the cumulative conditions stated in the immediately following phrases of the section have been satisfied. By the proviso, in the application of the section to an obligation under a bill of exchange or promissory note, only the first condition need be satisfied.

The general provisions as to computation of time contained in section 14 apply to section 7 as they do to extinction under section 6. For comments thereon see p. 72.

---

[70] *cf. Watson v. Fram Reinforced Concrete Co. and Winget*, 1960 S.C. (H.L.) 92.
[71] As amended by the Prescription and Limitation (Scotland) Act 1984, Sched. 2.
[72] *Beard v. Beveridge, Herd & Sandilands*, 1990 S.L.T. 609.

"(a) without any relevant claim having been made in relation to the obligation"

For comments on this phrase, see p. 66, above.

"and (b) without the subsistence of the obligation having been relevantly acknowledged"

For comments on this phrase, see p. 69, above.

It has to be noted that by the proviso to the subsection this paragraph is to be omitted in the application of the section to an obligation under a bill of exchange or promissory note. In such a case accordingly the obligation to pay is extinguished if 20 years have elapsed without a relevant claim having been made in relation to the obligation.

Under the former law it was held that prescription of a bond might be interrupted by payments of interest, but that these could not be proved by parole,[73] and also that payment of interest on a bond would not prevent the extinction by prescription of the obligation in a bond of corroboration accessory thereto.[74] It has also been held[75] that the inclusion of a bond as a debt in the inventory of a deceased debtor's estate and admission in correspondence between the debtor's trustee and solicitor and the creditor that the latter was in right of the bond were acknowledgments that the debt existed and interrupted prescription. It was even observed[76] that it was sufficient to interrupt prescription that there should be evidence inconsistent with abandonment of the debt by the creditor. The decision and dictum are not now good law. Such facts do not amount to "relevant acknowledgement."

Under this section it has been held[77] that whether performance amounted to "relevant acknowledgment" within the meaning of section 10 was a question of fact and degree in each case and must be of such a kind as could reasonably be explained only by reference to the particular obligation in question, and that the intention of Part I of the 1973 Act was to extinguish separate and independent obligations.

The effect of either the making of a relevant claim or a relevant acknowledgment of the subsistence of the obligation is to interrupt the prescriptive period and require it to recommence from the date of the last act which is part of the claim or acknowledgment.

In the former law "the tendency of the law has been to put a benignant construction upon evidence of interruption."[78] But by no means all the kinds of acts accepted in the older cases as interrupting prescription would now amount to "relevant claim" or "relevant acknowledgment."

"then as from the expiration of that period the obligation shall be extinguished"

This clause states that the effect of the lapse of a continuous period of 20 years without either relevant claim by the creditor or, save in the case of

---

[73] Stair, II, 12, 26; Bell, *Prin.*, § 616; *Nicolson v. Philorth* (1667) Mor. 11233; *Garden v. Rigg* (1743) Mor. 11274; *Kermack v. Kermack* (1874) 2 R. 156.

[74] *Yuill's Trs. v. Maclachlan's Trs.*, 1939 S.C. (H.L.) 40.

[75] *Marr's Exx. v. Marr's Trs.*, 1936 S.C. 64.

[76] *ibid.*, at p. 76, *per* Lord Murray.

[77] *Gibson v. Carson*, 1980 S.C. 356 at p. 360.

[78] *Marr's Exx.*, *supra*, at p. 76, *per* Lord Murray citing older cases.

bills or notes, relevant acknowledgment by the debtor, is wholly to extinguish the obligation. Therefore it cannot be sued on or enforced in any way.

It should be noted that under section 7 there is no counterpart to section 6(4) providing that in the computation of a prescriptive period, periods during which the creditor was induced by fraud or error induced by the debtor or was under legal disability are not to be reckoned. Accordingly under section 7 there is no extension of time by reason of allegation of fraud, induced error or legal disability affecting the creditor. Moreover by section 14(1)(*b*) any time during which any person against whom a provision of Part I of the 1973 Act is pled was under legal disability is, save under section 6(4), to be ignored. If A agreed to buy a house from B but did not obtain a disposition, then became of unsound mind and remained so until more than 20 years after the agreement, the obligation to grant a disposition would be extinguished.[79]

EXTINCTION OF RIGHTS RELATING TO PROPERTY

The next application of the long negative prescription is to extinguish certain rights relating to property.

Section 8 enacts—

Extinction of other rights relating to property by prescriptive periods of twenty years

8.—(1) If, after the date when any right to which this section applies has become exercisable or enforceable, the right has subsisted for a continuous period of twenty years unexercised or unenforced, and without any relevant claim in relation to it having been made, then as from the expiration of that period the right shall be extinguished.

(2) This section applies to any right relating to property, whether heritable or moveable, not being a right specified in Schedule 3 to this Act as an imprescriptible right or falling within section 6 or 7 of this Act as being a right correlative to an obligation to which either of those sections applies.

VERBAL COMMENTARY ON SECTION 8

"If... any right to which this section applies"

By subsection (2) the section is stated to be applicable to "any right relating to property, whether heritable or moveable." This can include, in relation to heritable property, a personal unfeudalised right to lands,[80] the right of the creditor in a ground-annual, both as to arrears and for the future, any personal right against the owner relating to the particular heritable property,[81] the right of a tenant, occupier or licensee, the right of a party in right of a servitude over the land and similar rights, the right of an adjacent proprietor to object to a use of land amounting to an actionable nuisance.[82]

---

[79] Example founded on *Gibson v. Carson*, 1980 S.C. 356.

[80] Hume *Lectures* IV, 535–6; *Robertson v. Robertson* (1770) Mor. 10694; *Paul v. Reid,* Feb. 8, 1814, F.C.; *Pettigrew v. Harton,* 1956 S.C. 67 at p. 77.

[81] *Paterson v. Wilson* (1859) 21 D. 322; *Skinner v. Skinner*, 1953 S.L.T. (Notes) 83; *Pettigrew v. Harton*, 1956 S.C. 67.

[82] *Harvie v. Robertson* (1903) 5 F. 338; *Webster v. Lord Advocate*, 1985 S.C. 173.

In relation to moveable property it can include any personal right against the possessor, such as of a lessor, lender, or depositor to recover a thing let, lent or deposited,[83] the right of a buyer to have delivery of goods bought, and similar rights, and rights in succession.

The section seems to apply to corporeal and incorporeal property, but not to incorporeal intellectual property where the property consists only in rights, such as the various rights comprehended in the copyright in a work, which are mostly regulated by special statutory provisions.

The section does not, however, apply to (a) a right specified in Schedule 3 as an imprescriptible right,[84] nor to (b) a right falling within section 6 or 7 as being "a right correlative to an obligation to which either of those sections applies." This latter phrase refers to the analysis of the term "right" and the related terms "privilege" or "liberty," "power" and "immunity", and of the term "duty," and the related terms "no-right," "liability" and "disability" worked out by such jurists as Windscheid, Thon, Bïerling and Salmond,[85] and most notably by Hohfeld,[86] whereby the terms "right" and "duty" and the other pairs of legal terms were defined as jural correlatives of each other. This relationship imports that the existence of a legal right in one person implies the existence of a legal duty in another person. Thus in the case of sale of goods to say that the buyer has a right to delivery of the goods implies as its correlative that the seller has a duty to deliver, and to say that the buyer has a duty to pay the price implies as its correlative that the seller has a right to obtain payment of the price. In *Macdonald v. North of Scotland Bank*[87] Lord Justice-Clerk Cooper said: "the principle clearly emerges that the non-enforcement by a creditor of a contractual right for the prescriptive period infers an irrebuttable presumption that the right has been abandoned, and therefore that the correlative obligation [*i.e.* the duty to pay] has been extinguished...."

An "obligation to which either of those sections [6 or 7] applies" includes obligations to pay, to make reparation, etc. (section 6) and obligations of any kind not being imprescriptible (section 7). Accordingly a "right correlative to an obligation to which either of those sections applies" is a right to exact payment, to exact reparation, etc. (section 6) or a right to enforce an obligation of any kind not being imprescriptible (section 7).

"If, after the date when any right... has become exercisable or enforceable"

This phrase fixes the starting date of the running of the long negative prescription of property rights.

When a particular right relating to property, whether heritable or moveable, has become exercisable or enforceable depends on what the

---

[83] *cf.* Ersk, III, 7, 7; *Minister of Aberscherder v. Minister of Gemrie* (1633) M. 10972; *Taylor v. Nisbet* (1901) 4 F. 79; *Bertram Gardner & Co.'s Tr. v. King's and Lord Treasurer's Remembrancer*, 1920 S.C. 555; *Webster v. Lord Advocate*, 1985 S.C. 173.

[84] For Sched. 3 and explanation thereof, see p. 77, *supra.*

[85] *Jurisprudence* (7th ed., 1924), ss. 76–77.

[86] *Fundamental Legal Conceptions* (1913) 23 Yale L.J. 16 and (1917) 26 Yale L.J. 710, reprinted, ed. W. W. Cook, 1923. See also Corbin, "Legal Analysis and Terminology" (1919) 29 Yale L.J. 165.

[87] 1942 S.C. 369 at p. 373.

kind of right is, and how it has come to be vested in the party entitled thereto. Thus it has been observed that a right of action to restrain a nuisance begins when the nuisance begins.[88] If a nuisance, though of the same general kind, is materially altered, it is treated as a fresh nuisance giving rise to a new right of action.[89]

"the right has subsisted for a continuous period of twenty years unexercised or unenforced"

The conditions of the extinction of the right by the long negative prescription are (a) that it has subsisted for 20 years continuously, and (b) throughout that time it has been unexercised or unenforced, and (c), as stated in the phrase next to be considered, that no relevant claim in relation thereto has been made. The infringement of the right need not have been continuous if it was periodical and regular, *e.g.* every year.[89]

It appears to be implied that if there is exercise or enforcement of the right in question within the prescriptive period that breaks the continuity of the 20-year period and requires the prescriptive period to commence running again.

"and without any relevant claim in relation to it having been made"

This phrase states the final condition which must be satisfied before the extinctive power of this section can take effect. It is implied that if a relevant claim be made by or on behalf of the creditor the prescriptive period is interrupted and must start to run again.

By section 9:

(1) ...

(2) In section 8 of this Act the expression "relevant claim," in relation to a right, means a claim made in appropriate proceedings by or on behalf of the creditor to establish the right or to contest any claim to a right inconsistent therewith.

(3) Where a claim which, in accordance with the foregoing provisions of this section, is a relevant claim for the purposes of section 6, 7, 8 or 8A of this Act is made in an arbitration, and the nature of the claim has been stated in a preliminary notice relating to that arbitration, the date when the notice was served shall be taken for those purposes to be the date of the making of the claim.

(4) In this section the expression "appropriate proceedings" and, in relation to an arbitration, the expression "preliminary notice" have the same meanings as in section 4 of this Act.[90]

It should be noted that the definition of "relevant claim" in relation to a right, under section 8, is by section 9(2), different from the definition of "relevant claim" in relation to an obligation, under sections 6, 7 and 8A.

Under section 8 there is no requirement that the subsistence of the right has not been "relevantly acknowledged" during the prescriptive period.

Under section 8 there is no provision, as there is under section 6(4), for excluding from the prescriptive period any period during which the creditor

---

[88] *Harvie v. Robertson* (1903) 5 F. 338 at p. 345.
[89] *Webster v. Lord Advocate*, 1985 S.C. 173 at p. 182.
[90] See p. 23, *supra*.

was induced to refrain from making a relevant claim by fraud or by error induced by the other party, or was under legal disability.

By section 14(1)(*b*) any time during which any person against whom the long negative prescription is pled was under legal disability, *i.e.* by section 15(1), legal disability by reason of nonage or unsoundness of mind, is to be reckoned as if the person were free from that disability. No addition accordingly falls to be made to the prescriptive period on account of disability of either kind.

Under the pre-1976 law it might be held that the period of the long negative prescription had not run where the claimant was held to have been *non valens agere cum effectu*,[91] unable to act with effect. This plea has not been expressly abolished, but it is doubtful if it survives.

"then as from the expiration of that period the right shall be extinguished"

This phrase states the effect of the lapse of the complete period of 20 years continuous, without exercise or enforcement, or relevant claim made in relation thereto, namely that the right is thereafter wholly extinguished.

Thus it was held that a right to dam up the water of a stream and control its flow, resting entirely on possession for the prescriptive period and acquired by such possession might equally be lost by non-user or non-possession for the subsequent prescriptive period.[92]

In a case of pollution of water though the right of objectors to complain may be excluded by prescription, and to that extent those responsible may have acquired a prescriptive right to pollute, that does not permit varying the conduct as to increase the pollution of the river.[93]

EXTINCTION OF OBLIGATIONS TO MAKE CONTRIBUTION BETWEEN WRONGDOERS

In the 1973 Act as originally passed a time-limit for claiming contribution between joint wrongdoers was enacted as a limitation of time provision by section 20. On the recommendation of the Scottish Law Commission this was, by the Prescription and Limitation (Scotland) Act 1984, s. 1, restated as an extinctive prescription provision and inserted in a more appropriate place, as section 8A, section 20 being repealed. Strictly speaking this is not a case of long negative prescription, but it is convenient to treat it at this place in the Act.

Section 8A enacts-

Extinction of obligations to make contribution between wrongdoers

8A. (1) If any obligation to make a contribution by virtue of section 3(2) of the Law Reform (Miscellaneous Provisions) (Scotland) Act 1940 in respect of any damages or expenses has subsisted for a continuous period of two years after the date on which the right to recover contribution became enforceable by the creditor in the obligation—

(*a*) without any relevant claim having been made in relation to the obligation; and

(*b*) without the subsistence of the obligation having been relevantly acknowledged;

then as from the expiration of that period the obligation shall be extinguished.

---

[91] See, *e.g. Pettigrew v. Harton*, 1956 S.C. 67.
[92] *Hunter & Aitkenhead v. Aitken* (1880) 7 R. 510.
[93] *McIntyre Bros. v. McGavin* (1893) 25 R. (H.L.) 49.

(2) Subsections (4) and (5) of section 6 of this Act shall apply for the purposes of this section as they apply for the purposes of that section.

VERBAL COMMENTARY

"If any obligation to made a contribution… in respect of any damages or expenses"

The Law Reform (Miscellaneous Provisions) (Scotland) Act 1940, s. 3(2) provides that where any person has paid any damages or expenses for which he was found liable in an action arising from any wrongful acts or negligent acts or omissions, he is entitled to recover from any other person who, if sued, might also have been held liable in respect of the loss or damage on which the action was founded such contribution, if any, as the court may deem just. Section 3(2) relates not to the case where the pursuer sued two or more defenders and obtained decree against them jointly and severally, in which case any one defender who pays more than the proportion of the damages or expenses which he has been judged justly liable to pay can recover from his co-defenders,[94] but to the case where one defender is pursued to judgment but has contended that another party, not called, might also have been held liable and seeks contribution or total relief from that other party.[95] A person who has been sued and found not liable, and is then sought to be brought in as a third party by another defender, is not a person who, "if sued, might have been held liable" under s. 3(2).[96] The defender's right to recover contribution cannot be defeated by a trick or device used by the pursuer.[97] Since the introduction of third party procedure this problem is less likely to occur[98] but it can still arise if a defender blames a third party but the pursuer does not bring that party in as a second defender.

"has subsisted for a continuous period of two years"

The period of two years was introduced by the Limitation Act 1963, s. 10(1).

"after the date on which the right to recover the contribution became enforceable by the creditor in the obligation"

This date, the starting date for the prescriptive period, can only be the date when a court grants decree in the action for contribution or relief for a contribution from a party, who, if he had also been sued in the original action against the party claiming contribution, might also then have been held liable in whole or in part. Until it has been decided that the party held liable in the first action is entitled to some contribution from the party not sued, but who might have been sued, in that action, that party has no right to recover contribution.

---

[94] This case is governed by s. 3(1). *e.g. Drew v. Western S.M.T. Co.*, 1947 S.C. 222; *Grant v. Sun Shipping Co.*, 1948 S.C. (H.L.) 73 at p. 100. In this case a claim for contribution will be cut off by the long negative prescription: *Campbell's Trs. v. Sinclair* (1878) 5 R. (H.L.) 119 at p. 131, *per* Lord Blackburn.
[95] e.g. *N. C. B. v. Thomson*, 1959 S.C. 353, doubted in *Corvi v. Ellis*, 1969 S.C. 312. See also *Taft v. Clyde Marine*, 1990 S.L.T. 170.
[96] *Travers v. Neilson*, 1967 S.C. 155.
[97] *Corvi, supra*, 320.
[98] e.g. *Carson v. Howard Doris*, 1981 S.C. 278.

"(a) without any relevant claim having been made in relation to the obligation"

"Relevant claim" is defined by section 9. For comment thereon see p. 66.

"and (b) without the subsistence of the obligation having been relevantly acknowledged;"

As in sections 6 and 7 both conditions must be satisfied if prescription is to operate.

On "relevant acknowledgment" see section 10 and comment on p. 69.

"then as from the expiration of that period the obligation shall be extinguished"

The effect of the lapse of two years without either relevant claim or relevant acknowledgment is totally to extinguish the obligation to make contribution.

"(2) Subsections (4) and (5) of section 6 of this Act shall apply ... that section."

The effect of this subsection is to apply to section 8A the provisions excluding from the computation of time periods during which the creditor was induced by the debtor's fraud or error induced by him to refrain from claiming, or during which he was under legal disability by reason of nonage or unsoundness of mind.

For comments on section 6(4) and (5) see p. 71.

Long prior to the 1973 Act it was held that where a defender's claim to contribution or relief from another party might be cut off by prescription it could be preserved by an action for declarator that, if the defender were held liable, he would have a claim against the other party.[99] This device may still be competent.

In *Dormer v. Melville Dundas & Whitson*[1] the defenders convened third parties after the triennium for a claim for personal injuries had expired, seeking a contribution under the 1940 Act, s. 3(2). The pursuer then sought to bring in the third party as additional defender and asked the court to allow this under section 19A. After a preliminary proof[2] the court dismissed the action against the third party. It then held that a defender who had been sued within the triennium could continue in the same process and, relying on the 1940 Act, s. 3(2), seek apportionment of damages between himself and the third party who had been convened even though the third party after being brought in had had the pursuer's case against him dismissed as time-barred.

AMENDMENT OF ACTIONS AFTER LAPSE OF PRESCRIPTIVE PERIOD

Where an action has been brought within the prescriptive period, amendment of that action outwith the five-year or 20-year period has been allowed

---

[99] *Central S.M.T. Co. v. Lanarkshire C.C.*, 1949 S.C. 450.
[1] 1989 S.L.T. 310; affd. 1990 S.L.T. 186.
[2] 1987 S.C.L.R. 655.

though it made substantial alteration of the averments of breach of contract and of fault,[3] or substituted one pursuer for another where it was a change of name rather than of identity,[4] or amended the defences to counter an alternative claim based on a breach of the same obligation,[5] but refused where the amendment sought to substitute a claim based on a different obligation,[6] or to substitute a claim based on breach of contract for one based on delict.[7] As with amendments in actions brought under section 17 or section 18 the question is whether the proposed amendment modifies or clarifies a case already made or seeks to substitute what is really a new case for the one originally averred.

Concluding Provisions of Part I

Savings

12.—(1) Where by virtue of any enactment passed or made before the passing of this Act a claim to establish a right or enforce implement of an obligation may be made only within a period of limitation in or determined under the enactment, and, by the expiration of a prescriptive period determined under section 6, 7 or 8 of this Act the right or obligation would, apart from this subsection, be extinguished before the expiration of the period of limitation, the said section shall have effect as if the relevant prescriptive period were extended so that it expires—

(*a*) on the date when the period of limitation expires, or

(*b*) if on that date any such claim made within that period has not been finally disposed of, on the date when the claim is so disposed of.

(2) Nothing in section 6, 7 or 8 of this Act shall be construed so as to exempt any deed from challenge at any time on the ground that it is invalid *ex facie* or was forged.

Section 12(1) appears to deal with the case where by a previous Act a claim may be made only within a period of limitation (not a prescriptive period) specified thereby, *e.g.* a claim under the Income and Corporation Taxes Act 1988, and, but for this subsection, it would be extinguished by the five-year prescription (s. 6) or the long negative prescription (s. 7 or s. 8) before the limitation period had run. In such a case section 6, 7 or 8 is to be extended to the date when the limitation period expires or the date when any claim made within the limitation period is finally disposed of.

Subsection (2) makes clear that, as under the older law, no extinctive prescription is to exclude challenge of a deed on the ground of *ex facie* invalidity or forgery.

In *Riddick v. Shaughnessy, Quigley & McColl*[8] the Lord Ordinary expressed the view that section 12 is not dealing with prescriptions properly so-called but with limitations.

Contracting out

Section 13 enacts:

---

[3] *Macleod v. Sinclair,* 1981 S.L.T. (Notes) 38.
[4] *Stewart v. Highlands and Islands Development Board,* 1991 S.L.T. 787.
[5] *Safdar v. Devlin,* 1995 S.L.T. 530.
[6] *Lawrence v. McIntosh & Hamilton,* 1981 S.L.T. (Sh. Ct.) 73.
[7] *Middleton v. Douglass,* 1991 S.L.T. 726.
[8] 1981 S.L.T. (Notes) 89.

Prohibition of contracting out

13.[9]—Any provision in any agreement purporting to provide in relation to any right or obligation that section 6, 7, 8 or 8A of this Act shall not have effect shall be null.

It is accordingly incompetent for a creditor to include in a contract a provision, or to provide by separate contract, that notwithstanding his failure for more than five years to exercise a claim his right is not to be extinguished. The only way to achieve this end is, within the prescriptive period, to make a "relevant claim" or obtain a "relevant acknowledgment."

This provision "assumes a deliberate intention on the part of the contracting parties to make an obligation which is enforceable not extinguishable by the lapse of a period of time. It does not in my judgment operate so as to make illegal an agreement by the parties to postpone the enforceability of an obligation".[10]

Section 16 enacts:

Amendments and repeals related to Part 1

16.—(1) The enactments specified in Part I of Schedule 4 to this Act shall have effect subject to the amendment there specified, being an amendment related to this Part of this Act.

(2) Subject to the next following subsection, the enactments specified in Part I of Schedule 5 to this Act (which includes certain enactments relating to the limitation of proof) are hereby repealed to the extent specified in column 3 of that Schedule.

(3) Where by virtue of any Act repealed by this section the subsistence of an obligation in force at the date of the commencement of this Part of this Act was immediately before that date, by reason of the passage of time, provable only by the writ or oath of the debtor the subsistence of the obligation shall (notwithstanding anything in sections 16(1) and 17(2) (a) of the Interpretation Act 1978,[11] which relates to the effect of repeals) as from that date be provable as if the said repealed Act had not passed.

GENERAL NOTE TO SECTION 16

This section effects the amendment of the statutes listed in Schedule 4, Part I, and the repeal of the statutes listed in Schedule 5, Part I, to the extent stated.

(3) "Where by virtue ... had not passed."

This provides in substance that where the subsistence of an obligation was until the commencement of Part I of the Act (ss. 1–16) (which, by s. 25(2), is on the expiration of three years from the date on which the Act was passed) provable only by the writ or oath of the debtor, notably obligations affected by the triennial, quinquennial, sexennial or vicennial prescriptions, the subsistence of the obligation after the commencement of Part I of the Act is provable without the restrictions on mode and onus of proof imposed by the relevant repealed Act, which then cease to affect such obligations. This appears to mean that if, for example, a tradesman's

---

[9] As amended by the Prescription and Limitation (Scotland) Act 1984, Sched. 1, para. 5.
[10] *McPhail v. Cunninghame D. C.*, 1985 S.L.T. 149 at p. 153. See also *Royal Bank v. Brown*, 1982 S.C. 89; *Ferguson v. McIntyre*, 1993 S.L.T. 1269.
[11] As amended by the Interpretation Act 1978, s. 25(2).

account was incurred in January 1974 and, not having been paid, became, by reason of triennial prescription, provable after January 1977 only by the debtor's writ or oath, after July 25, 1976 (the date of the commencement of this part of the Act), it will be provable in the ordinary way, by parole evidence, the onus being on the creditor, until January 1979 when it will be totally extinguished by the five-year prescription introduced by section 6.

Schedule 5 enacts:

Sections 16, 23   SCHEDULE 5

REPEALS

PART I

REPEALS COMING INTO FORCE ON EXPIRATION OF THREE YEARS FROM PASSING OF THIS ACT

Chapter	Short Title	Extent of Repeal
1469 c. 4.	The Prescription Act 1469.	The whole Act.
1474 c. 9.	The Prescription Act 1474.	The whole Act.
1579 c. 19.	The Prescription (Ejections) Act 1579.	The whole Act.
1579 c. 21.	The Prescription Act 1579.	The whole Act.
1594 c. 24.	The Prescription Act 1594.	The whole Act.
1617 c. 12.	The Prescription Act 1617.	The whole Act.
1617 c. 13.	The Reduction Act 1617.	The whole Act.
1669 c. 14.	The Prescription Act 1669.	The whole Act.
1669 c. 15.	The Interruptions Act 1669.	The whole Act.
1685 c. 14.	The Prescription Act 1685.	The whole Act.
1695 c. 7.	The Cautioners Act 1695.	The whole Act.
1696 c. 9.	The Prescription Act 1696.	The whole Act.
1696 c. 19.	The Interruptions Act 1696.	The whole Act.
12 Geo. 3. c. 72.	The Bills of Exchange (Scotland) Act 1772.	Sections 37, 39, 40.
31 & 32 Vict. c. 64.	The Land Writs Registration (Scotland) Act 1868.	Section 15.
45 & 46 Vict. c. 61	The Bills of Exchange Act 1882.	In section 100, the words from "this section shall not apply" to the end of the section.
14 & 15 Geo. 5. c. 27.	The Conveyancing (Scotland) Act 1924.	Sections 16, 17.
1 & 2 Geo. 6. c. 24.	The Conveyancing Amendment (Scotland) Act 1938.	Section 4.
1969 c. 39.	The Age of Majority (Scotland) Act 1969.	In Schedule 1, the entry relating to the Prescription Act 1617.
1970 c. 35.	The Conveyancing and Feudal Reform (Scotland) Act 1970.	Section 8.

CHAPTER 5

PRESCRIPTION OF OBLIGATIONS UNDER THE CONSUMER PROTECTION ACT 1987

THE Consumer Protection Act 1987[1] was passed to comply with Directive 85/374 of the Council of the European Communities of 1985 on the approximation of laws of the member states concerning liability for defective products. The Directive is appended to the Act and may be used in the interpretation of the Act. It imposes liability, where any damage is caused wholly or partly by a defect in a product, on (a) the producer of the product; (b) any person who, by putting his name on the product or using a trade mark or other distinguishing mark in relation to the product, has held himself out to be the producer of the product; (c) any person who has imported the product into a member state from a place outside the member states in order, in the course of any business of his, to supply it to another. This statutory liability is without prejudice to any liability arising otherwise than by virtue of Part I of the Act.[2] Liability is strict and fault need not be proved, but only production or supply by the defender, defect, actionable damage and causation. By the Act section 5 provides six specific defences to liability. It may not be limited or excluded by any contract term, by any notice or by any other provision.[3] "Damage" is defined as "death or personal injury or any loss of or damage to any property (including land)".[4]

By Schedule 1, Part II to the 1987 Act, various amendments were made to the Prescription and Limitation (Scotland) Act 1973.[5] Schedule I, Part II, paragraph 10, effected the insertion of a new Part IIA into the 1973 Act, dealing with prescription of obligations and limitation of actions under Part I of the Consumer Protection Act 1987. The new section 22A deals with prescription, and section 22D deals with interpretation of the new Part IIA. The new sections 22B and 22C, to which section 22D also applies, deal with limitation of actions.[6]

Ten years' prescription of obligations

22A.—(1) An obligation arising from liability under section 2 of the 1987 Act (to make reparation for damage caused wholly or partly by a defect in a product) shall be extinguished if a period of 10 years has expired from the relevant time, unless a relevant claim was made within that period and has not been finally disposed of, and no such obligation shall come into existence after the expiration of the said period.

(2) If, at the expiration of the period of 10 years mentioned in subsection (1) above, a relevant claim has been made but has not been finally disposed of, the obligation to which the claim relates shall be extinguished when the claim is finally disposed of.

(3) In this section a claim is finally disposed of when—

---

[1] In this chapter "1987 Act" means the Consumer Protection Act 1987. It replaced the Consumer Safety Act 1978.
[2] ss. 1–2; *e.g.* common law liability under the principle of *Donoghue v. Stevenson*, 1932 S.C. (H.L.) 31.
[3] s. 7.
[4] s. 5.
[5] The minor amendments are taken into account in the appropriate sections of the 1973 Act.
[6] See Chapter 7, *infra*.

> (*a*) a decision disposing of the claim has been made against which no appeal is competent;
> (*b*) an appeal against such a decision is competent with leave, and the time limit for leave has expired and no application has been made or leave has been refused;
> (*c*) leave to appeal against such a decision is granted or is not required, and no appeal is made within the time limit for appeal; or
> (*d*) the claim is abandoned;

"relevant claim" in relation to an obligation means a claim made by or on behalf of the creditor for implement or part implement of the obligation, being a claim made—

> (*a*) in appropriate proceedings within the meaning of section 4(2) of this Act; or
> (*b*) by the presentation of, or the concurring in, a petition for sequestration or by the submission of a claim under section 22 or 48 of the Bankruptcy (Scotland) Act 1985; or
> (*c*) by the presentation of, or the concurring in, a petition for the winding up of a company or by the submission of a claim in a liquidation in accordance with the rules made under section 411 of the Insolvency Act 1986;

"relevant time" has the meaning given in section 4(2) of the 1987 Act.

(4) Where a relevant claim is made in an arbitration, and the nature of the claim has been stated in a preliminary notice (within the meaning of section 4(4) of this Act) relating to that arbitration, the date when the notice is served shall be taken for those purposes to be the date of the making of the claim.

GENERAL NOTE

Section 22A creates a new extinctive prescription of ten years for obligations arising from liability under the 1987 Act to make reparation for damage caused by defect in a product.

VERBAL COMMENTARY ON SECTION 22A

"An obligation arising from liability under section 2 of the 1987 Act ... defect in a product)"

Subject to certain qualifications, section 2 of the 1987 Act imposes liability for any damage *i.e.* by section 5, death or personal injury or any loss of or damage to any property (including land), which was caused wholly or partly by a defect (as defined in 1987 Act, section 3), on (*a*) the producer of the product, (*b*) a person who, by putting his name on the product or using a trade mark or other distinguishing mark in relation to the product, has held himself out to be the producer of the product; (*c*) any person who has imported the product into a member state from a place outside the member states in order, in the course of any business of his, to supply it to another. Where two or more persons are liable by virtue of this Part of the 1987 Act, their liability is joint and several. "Partly caused" presumably requires causation to a more than negligible extent.

"shall be extinguished"

The effect of the section is wholly to extinguish the obligation to make reparation.

"if a period of ten years has expired"

The prescriptive period is 10 years. The provisions in section 14 of the 1973 Act about computation of time do not apply; it applies to Part I of the 1973 Act and section 22A is in Part IIA.

"from the relevant time"

"Relevant time", as defined by the 1987 Act, s. 4(2), in relation to electricity, means the time at which it was generated, being a time before it was transmitted or distributed, and in relation to any other product, means (a) if the person proceeded against is a person to whom subsection (2) of section 2 of the 1987 Act applies in relation to that product, *i.e.* a "deemed" producer, the time when he supplied the product to another; (b) if that subsection does not apply to that person in relation to the product, the time when the product was last supplied by a person to whom that subsection does apply in relation to the product.

"unless a relevant claim was made within that period"

"Relevant claim" is defined in the 1987 Act, s. 4(3). Its subheads (*a*), (*b*) and (*c*) correspond to subheads (*a*), (*b*) and (*d*) of the definition of "relevant claim" for the purposes of sections 6, 7 and 8A given in section 9 of the 1973 Act as amended by the Prescription Act 1987, s. 1. The definitions in section 9 and section 22A are not identical. The effect of a "relevant claim" under this section, as under sections 6, 7 and 8A, is to interrupt the prescriptive period and make it start to run again.

"and has not been finally disposed of"

The 1987 Act, section 4(3) defines when a claim is "finally disposed of". Of these (a)—a decision disposing of the claim has been made against which no appeal is competent—will include the rejection of a claim by the House of Lords.

"and no such obligation shall come into existence after the expiration of the said period"

An obligation to make reparation for damage caused by a defective product cannot come into existence after the expiry of 10 years from the "relevant time". If accordingly a person first becomes aware of what he believes to be damage to himself caused by a defect in a product more than 10 years from the relevant time no obligation to make reparation will arise.

There is no provision in this section for a claim being suspended by fraud, error induced, or the creditor's legal disability as there is under sections 6 and 8A.

"(2) If, at the expiration of the period of 10 years ... when the claim is finally disposed of."

If a relevant claim is made before the period of 10 years has expired, the claim may be pursued to final disposal outwith that period. This provision may give rise to difficulties where a claim is made within the prescriptive period, but is then sought, outwith the prescriptive period, to be amended. Probably the answer is that, as under section 17, if an action is commenced within the prescriptive period it may with the leave of the court be amended or modified outwith that period but may not be so substantially changed or rewritten as to become in substance a new and different action. Into which class a particular case falls will depend on the circumstances and the pleadings of the particular case.

"(3) In this section a claim is finally disposed when ... abandoned."

The subsection lays down when a claim is to be deemed "finally disposed of". Head (*a*) will include rejection of a claim by the House of Lords.

"Relevant claim" is defined in terms similar to but not identical with those in section 9 of the 1973 Act as amended.

"Relevant time" is defined only in the 1987 Act, section 4(2).

"(4) Where a relevant claim is made in an arbitration ... the making of the claim."

This subsection corresponds to section 9(3) of the 1973 Act.

Interpretation of this Part

22D.—(1) Expressions used in this Part and in Part I of the 1987 Act shall have the same meanings in this Part as in the said Part I.

(2) For the purposes of section 1(1) of the 1987 Act, this Part shall have effect and be construed as if it were contained in Part I of that Act.

(3) In this Part, "the 1987 Act" means the Consumer Protection Act 1987.

VERBAL COMMENTARY ON SECTION 22D

"(1) Expressions used in this Part"

"This Part" is Part IIA of the 1973 Act, inserted by the 1987 Act, Sched. I, para. 10.

"and in Part I of the 1987 Act"

Part I of the 1987 Act (sections 1 to 9 thereof) deals with Product Liability. Expressions used therein are "agricultural produce", "producer", "product" and "the product liability Directive" (all defined by section 1(2)), "defect" (defined in section 3(1)) and "damage" (defined by section 5(1)).

"shall have the same meanings in this Part as in the said Part I"

The meanings assigned to words in Part I of the 1987 Act are accordingly to have the same meanings in Part IIA of the 1973 Act. Thus a "producer" for the purposes of section 22A (in Part IIA of the 1973 Act) means what the 1987 Act, section 1(2) defines it as meaning.

"(2) For the purposes of section 1(1) of the 1987 Act"

Section 1(1) of the 1987 Act states that Part I is to have effect for the purpose of making such provision as is necessary in order to comply with the Product Liability Directive and shall be construed accordingly.

"this Part shall have effect and be construed as if it were contained in Part I of that Act"

Although the prescription provisions have been incorporated in the law as additional sections added to the 1973 Act they are to have effect and be interpreted as if they had been included in Part I of the 1987 Act.

CHAPTER 6

LIMITATION OF ACTIONS FOR DAMAGES
OR SOLATIUM

PART II of the Prescription and Limitation (Scotland) Act 1973 deals with limitation of actions, that is with rules providing that after the lapse of a stated period of time an action claiming damages for personal injury or wrongful death may no longer be brought. The purpose doubtless was and is to secure that such claims are brought before the evidence is forgotten or lost, to encourage reasonable diligence in pursuing such claims and to avoid oppressing defenders with stale claims. As originally passed sections 17 to 19 re-enacted with modifications provisions first enacted as the Law Reform (Limitation of Actions, etc.) Act 1954, s. 6, later replaced by the Limitation Act 1963, ss. 8 to 9, limiting the time within which actions for personal injuries or wrongful death might be brought, themselves altered by the Law Reform (Miscellaneous Provisions) Act 1971, Sched. I. Sections 17 to 19 were extremely involved, difficult to understand and to apply in practice, and the results of their application seemed questionably fair or just in some of the cases which arose. The draftsmanship of these provisions was severely criticised.[1] The similar words in a provision applicable to England were criticised by the House of Lords[2]: "The obscurity of the Act has been frequently severely criticised; indeed I think the Act has a strong claim to the distinction of being the worst drafted Act on the statute book". Section 19A, introduced by the Law Reform (Miscellaneous Provisions) (Scotland) Act 1980, s. 23, gave a judicial discretion to dispense with the time limits when it seems to the court equitable to do so.

The Scottish Law Commission considered the problem of these complicated provisions and published a consultative memorandum (No. 45) on time-limits in personal injuries actions and a consultation paper on prescription and limitation in private international law. Having considered the responses to these papers they issued in November 1982, Report No. 74: Prescription and Limitation of Actions: Report on Personal Injuries Actions and Private International Law Questions, which recommended various changes and included a draft Bill to give effect to them.

A private member introduced a Bill based on the Scottish Law Commission's draft Bill, which received support from both sides of the House and was passed as the Prescription and Limitation (Scotland) Act 1984. The effect of the Act was very largely to supersede Part II of the 1973 Act, particularly the complicated sections 17 to 19, and to replace them with somewhat simpler sections 17 to 18. In consequence cases dealing with interpretation of the earlier sections 17 to 19 are superseded and can be disregarded. The provisions of the corresponding law in England, now

---

[1] *Kerr v. Stewart (Plant) Ltd.*, 1976 S.C. 120 at p. 131.
[2] *Central Asbestos Co. v. Dodd* [1972] 2 All E.R. 1135 at p. 1138, *per* Lord Reid.

the Limitation Act 1980, ss. 11 to 14, are very different and give no assistance in interpretation.

Even the replacement sections 17 to 18 are by no means simple or clear and it is hard to see why Parliament could not have devised a simpler wording. In particular, in view of the discretion conferred on courts by section 19A to extend the limit of time for suing when it seems equitable to do so, it is hard to see why there is any necessity for the provisions that the limitation of time is not to run until the pursuer has become aware of stated facts. Awareness or justifiable ignorance of relevant facts are matters which could equally well be considered in deciding whether it is equitable or not to allow an extension of the time-limit in particular circumstances.

The onus of averment that one of the sections 17 to 18A bars an action is on the defender; the onus of averment and proof that notwithstanding the *prima facie* barring of an action by one of these sections the pursuer should be allowed to proceed is on the pursuer. It is for the person seeking to rely on provisions for extension of time to aver and prove facts and circumstances relating not only to his first becoming aware, but also to the date when it would have been reasonably practicable for him to have become aware, of facts justifying him in suing.[3] It has been said that proof before answer is more satisfactory than a preliminary proof on a question of time-bar.[4]

If a claim of one of the kinds affected by sections 17 to 18A is not brought within the time-limit laid down or extended it subsists, though it is unenforceable by action; even after the lapse of 20 years it is not totally extinguished by section 7.

Similarly a claim to which none of sections 17 to 18A (nor 22B or 22C in Part IIA of the Act) applies, *e.g.* for property damage or economic loss, is not subject to limitation of time at all but subsists until totally extinguished by section 7 and Schedule I, paragraph 2(*g*), (*gg*) and (*ggg*).

Part II not to extend to product liability

16A. This Part of this Act does not apply to any action which section 22B or 22C of this Act applies.

GENERAL NOTE

This new section was inserted by the Consumer Protection Act 1987, Sched. 1, para. 9. Paragraph 10 thereof instructs the insertion after section 22 of the 1973 Act of a new Part IIA dealing with Prescription of Obligations and Limitation of Actions under Part I of the Consumer Protection Act 1987, and comprising sections 22A to 22D. Section 16A makes clear that Part II ("This Part") of the 1973 Act does not apply to limitation of actions in cases under the product liability provisions (sections 1 to 9) of the 1987 Act. Part IIA of the 1973 Act does. Section 22A (of Part IIA) dealing with prescription of product liability is discussed in Chapter 5 above; sections 22B to 22D (of Part IIA) are discussed in Chapter 7 below.

---

[3] *Provan v. Glynwed,* 1975 S.L.T. 192; *Hamill v. Newalls Insulation Co.,* 1987 S.L.T. 478.
[4] *Shaw v. Renton & Fisher,* 1975 S.L.T. (Notes) 60.

Actions in respect of personal injuries not resulting in death

17.—(1) This section applies to an action of damages where the damages claimed consist of or include damages in respect of personal injuries, being an action (other than an action to which section 18 of this Act applies) brought by the person who sustained the injuries or any other person.

(2) Subject to subsection (3) below and section 19A of this Act, no action to which this section applies shall be brought unless it is commenced within a period of 3 years after—

(*a*) the date on which the injuries were sustained or, where the act or omission to which the injuries were attributable was a continuing one, that date or the date on which the act or omission ceased, whichever is the later; or

(*b*) the date (if later than any date mentioned in paragraph (*a*) above) on which the pursuer in the action became, or on which, in the opinion of the court, it would have been reasonably practicable for him in all the circumstances to become, aware of all the following facts—

(i) that the injuries in question were sufficiently serious to justify his bringing an action of damages on the assumption that the person against whom the action was brought did not dispute liability and was able to satisfy a decree;

(ii) that the injuries were attributable in whole or in part to an act or omission; and

(iii) that the defender was a person to whose act or omission the injuries were attributable in whole or in part or the employer or principal of such a person.

(3) In the computation of the period specified in subsection (2) above there shall be disregarded any time during which the person who sustained the injuries was under legal disability by reason of nonage or unsoundness of mind.

GENERAL NOTE

The substituted section 17 limits the time within which actions of damages for personal injuries not resulting in death may be brought. It applies (1984 Act, section 5(1)) to rights of action accruing both before and after the commencement of that Act.

VERBAL COMMENTARY ON SECTION 17

"(1) This section applies ... personal injuries"

This section applies to claims of damages, whatever the legal ground of action (delict, breach of contract, breach of statutory duty, or other, but not product liability), where the damages consist of, or include damages in respect of "personal injuries", which are defined in section 22, as substituted by section 3 of the 1984 Act, as including any disease and any impairment of a person's physical or mental condition. They include injured feelings[5] and distress and inconvenience arising when the pursuer's house and it's contents were extensively damaged by flooding.[6] The standard elements of such a claim are solatium, patrimonial loss and outlays and expenses incurred by reason of the injuries. A claim against a solicitor for not having brought an action of damages for personal injuries within three years of an accident is not itself an action of damages for personal injuries, and is not affected by section 17.[7] Nor is a claim against a trade union for failing to

---

[5] *Barclay v. Chief Constable, Northern Constabulary,* 1986 S.L.T. 562.
[6] *Fleming v. Strathclyde R. C.,* 1992 S.L.T. 161.
[7] *Flynn v. Graham,* 1964 S.L.T. (Notes) 69.

take up a member's claim in time.[8] The claim may also include claims for property damage or other loss, but must not be solely for such other losses. A claim for such other losses is not affected by section 17 but is subject to the short negative prescription under section 6 and Schedule 1, paragraph 1(*d*) of the 1973 Act.

The section clearly applies where personal injuries, as defined, have been caused directly and immediately by the defender's breach of duty. It may also apply where the primary harm was other than personal injuries and the personal injuries were consequential. In *Drinnan v. Ingram*[9] a woman alleged that she had bought a house in reliance on a report from a firm of surveyors, had then been informed by the local authority that the house was unsafe and had had to leave it. She averred that her health had been damaged as a result of the forced removal and that she had sustained economic loss. It was held in the circumstances that the action was not time-barred. It is submitted that the section does apply to consequential as well as to immediate personal injuries. The issue of whether the personal injuries are too remote to be considered will also arise.[10]

When time bar was being considered at the stage of amendment it was held that a plea of time bar should not be added to the record after the court had considered the question of time-bar and allowed the amendment.[11]

In a case under section 17 amendment relative to time bar has been disallowed when it was proposed after proof and the witnesses had been examined.[12]

Where a case of time-bar under section 17 was raised in a minute of amendment by the defenders after a proof before answer had been allowed it was held that the Lord Ordinary could reconsider the mode of inquiry in the light of the amended pleadings and allow a preliminary proof before answer on the issue of time-bar.[13]

"being an action ... brought by the person who sustained the injuries or any other person."

The action must not be one to which section 18 applies, that is one brought where death has resulted from the injuries.

The action must be brought by either the injured person, or by another person on his behalf, *e.g.* a tutor on behalf of a pupil, or a curator or judicial factor claiming on behalf of an injured incapax, *e.g. Cole-Hamilton v. Boyd*,[14] or an assignee of an injured person's claim, or an executor bringing or continuing an action for patrimonial loss down to the time of the injured person's death, where the death followed in time but resulted from a cause other than the relevant personal injuries. In such a case the executor can claim for the deceased's patrimonial loss and for solatium which now

---

[8] *McGahie v. Union of Shop, Distributive and Allied Workers,* 1966 S.L.T. 74.
[9] 1967 S.L.T. 205.
[10] On this see Walker, *Law of Delict in Scotland* (2nd ed.), 231 *et seq.*
[11] *Gibson v. Droopy & Browns,* 1989 S.L.T. 172.
[12] *Gold v. Costain Concrete Co.,* 1988 S.C.L.R. 15.
[13] *Bendex v. James Donaldson & Sons,* 1990 S.L.T. 350.
[14] 1963 S.C. (H.L.) 1.

transmits on the injured person's death: Damages (Scotland) Act 1993, s. 3.

"(2) Subject to subsection (3) below and section 19A of this Act,"

These provisions both permit, in different circumstances, an extension of the period of time provided by subsection (2).

"no action to which this section applies shall be brought unless it is commenced"

An action is "commenced" on the date of citation of the defender.[15]

"within a period of three years after"

It must be assumed that common law principles apply to the computation of time and that time runs to midnight on the same-numbered day in the same-named month three years after the date of the incident.[16]

"(a) the date on which the injuries were sustained"

In many cases, *e.g.* a road accident, this can be precisely fixed. In cases of progressive disease or harm injuries may be said to have been sustained once any appreciable degree of injury is observable.[17]

"or, where the act or omission to which the injuries were attributable was a continuing one,"

This seeks to deal with the case of *e.g.* exposure, in breach of duty on the defender's part, to dust or fumes over a period. It must be averred, and later proved, that the injuries were attributable to the alleged act or omission.

"that date"

The date on which the injuries were sustained.

"or, the date on which the act or omission ceased, whichever is the later;"

The date of ceasing may be a date on which the work was discontinued, or effectual precautions against the danger were taken. "Ceased" presumably means ceased in relation to that pursuer, so that if he leaves the danger zone or leaves that employment, the act or omission has ceased in relation to him.

"or (b) the date (if later...) on which the pursuer in the action became ... aware of"

This alternative date, which is more appropriate where the fact of having sustained injury cannot be attributed to a specific date, is the date when the

---

[15] Ersk., III, 6, 3; Maclaren, *Court of Session Practice*, 317; *Alston v. McDougall* (1887) 15 R. 78; *Stewart v. North* (1890) 17 R. (H.L.) 60 at p. 63; *Miller v. N.C.B.*, 1960 S.C. 376; *McGraddie v. Clark,* 1966 S.L.T. (Sh.Ct.) 36; *Boyle v. Glasgow Corporation*, 1975 S.C. 238 at p. 247.

[16] *Cavers Parish Council v. Smailholm Parish Council*, 1909 S.C. 195 at p. 197.

[17] *Cartledge v. Jopling* [1963] A.C. 758 at pp. 774 and 781; *Avinou v. Scottish Insulation Co. Ltd.,* 1970 S.C. 128 at p. 133; *Wilson v. Morrinton Quarries Ltd.,* 1979 S.L.T. 82 at p. 86.

pursuer did become aware of certain facts, *e.g.* on being advised by a doctor that he had contracted a disease.

"the pursuer"

It is the pursuer's and not, if different, the injured person's awareness which is relevant. But in a case of assignation of a claim, it is by section 22(2) the assignor's and not the assignee's knowledge which is relevant.

"or on which… it would have been reasonably practicable for him in all the circumstances to become aware of…"

This alternative provides for time starting to run from the date when the pursuer could reasonably have acquired knowledge of certain facts, that is, when he must be deemed to have had constructive knowledge. If a person deliberately or carelessly neglects to seek professional advice after he should reasonably have done so, it may be held that he could have become aware of the relevant facts earlier than he did.

The pursuer has to make averments explaining why it was not reasonably practicable to become aware, and to prove them. In the absence of such averments a pursuer was held precluded from suing third parties but was allowed under section 19A to bring in third parties as further defenders.[18]

"in the opinion of the court"

It is for the court to decide on the evidence whether it would have been reasonably practicable for the pursuer to become aware earlier than he did, and at what date.

"reasonably practicable"

The standard for constructive knowledge is objective. Whether it was reasonably practicable or not depends on the facts and circumstances of each case.[19] An injured person cannot extend the running of time by failing to inquire or take advice; if he could have done so and would have been told that he had suffered injury time will run from the date when injury could have been diagnosed.

"aware of all the following facts—"

The pursuer must have been, or it be held that he should have become, aware of all the following facts. Awareness or ignorance is a matter of fact; what he is aware or ignorant of may be matters of fact or of law,[20] and it is only ignorance of all the stated facts that prevents time running. A belief is not knowledge merely because it turns out to be true.[21] If he is justifiably ignorant of one or more of the stated facts time will not begin to run against him. The onus is on the pursuer to prove which of the facts listed he was

---

[18] *Webb v. B.P. Petroleum Development*, 1988 S.L.T. 775.
[19] *Nicol v. British Steel Corporation (General Steels)*, 1992 S.L.T. 141.
[20] *cf. McIntyre v. Armitage Shanks Ltd.*, 1980 S.C. (H.L.) 46 at p. 56.
[21] *Comer v. James Scott (Electrical Engineers)*, 1978 S.L.T. 235.

not aware of until after the date in section 17(2)(a) and that the action was brought within three years of it being practicable to become aware of them.[22]

"(i) that the injuries in question ... bringing an action of damages"

Time does not run so long as injuries, even if known, would justifiably be regarded as negligible, but time does begin to run if and when the pursuer has or should have had knowledge that his injuries were significant and sufficiently serious to justify not merely a claim but the bringing of an action. Any injuries beyond the minimal or trivial would justify bringing an action even though quantification of damages would be difficult and an award might be small. The question is whether a reasonable claimant would consider that the facts known or ascertainable made an action worthwhile.[23] The injured person need not know the name or nature of his injuries, but only that he had sustained some kind of injuries, more serious than any which would be excluded by the principle *de minimis non curat praetor.*

"on the assumption ... able to satisfy a decree ..."

This proviso seems intended to exclude, from the decision of the question whether injuries justified bringing an action, the practical considerations that in some circumstances proof of liability against a defender might be long, difficult and expensive, and that a defender might be impecunious or in liquidation and not worth suing.

"(ii) that the injuries were attributable in whole or in part to an act or omission;"

The pursuer must know, or it be held that he should have known, that the injuries were attributable to somebody's act or omission. This is a matter of evidence. Attributable means "referable to or resulting from in fact", or "caused by"[24] because section 22(3) provides that knowledge that any act or omission was or was not, as a matter of law, actionable, is irrelevant. Whether injuries were attributable is a question of fact. Time will not run so long as he reasonably thinks that the injuries were attributable to natural causes, old age, excessive smoking, the weather, another accident or the like. To become aware that an accident might be attributable, as only one of several possibilities, to a particular act or omission is not enough to start the time bar period running.[25] It has been held in England[26] that a plaintiff first knew that his injury was attributable to an act or omission, when he first knew that it was capable of being so attributed, namely after a particular visit to hospital. A reasonable belief or suspicion that injuries were so attributable is not "knowledge". Where the acts or omissions can be described broadly as failure to provide a pursuer with safe working conditions he has knowledge, even if he cannot specify the precise acts or

---

[22] *McArthur v. Strathclyde Regional Council,* 1995 S.L.T. 1129.
[23] *Blake v. Lothian Health Board,* 1993 S.L.T. 1248; *Ferla v. Secretary of State for Scotland,* 1995 S.L.T. 662.
[24] *Pickles v. N.C.B.* [1968] 2 All E.R. 596 at p. 600; *Central Asbestos Co. v. Dodd* [1972] 2 All E.R. 1135 at p. 1149.
[25] *Nicol v. British Steel Corporation (General Steels),* 1992 S.L.T. 141.

omissions required to enable his solicitors to draft an adequately specific summons or instructions to counsel.[26]

"and (iii) that the defender ... of such a person."

The pursuer must also know that the defender was a person to whose act or omission the injuries were attributable. In some cases discovery of whom to sue has been a difficulty for pursuers.[27] The defender may be the person actually responsible or the employer or principal of the person actually responsible. The pursuer need not know whether the attributability has or has not the legal consequence of attaching legal liability.[28] Time-bar accordingly cannot run to protect a defender if the pursuer reasonably did not know that the defender was a person who was in fact responsible for the act or omission in issue. This head covers the case where the pursuer could not discover who was responsible for the injuries, such as a hit and run driver.[29]

"(3) In the computation of the period ... unsoundness of mind."

Even if time has begun to run under subsection (2) there is to be left out of account any time during which the injured person was a pupil or minor[30] (now under 16)[31] or of unsound mind. This probably includes the case where a person is rendered of unsound mind by the injuries in issue, and the case where a person is injured and subsequently becomes of unsound mind. It follows that time may never run, or never run completely. This subsection operates in favour of the injured person, but not in favour of another pursuer, such as an executor or assignee.

Actions where death has resulted from personal injuries

18.—(1) This section applies to any action in which, following the death of any person from personal injuries, damages are claimed in respect of the injuries or the death.

(2) Subject to subsections (3) and (4) below and section 19A of this Act, no action to which this section applies shall be brought unless it is commenced within a period of three years after—

(*a*)   the date of death of the deceased; or

(*b*)   the date (if later than the date of death) on which the pursuer in the action became, or on which, in the opinion of the court, it would have been reasonably practicable for him in all the circumstances to become, aware of both of the following facts—

(i) that the injuries of the deceased were attributable in whole or in part to an act or omission; and

(ii) that the defender was a person to whose act or omission the injuries were attributable in whole or in part or the employer or principal of such a person.

(3) Where the pursuer is a relative of the deceased, there shall be disregarded in the computation of the period specified in subsection (2) above any time during which the relative was under legal disability by reason of nonage or unsoundness of mind.

---

[26] *Wilkinson v. Ancliff Ltd.* [1986] 3 All E.R. 427.

[27] *e.g. Simpson v. Norwest Holst Southern Ltd.* [1980] 2 All E.R. 417.

[28] The legal consequences of facts are not themselves facts. *cf. McIntyre v. Armitage Shanks Ltd.,* 1980 S.C. (H.L.) 46 at pp. 61 and 66.

[29] *McHardy v. Bowden International,* 1993 S.C.L.R. 893.

[30] *Forbes v. House of Clydesdale,* 1988 S.L.T. 594.

[31] Age of Legal Capacity (Scotland) Act 1991, s. 1(2).

(4) Subject to section 19A of this Act, where an action of damages has not been brought by or on behalf of a person who has sustained personal injuries within the period specified in section 17(2) of this Act and that person subsequently dies in consequence of those injuries, no action to which this section applies shall be brought in respect of those injuries or the death from those injuries.

(5) In this section "relative" has the same meaning as in Schedule 1 to the Damages (Scotland) Act 1976.

GENERAL NOTE

Section 18 deals with the limitation of claims where a person has either been killed outright or has been personally injured and has subsequently died as a result of the injuries (except claims arising from product liability). In either case claims will be made by one or more "relatives" entitled to sue under the Damages (Scotland) Act 1976, section 1 and Schedule 1, as amended, claiming for loss of society award and/or loss of support, and possibly for loss of personal services under the Administration of Justice Act 1982, section 9. It will also apply to claims made by a tutor, curator or judicial factor on behalf of an entitled relative, or to the assignee of a relative. Section 18 however is inapplicable where a person has been injured and has subsequently died from natural causes or for other reasons and where no claim is competent under the 1976 Act.

"Personal injuries" are defined by section 22(1).

The general principle is that a claim by an entitled surviving relative must be brought within three years of the death or three years from the time the pursuer learned or should have learned that the injuries which caused the death were attributable to the defender.

VERBAL COMMENTARY ON SECTION 18

"(1) This section applies ... or the death"

An action in which, following the death of any person from personal injuries, damages are claimed in respect of the injuries or the death may be one brought by his executor for the deceased's ante-mortem patrimonial loss[32] and for solatium for his ante-mortem injuries[33] and/or by one or more of the surviving relatives of the deceased under the Damages (Scotland) Act 1976, as amended. The death may have been caused instantly, or have followed after some time on injuries; in the latter case a claim by the executor and claims by surviving relatives are both competent.[34] "Any person" includes a child as soon as born, and a claim may be brought for the death of a child after its birth in consequence of ante-natal injuries.[35] "Personal injuries" are defined in section 22(1). The death may have been caused instantly by the personal injuries or have followed after some time. A question may arise whether a death following upon personal injuries was or was not caused thereby. If it was not "death... *from* personal injuries" a claim cannot be brought under the Damages (Scotland) Act 1976, which

---

[32] At common law.
[33] Damages (Scotland) Act 1993.
[34] *Dick v. Burgh of Falkirk*, 1976 S.C. (H.L.) 1.
[35] *Hamilton v. Fife Health Board*, 1993 S.L.T. 624.

deals with the case where "a person dies in consequence of personal injuries sustained by him as a result of an act or omission ... giving rise to liability" and section 18 is inapplicable, but a claim might be brought by the deceased's executor and section 17 might bar it.

"(2) Subject to subsections (3) and (4) below and section 19A of this Act"

These provisions provide for extension in particular circumstances of the time-limit beyond the period laid down by the next words.

"no action... shall be brought"

This is the basic limitation of time.

"unless it is commenced"

On "commenced" see note to section 17(2).

"within a period of three years after—"

This states the basic period allowed for bringing an action. A stepdaughter's claim has been held barred though she acquired title to sue less than three years before the action.[36]

"(a) the date of death of the deceased"

This is the first possible starting date for the time for suing; it is usually readily ascertainable. The date of the injuries causing the death is irrelevant save that, if the deceased survived the inflicting of the injuries by more than three years the question would arise of whether his claims for those injuries were not cut off by section 17. No liability to surviving relatives arises if the liability to the deceased or his executor in respect of the act or omission had been excluded or discharged by the deceased before his death, or was excluded by virtue of any enactment: Damages (Scotland) Act 1976, section 1(2). If he could not himself have sued before his death, his relatives cannot sue after his death.

"or (b) the date (if later than the date of death) on which the pursuer in the action became, ... aware"

The next possible starting date for the running of time is the date when the pursuer, not the deceased, became aware of certain facts. The test of knowledge is applicable to each pursuer separately, so that some relatives pursuing under the Damages (Scotland) Act 1976, may be barred but not others. The court may have to determine how far facts disclosed to an injured person should be deemed known by any particular surviving relative after his death.

"or on which, ... it would have been reasonably practicable for him in all the circumstances to become, aware"

The court must consider whether the pursuer could by inquiries have become aware of the relevant facts. A pursuing relative cannot prolong the

---

[36] *Cunningham v. N.C.B.*, 1981 S.L.T. (Notes) 74.

running of time by taking no action if reasonably practicable inquiries could have been made and would have produced awareness of the relevant facts. It is for a person seeking to rely on section 18(2)(*b*) to aver and prove facts and circumstances as to the date when he first became aware that death was attributable to the defenders' act or omission and also to the date when it would have been reasonably practicable to have become aware of the necessary facts.[37]

"in the opinion of the court"

The decision on practicability is for the court.

"aware of both of the following facts"

The pursuer must have become aware of both, not merely one of the facts.

"(i) that the injuries of the deceased were attributable in whole or in part to an act or omission;"

"Attributable" means "referable to or in fact resulting from". The pursuer must have discovered that the injuries and the consequent death were not brought about by old age, natural causes or extraneous factors.

"and (ii) that the defender was a person to whose act or omission the injuries were attributable in whole or in part or the employer or principal of such a person."

The other fact, knowledge of which is essential for time to start running, is the fact that the act or omission which caused the injuries leading to the death was brought about by the defender. He may be responsible personally or vicariously.

"(3) Where the pursuer is a relative... unsoundness of mind."

By subsection (5) "relative" has the same meaning as in the Damages (Scotland) Act 1976, Sched. 1, as amended by the Administration of Justice Act 1982, s. 14. Time does not run against a pursuer who is such a "relative" so long as he is a pupil or minor[38] (now under 16)[39] or of unsound mind. There need be no causal connection between the period of nonage and the delay.[40] Difficulties may arise where there are several relatives pursuing and some are under disability. It seems that each pursuer has to be considered separately and that time cannot start to run against any particular one until that one has emerged from legal disability.[41] Time may therefore run against a widowed mother but not against her children until each has emerged from minority and it will never run against a pursuer who is all the time of unsound mind. In case of supervening unsoundness of mind time does not run while that disability exists.

---

[37] *Hamill v. Newalls Insulation Co.*, 1987 S.L.T. 478.
[38] *Forbes v. House of Clydesdale*, 1988 S.L.T. 594.
[39] Age of Legal Capacity (Scotland) Act 1991, s. 1(2).
[40] *Paton v. Loffland Brothers North Sea*, 1994 S.L.T. 784.
[41] e.g. *Hamill v. Newalls Insulation Co., supra.*

"(4) Subject to section 19A of this Act,"

This reserves the court's power to extend the time for suing if it considers it equitable to do so.

"where an action of damages has not been brought ... and that person
  subsequently dies in consequence of those injuries, no action ...
  from those injuries."

If a person sustained injuries but allowed the triennium to elapse without suing, and later died from those injuries, his claim has been excluded by section 17 and neither a relative nor an executor can bring an action after his death.

ACTIONS FOR DEFAMATION

Limitation of defamation and other actions

18A.[42]—(1) Subject to subsections (2) and (3) below and section 19A of this Act, no action for defamation shall be brought unless it is commenced within a period of three years after the date when the right of action accrued.

(2) In the computation of the period specified in subsection (1) above there shall be disregarded any time during which the person alleged to have been defamed was under legal disability by reason of nonage or unsoundness of mind.

(3) Nothing in this section shall affect any right of action which accrued before the commencement of this section.

(4) In this section—

  (a) "defamation" includes *convicium* and malicious falsehood and "defamed" shall be construed accordingly; and

  (b) references to the date when a right of action accrued shall be construed as references to the date when the publication or communication in respect of which the action for defamation is to be brought first came to the notice of the pursuer.

GENERAL NOTE

This section creates a three year limitation of time for bringing actions for defamation, as defined in the section.

VERBAL COMMENTARY ON SECTION 18A

"(1) Subject to subsections (2) and (3) below and section 19A of this
  Act,"

These provisions provide for extension of the time limit in particular circumstances.

"no action for defamation shall be brought"

"Defamation" is defined by subsection (4) as including *convicium* and malicious falsehood. These are the three species of the generic wrong of verbal injury,[43] though defamation is the commonest and best known. It includes both oral slander and libel in permanent form, including broadcasting.

---

[42] Inserted with effect from December 30, 1985, by the Law Reform (Miscellaneous Provisions) (Scotland) Act 1985, s. 12(2).
[43] Walker, *Law of Delict in Scotland* (2nd ed.), 730 *et seq.*

"unless it is commenced within a period of three years"

On "commenced" see commentary on section 17(2).

The common law principles relative to computation of the period of "three years" apply; section 14 does not apply as it relates only to Part I of the 1973 Act. At common law a claim for defamation was not subject to limitation of time but only to the long negative prescription and it is still subject to the short negative prescription by virtue of section 6 and Schedule I, paragraph 1(*d*).

By subsection 4(*b*) a right of action is deemed to accrue on the date when the publication or communication in respect of which the action for defamation is to be brought first came to the notice of the pursuer. If, accordingly, matter alleged to be defamatory of a person is published in an obscure journal or local newspaper and does not come to his notice until weeks later, the later date and not the date of publication is the date when the right of action accrues. It follows also that no right of action accrues so long as defamatory matter has not been published but has come to the notice only of an editor, secretaries, printers and the like.

"(2) In the computation of the period ... unsoundness of mind."

The subsection provides for extension of the time limit where the person aggrieved was a pupil, minor (now one under 16)[44] or suffered from unsoundness of mind to three years from the time when the disability ended.

"(3) Nothing in this section ... this section."

The section does not have retrospective effect.

"(4) In this section ... the pursuer."

The explanations of "defamation" and the date when a right of action accrued are taken into account in the commentary on subsection (1) above.

Section 19 of the 1973 Act was repealed by the Prescription and Limitation (Scotland) Act 1984, s. 2.

JUDICIAL POWER TO OVERRIDE TIME-LIMITS

It was apparent soon after the 1973 Act was passed that Part II was extremely difficult to understand and to apply, and that the results of its application seemed sometimes to be questionably just. The Law Reform (Miscellaneous Provisions) (Scotland) Act 1980 provided by section 23 for the introduction of a judicial discretion to dispense with the limitation of time rules when it seemed to the court equitable to do so. This was done by incorporating a new section 19A into the 1973 Act. When the new versions of sections 17 and 18 were substituted by the 1984 Act, section 19A was left in, to cater for any case of hardship not covered by the provisions of the new sections.

---

[44] Age of Legal Capacity (Scotland) Act 1991, s. 1(2).

Power of court to override time-limits, etc.

19A.[45]—(1) Where a person would be entitled, but for any of the provisions of section 17 or section 18 and 18A of this Act, to bring an action, the court may, if it seems to it equitable to do so, allow him to bring the action notwithstanding that provision.

(2) The provisions of subsection (1) above shall have effect not only as regards rights of action accruing after the commencement of this section but also as regards those, in respect of which a final judgment has not been pronounced, accruing before such commencement.

(3) In subsection (2) above, the expression "final judgment" means an interlocutor of a court of first instance which, by itself, or taken along with previous interlocutors, disposes of the subject matter of a cause notwithstanding that judgment may not have been pronounced on every question raised or that the expenses found due may not have been modified, taxed or decerned for; but the expression does not include an interlocutor dismissing a cause by reason only of a provision mentioned in subsection (1) above.

(4) An action which would not be entertained but for this section shall not be tried by jury.

GENERAL NOTE

This section gives the court dealing with a case power, if it seems to it equitable to do so, to allow a person to bring an action notwithstanding a limitation provision in any of sections 17, 18 or 18A.

The discretion is unfettered, save by any guidance which may be given in decisions by the superior courts. It may be exercised in favour of an injured pursuer, or of a surviving relative or executor making a claim in consequence of the death of a victim, or of a person defamed.

It has been judicially asserted repeatedly that the discretion should be exercised sparingly and with restraint[46] and that the onus is on the pursuer to satisfy the court that it was equitable that the action be allowed to proceed.[47] The question is, whether it would be fair and just to allow the extension. The interests of all parties have to be considered.[48]

VERBAL COMMENTARY ON SECTION 19A

"(1) Where a person would be entitled, but for ... to bring an action,"

The power applies in cases where a pursuer would be entitled to bring an action for personal injuries (section 17), or for wrongful death of a relative (section 18) or for defamation (section 18A) but is being prevented from doing so by the expiry of a limitation of time provision in the relevant section.

"the court may ... allow him to bring the action notwithstanding that provision."

The court may override the effect of an otherwise applicable limitation provision, and allow the action to be brought. To do so should not be

---

[45] As amended by the Prescription and Limitation (Scotland) Act 1984, Sched. 1, para. 8 and, with effect from December 30, 1985, by the Law Reform (Miscellaneous Provisions) (Scotland) Act 1985, s. 12(3).

[46] *McCullough v. Norwest Socea,* 1981 S.L.T. 201; *Carson v. Howard Doris,* 1981 S.C. 278; *Black v. B. R. Board,* 1983 S.L.T. 146; *Whyte v. Walker,* 1983 S.L.T. 441.

[47] *Donald v. Rutherford,* 1983 S.L.T. 253; 1984 S.L.T. 70.

[48] *Carson, supra,* 282.

automatic or regular because doing so is overriding the *prima facie* rule established by the three sections intended to protect defenders from stale claims and will always, to some extent, prejudice the defender. It should be exceptional.

"if it seems to it equitable to do so"

"Equitable" means "just", "fair", "reasonable" and the decision to grant or refuse permission for the case to proceed can only be a matter of impression in the whole circumstances of the case. The court's discretion is unfettered[49] save by any guidelines laid down by superior courts or deducible from the trend of decisions.

It is for the pursuer seeking an extension of time to satisfy the court that in the circumstances it is equitable to allow the extension.[50] The pursuer must accordingly aver and prove facts and circumstances which convince the judge that on balance an extension of time should be allowed. Accordingly the reasons for the delay must be explained and what prejudice would be suffered if the discretion is not exercised and the action dismissed. The defender must show what prejudice would be suffered by the action being allowed to continue.

The issue of whether it is "equitable" or not may be reserved by the court allowing a proof before answer or it may require investigation by a preliminary proof on that issue only.[51]

The court's equitable discretion to allow an extension of time has been invoked far more frequently than their powers to extend the time under sections 17(2)(*b*), and 18(2)(*b*). Even where the pursuer has failed to justify an extension of time under section 18 the court held that it could allow an action to proceed under section 19A.[52]

It has been said that the discretion should be exercised sparingly[53] but the courts have in practice frequently exercised it in favour of pursuers. Courts have frequently weighed the prejudice to the pursuer by having his action dismissed against the prejudice to the defender by having to defend a case long after the material facts had happened.[54] Accordingly the pursuer's reasons for not having sued within the triennium must be stated and whether they are attributable to the pursuer, or to a third party such as an adviser. When an adviser appears to have been in fault the court is less willing to extend the time for suing where it appears that the pursuer has a good or reasonable ground of action against the adviser for having misled the pursuer or not been properly diligent in bringing the pursuer's action within the time.[55]

---

[49] *cf. Thompson v. Brown Construction (Ebbw Vale) Ltd.* [1981] 2 All E.R. 296 (H.L.); see also *Taft v. Clyde Marine Motoring Co.,* 1990 S.L.T. 170.

[50] *Munro v. Anderson-Grice Engineering Co.,* 1983 S.L.T. 295.

[51] *e.g. Dormer v. Melville, Dundas & Whitson,* 1989 S.L.T. 310.

[52] *Black v. B. R. Board,* 1983 S.L.T. 146.

[53] *McCullough v. Norwest Socea,* 1981 S.L.T. 201; *Carson v. Howard Doris,* 1981 S.C. 278; *Black, supra; Whyte v. Walker,* 1983 S.L.T. 441.

[54] *Donald v. Rutherford,* 1983 S.L.T. 253.

[55] *Donald, supra.*

Cases where extension of time allowed

The discretion has been exercised in favour of pursuers where the pursuer's inaction was excusable and the defenders would not be prejudiced;[56] where the pursuer was not at fault, the defenders had had early notice of the claim and the pursuer would be prejudiced if required to proceed against dilatory solicitors;[57] where second defenders, cited late, had had early opportunity to investigate the claim and it would avoid the need for the pursuer also to sue his solicitors;[58] where despite six years' delay the pursuer had been ignorant of the possibility of taking legal action;[59] where the pursuer had a probable remedy against his solicitors and would be prejudiced by possible third party proceedings against messengers at arms;[60] where though the deceased was aware that he had contracted an industrial disease due to working conditions he had been unaware that he had a prospective right of action against his former employers;[61] where an error in the summons had been trivial, and immediately corrected and the defenders had fully investigated the claim before the summons had been served;[62] where the balance of the equities favoured allowing the action to proceed;[63] where the delay arose because the defender had been struck off the Register of Companies and the chance of an alternative remedy against the pursuer's solicitors was slim;[64] where the pursuer was old and infirm and was prejudiced by the defender company having been struck off the Companies Register;[65] where the equities would have been narrowly in favour of allowing the pursuer to proceed;[66] where the delay had not seriously affected evidence on the issues in dispute;[67] where the pursuer had not been responsible for the delay or the action being raised in the wrong forum and to claim against his solicitors would cause further delay;[68] where an action had been served in time but had gone off the rails procedurally, but the defender had not been prejudiced;[69] where the pursuer had received unfortunate medical and legal advice and the defender could not offer to prove prejudice.[70]

Cases where extension of time refused

Courts have however declined to exercise the discretion to extend the time where it would merely be unfortunate for the pursuer, there had been no reasonable explanation or excuse for the delay and the defenders would be prejudiced by the delay;[71] where the delay was not adequately explained,

[56] *Black v. B.R. Board*, 1983 S.L.T. 146.
[57] *Henderson v. Singer (U.K.)*, 1983 S.L.T. 198.
[58] *Anderson v. City of Glasgow District Council*, 1987 S.L.T. 279.
[59] *Comber v. Greater Glasgow Health Board*, 1989 S.L.T. 639.
[60] *Elliot v. J. & C. Finney*, 1989 S.L.T. 605.
[61] *McLaren v. Harland and Wolff*, 1991 S.L.T. 85.
[62] *Ferguson v. McFadyen*, 1992 S.L.T. 44.
[63] *Nicol v. British Steel Corporation (General Steels)*, 1992 S.L.T. 141.
[64] *Percy v. Glenburnie Securities Services*, 1993 S.L.T. (Sh.Ct.) 78.
[65] *Griffen v. George MacLellan Holdings Ltd.*, 1994 S.L.T. 336.
[66] *Blake v. Lothian Health Board*, 1993 S.L.T. 1248.
[67] *Kidd v. Grampian Health Board*, 1994 S.L.T. 267.
[68] *MacFarlane v. Breen*, 1994 S.C.L.R. 382.
[69] *McCluskey v. Sir Robert McApline & Sons*, 1994 S.C.L.R. 650.
[70] *Ferla v. Secretary of State for Scotland*, 1995 S.L.T. 662.
[71] *Williams v. Forth Valley Health Board*, 1983 S.L.T. 376.

the defenders would suffer greater prejudice and the defender's insurers be severely prejudiced;[72] where the failure to bring an action was the fault of the pursuer's former solicitors but the parties had completed their inquiries before the expiry of the triennium;[73] where the pursuer's solicitors were in fault but the pursuer had a good right of action against them;[74] where the pursuer had been misadvised but her delay was unjustified and she might well succeed in a claim against her solicitors;[75] where the delay was the pursuer's own fault;[76] where solicitors had inadvertently failed to raise an action and the defender would be more prejudiced than the pursuer;[77] where solicitors failed to serve an action properly and the defenders would be more prejudiced;[78] where the pursuer had grounds for a claim against his agents but the defenders would be seriously prejudiced by the action continuing;[79] where a second defender, cited after the triennium had expired, would be prejudiced by the action proceeding against him;[80] where the defenders would be prejudiced by the action continuing but there was a clear case against the pursuer's solicitors for failure to raise the action timeously;[81] where 11 years had elapsed and the pursuer could claim against her solicitors.[82]

It appears accordingly that the main factors relevant to the decision to exercise the discretion or not are (a) the duration of the delay; (b) who was responsible for it, including the pursuer's state of knowledge of his injuries and his right to sue; (c) the prejudice which would be suffered by the pursuer if his action were dismissed, including the chance that he could in separate proceedings recover from a negligent adviser; (d) the prejudice which would be suffered by the defender by having to defend when the facts had happened more than three years ago, including his prospective liability in expenses; and (e) the balance of the equities in the whole circumstances.

Similar principles apply to a counterclaim raised only after the time-limit has expired.[83]

As the decision in applications under section 19A is entirely discretionary an appellate court will not interfere with the exercise of the judge's discretion unless he has gone seriously wrong.[84] If he has the exercise of discretion is for the appellate court.[85]

"(2) The provisions of subsection (1) above shall have effect ... before such commencement."

The power exists in relation to cases in which final judgment had not been pronounced by 29 October, 1980.

[72] *Whyte v. Walker,* 1983 S.L.T. 441.
[73] *Donald v. Rutherford,* 1984 S.L.T. 70.
[74] *Forsyth v. A. F. Stoddard & Co.,* 1985 S.L.T. 51.
[75] *Forbes v. House of Clydesdale,* 1987 S.C.L.R. 136.
[76] *Millar v. Newalls Insulation Co.,* 1988 S.C.L.R. 359 (Sh. Ct.).
[77] *Craw v. Gallagher,* 1988 S.L.T. 204.
[78] *Bell v. Greenland,* 1988 S.L.T. 215.
[79] *Anderson v. John Cotton (Colne),* 1991 S.L.T. 696.
[80] *McCabe v. McLellan,* 1994 S.L.T. 346.
[81] *Beaton v. Strathclyde Buses,* 1993 S.L.T. 931.
[82] *Clerk v. McLean,* 1995 S.L.T. 235.
[83] *Henshaw v. Carnie,* 1988 S.C.L.R. 305.
[84] *cf. Conry v. Simpson* [1983] 3 All E.R. 369. See also *Tuft v. Clyde Marine Motoring Co.,* 1990 S.L.T. 170.
[85] *Anderson v. City of Glasgow D. C.,* 1987 S.L.T. 279.

"(3) In subsection (2) above, the expression "final judgment" means ...
   subsection (1) above."

This subsection defines "final judgment" for the purposes of subsection
(2). It does not include an interlocutor dismissing a cause by reason only of
the lapse of the time-limit fixed by one of sections 17, 18 or 18A.

"(4) An action which would not ... tried by jury."

This means that if an action has been allowed to proceed, notwithstanding
the expiry of a relevant time-limit, only by virtue of this section, it is not to
be tried by jury. The reason doubtless is that it is the court which has to
consider whether the averments that it was equitable to allow the case to
proceed have been established by the evidence and that if the court allows
it, the evidence will be at least three years old.

AMENDMENT OF ACTIONS SUBJECT TO TIME LIMIT

A problem which has arisen many times is whether and to what extent an
action, which is subject to a limitation of time for its commencement, and
has been raised within that time, can be amended after the time-limit has
expired. To allow amendment or not is in the discretion of the court.[86] The
vital point of time is when the motion to allow the minute of amendment to
be received and answered is made, because then the defender has notice of
the new or altered case being made against him.[87] The leading principle is
that a pursuer is not entitled to change the basis of his case by amendment
at a time when he would have been time-barred from raising an action.[88]
But the courts have sometimes allowed the amendment, such as to introduce
a fresh ground of liability, where the substantial basis of the action was not
altered, outwith the time limit.[89] On the other hand they have frequently
refused to allow amendment where in substance the pursuer was seeking
to make fundamental change or really make a new case.

"Our reports contain many decisions showing that the court will not in
general allow a pursuer by amendment to cure a radical incompetence in
his action, or to change the basis of his case if he seeks to make such
amendment only after the expiry of a time limit which would have prevented
him at that stage from raising proceedings afresh".[90]

"The decisions show that the court will not in general allow a pursuer by
amendment to substitute the right defender for the wrong defender, or to
cure a radical incompetence in his action, or to change the basis of his case,
if he seeks to make such amendments only after the expiry of a time limit
which would have prevented him at that stage from raising proceedings
afresh".[91]

---

[86] No such problem arises where a record is being adjusted, not amended. It can be adjusted without requiring the
court to exercise discretion : *Sellars v. I.M.I. Yorkshire Imperial,* 1986 S.L.T. 629.

[87] *Boyle v. Glasgow Corporation,* 1975 S.C. 238 at p. 251.

[88] *Pompa's Trs. v. Edinburgh Mags.,* 1942 S.C. 119 at p. 125 *per* L.J.-C. Cooper; *Boyle v. Glasgow Corporation,*
1975 S.C. 238 at p. 245, *per* Lord Dunpark.

[89] *McCluskie v. N.C.B.,* 1961 S.C. 87; *Jones v. McDermott (Scotland),* 1986 S.L.T. 551.

[90] *Pompa's Trs., supra.*

[91] *McPhail v. Lanarkshire C.C.,* 1951 S.C. 301 at p. 309, *per* L.P. Cooper.

The test is accordingly whether an amendment outwith the time-limit for commencing the action has "changed the basis of the pursuer's case"[92] or merely altered, amplified or restated what is fundamentally the same case. Is it reinforcing an attack or attacking on a new front? Whether a particular case falls into the category of allowable amendment or fundamental change of the basis of claim, which should be rejected, is a question of degree in each case[93] or of balancing the equities.[94]

The court has accordingly allowed amendment after the time-limit has expired where it sought to effect service on the proper officer of the defenders,[95] or correct an error in the defender's Christian name,[96] or to add statutory grounds of fault to a common law case,[97] or new grounds of fault were substituted,[98] or an additional omission by the defenders was averred,[99] or an additional averment of direct liability was made as well as vicarious liability,[1] or deleted the pursuer's common law case and substituted a case of vicarious liability,[2] or was designed to make an action relevant,[3] or sought to bring in third parties, in effect incorporating an action of relief in the defences,[4] or changed the averments as to duties and breaches of duty,[5] or deleted averments against one defender,[6] or added additional representatives of the deceased defender's estate and amended a conclusion to remove a technical irregularity,[7] or to found on a different statutory provision as breach of statutory duty,[8] or to add a case of faulty system and averments of practice,[9] or to make a case against a third party, to whom the action had been intimated in time,[10] or to make non-material changes in facts averred,[11] or to substitute a case of defective system for a case of fault by the defender's employee,[12] or to substitute new averments of fault but leaving the factual basis of the case unchanged,[13] or to modify averments as to one defender,[14] or to allow the trustee in sequestration to be sisted as additional pursuer in a bankrupt's claim for personal injuries,[15]

---

[92] *Greenhorn v. Smart*, 1979 S.C. 427 at p. 430; *Jones v. Lanarkshire Health Board*, 1991 S.L.T. 714.

[93] *Hynd v. West Fife Cooperative Society Ltd.*, 1980 S.L.T. 41. *Greenhorn, supra*, 431.

[94] *Nicol v. British Steel Corporation (General Steels)*, 1992 S.L.T. 141.

[95] *Pompa's Trs., v. Edinburgh Mags.*, 1942 S.C. 119.

[96] *Ferguson v. McFadyen*, 1992 S.L.T. 44.

[97] *McCluskie v. N.C.B.*, 1961 S.C. 87.

[98] *Coyle v. N.C.B.*, 1959 S.L.T. 114.

[99] *Kelly v. Holloway Bros. (London) Ltd.*, 1960 S.L.T. (Notes) 69; *Keatings v. Secretary of State for Scotland*, 1961 S.L.T. (Sh.Ct.) 63.

[1] *Mackenzie v. Fairfields Shipbuilding and Engineering Co.*, 1964 S.C. 90.

[2] *O'Hare's Exx. v. Western Heritable Investment Co.*, 1965 S.C. 47.

[3] *Mowatt v. Shore Porters Society*, 1965 S.L.T. (Notes) 10.

[4] *Findlay v. N.C.B.*, 1965 S.L.T. 328.

[5] *Wright v. British Insulated Callenders Construction Co.*, 1968 S.L.T. (Sh.Ct.) 13.

[6] *Emslie v. Tognarelli's Exrs.*, 1969 S.L.T. 20 (disapproved on another point in *Gray v. N.B. Steel Foundry Co.*, 1969 S.C. 231).

[7] *Stevens v. Thomson*, 1971 S.L.T. 136.

[8] *Smith v. Laidlaw & Fairgrieve*, 1973 S.L.T. (Notes) 76.

[9] *Anderson v. B.R. Board*, 1973 S.L.T. (Notes) 20.

[10] *Cross v. Noble*, 1975 S.L.T. (Notes) 33.

[11] *Mazs v. Dairy Supply Co.*, 1978 S.L.T. 208.

[12] *Hynd v. West Fife Cooperative Society*, 1980 S.L.T. 41.

[13] *McGrattan v. Renfrew D.C.*, 1983 S.L.T. 678.

[14] *Meek v. Milne*, 1985 S.L.T. 318.

[15] *Grindall v. John Mitchell (Grangemouth)*, 1987 S.L.T. 137; *Dormer v. Melville Dundas & Whitson*, 1987 S.L.C.R. 655.

or to allow a third party to be called as an additional defender,[16] or to identify the correct defender.[17]

The court has, however, declined to allow amendment after the time-limit had expired where an additional defender was only served with amended pleadings implicating him after the time,[18] where a pursuer sought to substitute a case founded on the fault of a fellow servant for a case of unsafe plant,[19] where the pursuer sought to delete his statutory case, substitute a common law case of fault of a fellow servant and modify the original case of faulty system,[20] where a widow sought to add her children as additional pursuers,[21] where the pursuer proposed to bring in a third party as a second defender,[22] where a case of unsafe system was to be changed to one of failure to provide a safe working place and access thereto and including alleged breaches of statutory duty,[23] where an amendment proposed to abandon all the grounds of fault and substitute new ones,[24] where an amendment sought to change the locus of the accident, the alleged cause and the ground of fault alleged,[25] where it was proposed to add a further relative pursuer,[26] where it was proposed to add three children as pursuers and add conclusions for awards to them,[27] where substantial alterations in the case were proposed and the amendments were long delayed,[28] where the pursuer changed his first ground of fault and deleted his second completely,[29] where a new case was sought to be made after the proof.[30]

Whether to allow amendment or not is a matter for the discretion of the judge of first instance and an appellate court will be slow to interfere with his exercise of discretion.[30a]

When time bar is being considered at the stage of amendment, the plea of time bar should not be added to the record after the court has considered the question of time bar and allowed the amendment.[31]

CONCLUDING PROVISIONS

Sections 20 and 21 of the 1973 Act were repealed by the Prescription and Limitation (Scotland) Act 1984, Sched. 2.

---

[16] *Webb v. B.P. Petroleum Development*, 1988 S.L.T. 775.
[17] *Dailly v. Wilson*, 1990 S.L.T. 106; *McHardy v. Bawden International Ltd.*, 1993 S.C.L.R. 893 (Sh. Ct.); *Gibson v. Wilcox*, 1994 S.C.L.R. 174.
[18] *Miller v. N.C.B.*, 1960 S.C. 376.
[19] *Clark v. India Tyre Co.*, 1960 S.L.T. (Sh.Ct.) 37.
[20] *Dryburgh v. N.C.B.*, 1962 S.C. 485. This case turned partly on the fact that the amendment was proposed only a few days before the proof.
[21] *Maclean v. B.R. Board*, 1965 S.L.T. (Notes) 94.
[22] *Aitken v. Norrie*, 1966 S.C. 168.
[23] *Greenhorn v. Smart*, 1979 S.C. 427.
[24] *Davies v. B.I.C.C.*, 1980 S.L.T. (Sh.Ct.) 17.
[25] *Rollo v. B.R. Board*, 1980 S.L.T. (Notes) 103.
[26] *McArthur v. Raynesway Plant*, 1980 S.L.T. 74.
[27] *Marshall v. Black*, 1981 S.L.T. 228.
[28] *Brady v. Clydeport Stevedoring Services*, 1987 S.L.T. 645.
[29] *Grimason v. N.C.B.*, 1987 S.L.T. 714.
[30] *Gold v. Costain Concrete Co.*, 1988 S.C.L.R. 15.
[30a] *Grimason v. N.C.B.*, supra.
[31] *Gibson v. Droopy & Browns*, 1989 S.L.T. 172.

Section 22 enacts:

Interpretation of Part II and supplementary provisions

22.[32]—(1) In this Part of this Act—

"the court" means the Court of Session or the sheriff court; and "personal injuries" includes any disease and any impairment of a person's physical or mental condition.

(2)[33] Where the pursuer in an action to which section 17, 18 or 18A of this Act applies is pursuing the action by virtue of the assignation of a right of action, the reference in subsection (2)(*b*) of the said section 17 or of the said section 18 or, as the case may be, subsection (4)(*b*) of the said section 18A to the pursuer in the action shall be construed as a reference to the assignor of the right of action.

(3) For the purposes of the said subsection (2)(*b*) knowledge that any act or omission was or was not, as a matter of law, actionable, is irrelevant.

(4) An action which would not be entertained but for the said subsection (2)(*b*) shall not be tried by jury.

Amendments and repeals related to Part II

By the Consumer Protection Act 1987, Sched. 1, para. 11, section 23 is to cease to have effect, but for the avoidance of doubt it is declared that the amendments in Part II of Schedule 4 shall continue to have effect. These are taken account of in the appropriate places.

Section 23(2) repealed the enactments in Part II of Schedule 5, as follows.

PART II

REPEALS COMING INTO FORCE ON PASSING OF THIS ACT

Chapter	Short Title	Extent of Repeal
2 & 3 Eliz. 2 c. 36	The Law Reform (Limitation of Actions &c.) Act 1954.	Section 6.
1963 c. 47	The Limitation Act 1963.	Part II.
1971 c. 43	The Law Reform (Miscellaneous Provisions) Act 1971.	Part I. In Schedule 1, Part II. Schedule 2.

---

[32] As substituted by the Prescription and Limitation (Scotland) Act 1984, s. 3.

[33] As amended by the Law Reform (Miscellaneous Provisions) (Scotland) Act 1985, s. 12(4) with effect from December 30, 1985.

CHAPTER 7

LIMITATION OF ACTIONS UNDER THE CONSUMER PROTECTION ACT 1987

THE main principles of the Consumer Protection Act 1987 have been outlined in Chapter 5.

The 1987 Act, by Sched. I, Part II, para. 10, provides for the insertion in the 1973 Act, after section 22, of a new Part IIA headed "Prescription of Obligations and Limitations of Actions under Part I of the Consumer Protection Act 1987". In the new Part IIA sections 22A and 22D are prescription provisions and examined in Chapter 5 hereof. Sections 22B, 22C and 22D deal with limitation of actions and are here considered.

Three-year limitation of actions

22B.—(1) This section shall apply to an action to enforce an obligation arising from liability under section 2 of the 1987 Act (to make reparation for damage caused wholly or partly by a defect in a product), except where section 22C of this Act applies.

(2) Subject to subsection (4) below, an action to which this section applies shall not be competent unless it is commenced within the period of three years after the earliest date on which the person seeking to bring (or a person who could at an earlier date have brought) the action was aware, or on which, in the opinion of the court, it was reasonably practicable for him in all the circumstances to become aware, of all the facts mentioned in subsection (3) below.

(3) The facts referred to in subsection (2) above are—
    (*a*) that there was a defect in a product;
    (*b*) that the damage was caused or partly caused by the defect;
    (*c*) that the damage was sufficiently serious to justify the pursuer (or other person referred to in subsection (2) above) in bringing an action to which this section applies on the assumption that the defender did not dispute liability and was able to satisfy a decree;
    (*d*) that the defender was a person liable for the damage under the said section 2.

(4) In the computation of the period of three years mentioned in subsection (2) above, there shall be disregarded any period during which the person seeking to bring an action was under legal disability by reason of nonage or unsoundness of mind.

(5) The facts mentioned in subsection (3) above do not include knowledge of whether particular facts and circumstances would or would not, as a matter of law, result in liability for damage under the said section 2.

(6) Where a person would be entitled, but for this section, to bring an action of reparation other than one in which the damages claimed are confined to damages for loss of or damage to property, the court may, if it seems to it equitable to do so, allow him to bring the action notwithstanding this section.

GENERAL NOTE ON SECTION 22B

This section imposes a time limit of three years for bringing an action seeking damages for personal injuries or property damage arising from liability to make reparation for damage caused by a defect in a product.

VERBAL COMMENTARY ON SECTION 22B

"(1) This section shall apply ... defect in a product)."

Section 2 of the 1987 Act provides that where any damage (defined in section 5(1) thereof as death or personal injury or any loss of or damage to any property (including land)) is caused wholly or partly by defect (defined in section 3 thereof) in a product (defined in section 1(2) thereof) the persons listed in section 2(2) thereof shall be liable for the damage.

"except where section 22C of this Act applies."

Section 22C deals with actions under the 1987 Act where death has resulted from personal injuries caused by defect in a product. Accordingly section 22B deals with personal injuries not resulting in death and damage to property (including land).

"(2) Subject to subsection (4) below an action to which this section applies shall not be competent"

Subsection (4) provides for an extension of the time-limit in particular circumstances; apart from that an action raised after the time-limit is incompetent.

"unless it is commenced within the period of three years"

On "commenced" see commentary on section 17(2).
The time limit is fixed as three years.

"after the earliest date on which the person seeking to bring ... the action"

This defines the starting date for the time-limit.

"(or a person who could at an earlier date have brought) the action"

This seems designed to deal with the case where damage is done to property and the property is transmitted to another; though the latter may have the title to sue the starting date for the time-limit is the date when the former owner was aware of the facts.

"was aware, or on which, in the opinion of the court, it was reasonably practicable for him in all the circumstances to become aware"

Time starts to run from the earliest date on which complainer was actually aware, or in the opinion of the court, should reasonably have become aware, of certain facts. By virtue of the second alternative date (deemed awareness) a complainer may find that time has run and excluded his claim if he remained stubbornly or negligently ignorant or wilfully blind by failing to inspect, to take skilled opinion or advice, or otherwise not become aware in circumstances where it was reasonably practicable to become aware.

"of all the facts mentioned in subsection (3) below."

To start the limitation period it is necessary for the complainer to have become aware of all the four facts mentioned, not merely one or more.

"(3) The facts referred to in subsection (2) above are (a) that there was a defect in a product;"

"Defect" is defined by the 1987 Act, s. 3. A defect which does not affect safety, such as a piece of cloth which quickly fades, is not a defect within the 1987 Act (though it may be for the purposes of the Sale of Goods Act 1979).

"(b) that the damage was caused or partly caused by the defect;"

Whether the damage alleged was or was not caused by the defect alleged is a question of fact and evidence.

"(c) that the damage was sufficiently serious ... to which this section applies"

Time does not start to run until the complainer has also become aware that the damage (*i.e.* by section 5(1) death or personal injury or any loss or damage to any property (including land)) was serious enough to justify an action. When this time has arrived may be a matter of dispute.

"on the assumption that ... satisfy a decree;"

The decision whether damage was serious enough to justify an action is to ignore the possibility that the defender would dispute liability and that in consequence the time and expense of a proof would be incurred, and also the possibility that the defender is impecunious or on the point of liquidation.

"(d) that the defender was a person liable for the damage under the said section 2."

The complainer must also have been aware that the person whom he calls as defender was liable under the 1987 Act, s. 2, as, being the producer of the product, a person who by putting his name, trade mark or other distinguishing mark on the product has held himself out to be the producer, or a person who has imported the product into a member state from a place outside the European Communities in order to supply it to another.

"(4) In the computation of the period of three years ... unsoundness of mind."

Time is not to run against a person so long as that person is a pupil, minor (now aged under 16)[1] or of unsound mind.

"(5) The facts mentioned in subsection (3) above do not include knowledge of whether particular facts and circumstances would or would not, as a matter of law, result in liability for damage under the said section 2."

Awareness of facts, which after three years will bar an action, does not include knowledge of whether particular facts, if admitted or held proved, would result in liability. Such knowledge cannot exist until a defender has admitted liability or been held liable by a court; till then it is belief only.

---

[1] Age of Legal Capacity (Scotland) Act 1991, s. 1(2).

"(6) Where a person would be entitled ... loss of or damage to property,"

This deals with the case where a person is barred by this section from bringing an action for reparation, and the action is one for personal injuries, or personal injuries and property damage, but not for loss of or damage to property alone.

"the court may, if it seems to it equitable to do so, allow him to bring the action notwithstanding this section."

If the court thinks it equitable it may, despite the time limit having expired, allow the person to bring the action. Compare section 19A.

Actions under the 1987 Act where death has resulted from personal injuries

22C.—(1) This section shall apply to an action to enforce an obligation arising from liability under section 2 of the 1987 Act (to make reparation for damage caused wholly or partly by a defect in a product) where a person has died from personal injuries and the damages claimed include damages for those personal injuries or that death.

(2) Subject to subsection (4) below, an action to which this section applies shall not be competent unless it is commenced within the period of three years after the later of—

    (*a*) the date of death of the injured person;

    (*b*) the earliest date on which the person seeking to make (or a person who could at an earlier date have made) the claim was aware, or on which, in the opinion of the court, it was reasonably practicable for him in all the circumstances to become aware—

        (i) that there was a defect in the product;

        (ii) that the injuries of the deceased were caused (or partly caused) by the defect; and

        (iii) that the defender was a person liable for the damage under the said section 2.

(3) Where the person seeking to make the claim is a relative of the deceased, there shall be disregarded in the computation of the period mentioned in subsection (2) above any period during which that relative was under legal disability by reason of nonage or unsoundness of mind.

(4) Where an action to which section 22B of this Act applies has not been brought within the period mentioned in subsection (2) of that section and the person subsequently dies in consequence of his injuries, an action to which this section applies shall not be competent in respect of those injuries or that death.

(5) Where a person would be entitled, but for this section, to bring an action of reparation other than one in which the damages claimed are confined to damages for loss or damage to property, the court may, if it seems to it equitable to do so, allow him to bring the action notwithstanding this section.

(6) In this section "relative" has the same meaning as in the Damages (Scotland) Act 1976.

(7) For the purposes of subsection (2)(*b*) above there shall be disregarded knowledge of whether particular facts and circumstances would or would not, as a matter of law, result in liability for damage under the said section 2.

General Note

Section 22C deals with cases where liability has arisen under section 2 of the 1987 Act to make reparation for damage (1987 Act, s. 5(1)) caused by a defect (1987 Act, s. 3) in a product (1987 Act, s. 1(2)) and a person injured has died in consequence. Claims for the losses resulting from the death will have to be made by one or more relatives entitled to sue under the Damages (Scotland) Act 1976, Sched. 1, as amended by the Administration of Justice Act 1982, s. 14.

VERBAL COMMENTARY ON SECTION 22C

"(1) This section shall apply ... where a person has died from personal injuries"

The claim will have to be brought by one or more relatives within the meaning of the Damages (Scotland) Act 1976, as amended, claiming for loss of society and/or loss of support and possibly also outlays and expenses. The person must have died "from personal injuries", not from unconnected causes.

"and the damages claimed include damages for those personal injuries or that death."

This clause is obscure; if the victim has died his relatives claim for the losses sustained by them severally by reason of the death, but nobody can claim for the personal injuries which brought about his death. His executor can claim for any patrimonial loss sustained by the deceased by reason of the injuries between the date of the injuries and the date of death:[2] and now also for the deceased's solatium for his ante-mortem personal injuries.[3]

"(2) Subject to subsection (4) below, an action to which this section applies shall not be competent"

These words introduce the restriction of competency by the time-limit for suing. The reference to subsection (4) is apparently a mistake, as subsection (3) allows a possible extension of time.

"unless it is commenced within the period of three years"

On "commenced" see commentary on section 17(2).

"after the later of—"

There are two alternative starting dates for the time-limit, and the later is the effective one.

"(a) the date of death of the injured person;"

The death of the injured person may be considerably later than the personal injuries initially caused by the defect in the product, but it must be shown to have been caused wholly or partly thereby. If the death took place more than three years after the personal injuries, subsection (4) applies.

"(b) the earliest date on which the person seeking to make (or a person who could at an earlier date have made) the claim was aware,"

The alternative starting date for the time-limit is the earliest date on which a pursuer, *i.e.* an entitled relative, or an executor seeking to recover post-injuries but pre-death patrimonial loss sustained by the deceased, became

[2] *McGhie v. B.T.C.*, 1964 S.L.T. 25; *Gray v. N.B. Steel Foundry Ltd.*, 1969 S.C. 231; *Dick v. Burgh of Falkirk*, 1976 S.C. (H.L.) 1.
[3] Damages (Scotland) Act 1993, s. 2, reversing Damages (Scotland) Act 1976, s. 2(3).

aware of certain facts. The words in parentheses seem to refer to the possible case where one relative became aware of facts and could have sued but did not, and later another relative does actually sue; in that event the starting date is the date which the former relative was affected by knowledge.

"was aware, or on which, in the opinion of the court, it was reasonably practicable for him in all the circumstances to have become aware"

The starting date is the time when the earlier of the persons referred to in (*b*) above actually became aware, or could reasonably have become aware, of certain facts. Accordingly persons must, if they have any suspicions, make inquiries and take advice and cannot have the time-limit extended by deliberately or negligently failing to inquire.

"(i) that there was a defect in the product"

"Defect" is defined by the 1987 Act, s. 3.
"Product" is defined by the 1987 Act, s. 1(2).

"(ii) that the injuries of the deceased were caused (or partly caused) by the defect;"

This is a question of evidence.

"(iii) that the defender was a person liable for the damage under the said section 2."

The persons liable are producers, deemed producers and importers: 1987 Act, s. 2.

"(3) Where the person seeking to make the claim is a relative ... unsoundness of mind."

This subsection allows for extension of time in the cases where the relative is a pupil or minor (now one aged under 16)[4] or of unsound mind. In the case of a claim by several relatives this must be applied to each pursuer individually, so that some claiming relatives may have the starting-dates for their claims deferred but others may not.

"(4) Where an action to which section 22B ... or that death"

Where a person has suffered personal injuries by reason of defect in a product and has allowed the limit of time under section 22B to expire without having commenced an action, and has subsequently died in consequence of these injuries, a claim cannot be brought for his death. Immediately before his death he could not have sued, and accordingly the cause of action is exhausted.

"(5) Where a person would be entitled ... notwithstanding this section."

This subsection gives the court power, if it seems to it equitable to do so in the circumstances, to allow an action for loss, other than solely for loss

---

[4] Age of Legal Capacity (Scotland) Act 1991, s. 1(2).

of or damage to property, to be brought even though the time-limit has expired. A claim by an executor for post-injuries but pre-death patrimonial loss sustained by the deceased is a claim for loss of property. Compare section 19A.

"(6) In this section 'relative' ... Damages (Scotland) Act 1976."

"Relative" is defined by the Damages (Scotland) Act 1976, s. 1 and Sched. 1, amended by the Administration of Justice Act 1982, s. 14.

"(7) For the purposes of subsection 2(b) above ... the said section 2."

The facts, awareness or deemed awareness of which are relevant to the running of time which may bar the action, are not to include knowledge of whether particular facts and circumstances would or would not result in legal liability to make reparation. That is a matter for the court.

Interpretation of this Part

22D.—(1) Expressions used in this Part and in Part I of the 1987 Act shall have the same meanings in this Part as in the said Part I.

(2) For the purposes of section 1(1) of the 1987 Act, this Part shall have effect and be construed as if it were contained in Part I of that Act.

(3) In this Part, "the 1987 Act" means the Consumer Protection Act 1987.

GENERAL NOTE

This section deals with the interpretation of Part IIA of the 1973 Act.

VERBAL COMMENTARY ON SECTION 22D

(1) *"This part"* is Part IIA of the 1973 Act, inserted by the 1987 Act, Sched. 1, para. 10.

"Part I of the 1987 Act" is the Part dealing with Product Liability and creating statutory liability to make reparation for harm caused by defect in a product.

(2) This Part IIA of the 1973 Act is to have effect and be construed as if it were contained in Part I of the 1987 Act.

CHAPTER 8

SUPPLEMENTAL PROVISIONS

PART III of the 1973 Act contains certain supplemental sections.

Private international law application

23A.[1]—(1) Where the substantive law of a country other than Scotland falls to be applied by a Scottish court as the law governing an obligation, the court shall apply any relevant rules of law of that country relating to the extinction of the obligation or the limitation of time within which proceedings may be brought to enforce the obligation to the exclusion of any corresponding rule of Scots law.

(2) This section shall not apply where it appears to the court that the application of the relevant foreign rule of law would be incompatible with the principles of public policy applied by the court.

(3) This section shall not apply in any case where the application of the corresponding rule of Scots law has extinguished the obligation, or barred the bringing of proceedings prior to the coming into force of the Prescription and Limitation (Scotland) Act 1984.

GENERAL NOTE

The need for this new provision arises from the fact that some rules dealing with the effect of lapse of time are deemed rules of substantive law, as where they extinguish the obligation, and some are deemed rules of a procedural character, as where they render an obligation unenforceable after a stated lapse of time or change the onus or mode of proof of the substance of the obligation after a lapse of time. Difficulty arises where an obligation is governed in principle by the law of another territory; in such a case previously a Scottish court would have had regard to a substantive rule of the foreign *lex causae*; if by that system the obligation was extinguished, no action was competent thereon in Scotland: *Higgins v. Ewing's Trustees*, 1925 S.C. 440; if by the other system there is merely a time after which no action on the obligation is competent, the Scottish courts would disregard the foreign limitation as procedural and allow an action in Scotland subject to the limitation, procedural and evidential rules of Scots law: *e.g. Westminster Bank Ltd. v. McDonald*, 1955 S.L.T. (Notes) 73; *Stirling's Trustees v. Legal and General Assurance Society*, 1957 S.L.T. 73. Particular difficulties arose where one or both of Scots law and the other legal system involved applied rules which are procedural in nature. The best solution, it seemed to the Scottish Law Commission, was to enact that the rules of prescription or limitation of the *lex causae*, including any relevant rules of suspension and interruption should be applied by a Scottish court, however they might be classified for choice of law purposes under the *lex causae*, to the exclusion of any corresponding rules of Scots law. The new section 23A seeks to give effect to this recommendation. It effects a considerable simplification of the law.

[1] Inserted by the Prescription and Limitation (Scotland) Act 1984, s. 4, as regards proceedings commenced on or after September 26, 1984.

VERBAL COMMENTARY ON SECTION 23A

"(1) Where the substantive law ... governing an obligation"

This makes the section applicable to a case where a Scottish court has jurisdiction but has reached the conclusion that by Scots rules of choice of law another legal system is the *lex causae* or appropriate system of substantive law to determine the rights and duties of parties to the case, *e.g.* as being the proper law of a contract.

"the court shall apply any relevant rules ... proceedings may be brought"

In such circumstances the Scottish court is directed to apply the rules as to the effect of lapse of time of the foreign legal system (*lex causae*), whether extinctive in effect, *i.e.* a prescription, or limiting as to time for suing, *i.e.* a limitation.

"to the exclusion of any corresponding rule of Scots law."

The foreign law rule is to be applied and the corresponding Scottish rule, if any, disregarded.

"(2) This section shall not apply ... public policy applied by the court."

This reserves the liberty of the court to decline to apply the rule of section 23A if to do so would be incompatible with the court's view of the requirements of public policy. In the Scottish Standing Committee the instance was quoted of a possible prescriptive or limiting rule of a foreign system which applied differently and less favourably to certain pursuers, *e.g.* coloured persons or foreigners, than to others. If the court declines on this ground to apply section 23A it will have to determine and apply the existing common law rule.

"(3) This section shall not apply ... Prescription and Limitation (Scotland) Act 1984.

This makes clear that the operation of section 23A is not to reopen any cause extinguished or barred from being a cause of action by the lapse of time prior to this Act coming into force.

The Crown

24.—This Act binds the Crown.

GENERAL NOTE

By virtue of this section the Crown, including departments of state and bodies having the privilege of the Crown, is affected by all the provisions of the 1973 Act. Accordingly provisions of the 1973 Act may be pleaded by or against the Crown. But certain claims by or against the Crown, such as for recovery of tax, are governed by special provisions. The Consumer Protection Act 1987, Part I, which is affected by Part IIA of the 1973 Act, by section 9, thereof, also binds the Crown but only so far as the Crown is made liable in reparation under the Crown Proceedings Act 1947, as that Act has effect from time to time.

Short title, commencement and extent

25.—(1) This Act may be cited as the Prescription and Limitation (Scotland) Act 1973.

(2)[2] This Act shall come into operation as follows:—

    (*a*) Parts II and III of this Act, Part II of Schedule 4 of this Act and Part II of Schedule 5 to this Act shall come into operation on the date on which this Act is passed;

    (*b*) except as aforesaid this Act shall come into operation on the expiration of three years from the said date.

(3)[3]...

(4) This Act extends to Scotland only.

GENERAL NOTE

The Act was passed on July 25, 1973 and Parts II and III, and parts of the Schedules, came into force then. Part I and the remainder of the Schedules came into force on July 25, 1976.

The Schedules are not reproduced herein but in the context of the sections to which they are severally relevant.

---

[2] As amended by the Prescription and Limitation (Scotland) Act 1984, Sched. 2.
[3] Repealed by the Prescription and Limitation (Scotland) Act 1984, Sched. 2.

CHAPTER 9

THE LIMITATION (ENEMIES AND WAR PRISONERS) ACT
1945

THE text of this Act, as applicable to Scotland and as amended by the Prescription and Limitation (Scotland) Act 1973 and certain later Acts is as follows:

Suspension of limitation period where party was an enemy or detained in enemy territory

1.—(1) If, during any period of less than ten years prescribed by any of the enactments hereinafter referred to as the period within which any action or diligence must be raised or executed or on the expiry of which any limitation on the mode of proof in any action becomes operative or any obligation is extinguished, any person who would have been a necessary party to such action or who was a party to such obligation was an enemy or was detained in enemy territory, the period so prescribed shall be deemed not to have run while the said person was an enemy or was so detained and shall in no case expire before the end of twelve months from the date when he ceased to be an enemy or to be so detained or from the date of the passing of this Act whichever is the later:

Provided that where any person was only an enemy as respects a business carried on in enemy territory, this section shall only apply so far as that person is concerned to actions or obligations arising in the course of that business.

The enactments hereinbefore referred to are—

    section six of the Prescription and Limitation (Scotland) Act 1973,

    section eight of the Maritime Conventions Act 1911,

    Rule 6 of Article III of the Schedule to the Carriage of Goods by Sea Act 1971,[1]

    sections 8A and 17 of the Prescription and Limitation (Scotland) Act 1973.

(2) If it is proved in any action that any person was resident or carried on business or was detained in enemy territory at any time, he shall for the purposes of this Act be presumed to have continued to be resident or to carry on business or to be detained, as the case may be, in that territory until it ceased to be enemy territory, unless it is proved that he ceased to be resident or to carry on business or to be detained in that territory at an earlier date.

(3) If two or more periods have occurred in which any person who would have been such a necessary party as aforesaid was an enemy or was detained in enemy territory, those periods shall be treated for the purposes of this Act as one continuous period beginning with the beginning of the first period and ending with the end of the last period.

Interpretation

2.—(1) In this Act the following expressions have the meanings hereby respectively assigned to them, that is to say:—

    "action" means civil proceedings before any court or tribunal and includes arbitration proceedings;

    "enemy" means any person who is, or is deemed to be, an enemy for any of the purposes of the Trading with the Enemy Act 1939 except that in ascertaining whether a person is such an enemy the expression "enemy

---

[1] As substituted by virtue of Interpretation Act 1978, s. 17(2)(*a*).

territory" in section two of the said Act shall have the meaning assigned to that expression by this section[2];

"enemy territory" means:

(*a*) any area which is enemy territory as defined by subsection (1) of section fifteen of the Trading with the Enemy Act 1939;

(*b*) any area in relation to which the provisions of the said Act apply, by virtue of an order made under subsection (1A) of the said section fifteen, as they apply in relation to enemy territory as so defined; and

(*c*) any area which, by virtue of Regulation six or Regulation seven of the Defence (Trading with the Enemy) Regulations 1940, or any order made thereunder, is treated for any of the purposes of the said Act as enemy territory as so defined or such territory as is referred to in the last foregoing paragraph;

"statute of limitation" [not applicable to Scotland].

(2) References in this Act to any person who would have been a necessary party to an action shall be construed as including references to any person who would have been such a necessary party but for the provisions of section seven of the Trading with the Enemy Act 1939, or any order made thereunder.

(3) References in this Act to the period during which any person was detained in enemy territory shall be construed as including references to any period immediately following the period of such detention during which that person remained in enemy territory.

(4) Subsection (2) of section fifteen of the Trading with the Enemy Act 1939 (which provides that a certificate of a Secretary of State shall, for the purposes of proceedings under or arising out of that Act, be conclusive evidence of certain matters affecting the definition of "enemy territory") shall apply for the purposes of any action to which this Act relates.

(5) References in this Act to any enactment or to any Defence Regulation shall be construed as referring to that enactment or Regulations as amended by any subsequent enactment or Defence Regulation.

Application to the Crown

3. This Act shall apply to proceedings to which the Crown is a party, including proceedings to which His Majesty is a party in right of the Duchy of Lancaster and proceedings in respect of property belonging to the Duchy of Cornwall.

Application to Scotland

4. [Modifications made to the Act in relation to its application to Scotland have been taken account of above.]

5. [This section is not applicable to Scotland.]

Short title and date of operation

6. (1) This Act may be cited as the Limitation (Enemies and War Prisoners) Act 1945.

---

[2] Hence a person may not be an enemy for the purpose of suing, but yet be an enemy for the suspension of the running of time: see *The Atlantic Scout* [1950] P. 266.

CHAPTER 10

OTHER STATUTORY PRESCRIPTIONS OR LIMITATIONS ON TIME FOR BRINGING CIVIL ACTIONS

THE Prescription and Limitation (Scotland) Act 1973 is not completely comprehensive in that it does not repeal or supersede a large number of provisions contained in various statutes dealing with a wide variety of subjects, all providing in various terms that something must be done within a stated time, or may not be done after the lapse of a stated time or ceases to be valid after a stated time. This chapter attempts to collect the main such statutory provisions in force in private law and to group them under the appropriate legal headings. These provisions apply to a great variety of circumstances and are expressed in very varied terms. It is frequently difficult to say whether the provisions should be classified as of the nature of prescriptions or limitations in the proper sense of either term.

Adjudication

A creditor who obtains decree of adjudication against a debtor acquires only a defeasible right as the debtor may pay the debt and recover the property. But after 10 years the creditor may obtain declarator of the expiry of "the legal" [term of redemption] and convert his right into a right of property.[1] Alternatively a right of property can be obtained by possession for the prescriptive period of 10 years.[2]

Arrestments

Arrestments prescribe in three years, if not "pursued and insisted on" within that time, in the case of a future and contingent debt from the time when the debt shall become due and the contingency be purified.[3]

Carriage

(a) *Air.* No action against a carrier's servant or agent which arises out of damage to which the Convention scheduled to the Carriage by Air Act 1961 relates shall, if he was acting within the scope of his employment, be brought after more than two years from the date of arrival at the destination or from the date on which the aircraft ought to have arrived, or from the date on which the carriage stopped.[4]

The right to damages under the Convention is extinguished if an action is not brought within two years, reckoned from the date of arrival at the

---

[1] Diligence Act 1661; Adjudications Act 1672.
[2] G.L. Gretton "Prescription and the Foreclosure of Adjudications" 1983 J.R. 177.
[3] Debtors (Scotland) Act 1838, s. 22, reducing to three years the prescription of five years enacted by Prescription Act 1669; amended by Debtors (Scotland) Act 1987, Sched. 6; *Jameson v. Sharp* (1887) 14 R. 643.
[4] Carriage by Air Act 1961, s. 5(1). A new Schedule is substituted by the Carriage by Air and Road Act 1979, s. 1.

destination, or from the date on which the aircraft ought to have arrived, or from the date on which the carriage stopped. The method of calculating the period of limitation is determined by the law of the court seised of the case.[5]

(b) *Railway.*   The periods of limitation for actions of damages brought under the Convention incorporated by statute, are (a) in the case of the passenger who has sustained an accident, three years from the day after the accident; (b) in the case of other claimants, three years from the day after the death of the passenger, or five years from the day after the accident, whichever is the earlier. These periods may be suspended in certain cases: subject to these provisions the limitation of actions is governed by national law.[6]

(c) *Road.*   The period of limitation for an action arising out of carriage under the Convention enacted by the International Transport Conventions Act 1983 is one year, or in the case of a deliberate or reckless act or omission, two years, from starting dates specified.[7]

A carrier of passengers and luggage by road is liable for death or injury to a passenger or loss or damage to luggage. The period of limitation for death or injury is three years.[8]

(d) *Sea.*   Subject to provisions as to indemnity a carrier by sea and the ship are discharged from all liability whatsoever in respect of goods, unless suit is brought within one year of their delivery or of the date when they should have been delivered; the period may be extended if the parties so agree after the cause of action has arisen.[9]

A carrier of passengers by sea is liable for damage caused by the death of or injury to a passenger caused by the carrier's fault but such an action is time-barred after two years.[10]

Collisions at sea

A claim or lien against a vessel or her owners in respect of any damage or loss to another vessel, her cargo or freight or any property on board her, or damages for loss of life or personal injuries suffered by any person on board her, or in respect of any salvage services, must be brought within two years from the date when the damage or loss or injury was caused or the salvage services were rendered.[11]

An action to enforce any contribution in respect of an overpaid proportion of any damages for loss of life or personal injuries must be brought within one year from the date of payment.[12]

---

[5] *ibid.*, Sched. 1, Art. 29.

[6] International Transport Conventions Act 1983, s. 1.

[7] International Transport Conventions Act 1983, COTIF Convention, App. B, Art. 58.

[8] COTIF Convention, App. A, Arts. 49 and 51.

[9] Carriage of Goods by Sea Act 1971, Sched., Art. III, para. 6.

[10] Merchant Shipping Act 1979, ss. 14–16 and Sched. 3, incorporating Athens Convention of 1974 and Protocol of 1976.

[11] Maritime Conventions Act 1911, s. 8. The period may be extended by the court: *ibid.* See *Birkdale S.S. Co.*, 1922 S.L.T. 575; *"Reresby" v. "Cobetas,"* 1923 S.L.T. 492 at p. 719; *Dorie Steamship Co.,* 1923 S.C. 593; *Essien v. Clan Line Steamers,* 1925 S.N. 75; *Brown v. Devanha Fishing Co.,* 1968 S.L.T. (Notes) 4; *Taft v. Clyde Marine,* 1990 S.L.T. 170.

[12] Maritime Conventions Act 1911, s. 8. The period may be extended by the court: *ibid.*

Compensation

Notice of a claim for compensation under the Compensation (Defence) Act 1939 must be given to the prescribed authority within six months or such longer period as the Treasury may allow.[13]

Compulsory acquisition

An order for the compulsory acquisition of land under the Allotments Acts becomes void if notice to treat thereunder is not served by the acquiring authority within three months after the making of the order. [14]

The powers of the promoters of an undertaking may not be exercised after the expiry of the prescribed period, which, if no period be prescribed, is three years from the passing of the special Act.[15]

Copyright

Copyright in published literary, dramatic, musical or artistic works subsists until the end of 50 years from the end of the calendar year in which the author died.[16] Copyright in computer-generated works lasts for 50 years from the time it was made.[17]

Copyright in published editions of literary, dramatic or musical works subsists till 25 years from the end of the calendar year in which the edition was first published.[18]

Copyright in unpublished literary, dramatic, musical or artistic works subsists until the end of 50 years from the end of the calendar year in which the author died.[19]

Copyright in sound recordings subsists till the end of 50 years from the end of the calendar year in which the recording is first published.[20]

Copyright in broadcast and cable programmes subsists until 50 years from the end of the year in which the broadcast is made.[21]

Crown copyright lasts for 50 years from commercial publication or 125 years, whichever is shorter.[22] Parliamentary copyright lasts for 50 years from making.[23]

Death, presumption of

Where a person is missing and is not known to have been alive for at least seven years, declarator may be sought that he be presumed dead.[24] An order varying the effect of such a decree on property may be sought only within five years of the decree.[25]

---

[13] Compensation (Defence) Act 1939, s. 11.
[14] Allotments (Scotland) Act 1922, s. 13(1). No further order may be made within three years unless for special reasons: *ibid.*, s. 13(2).
[15] Lands Clauses Consolidation (Scotland) Act 1845, s. 116.
[16] Copyright, Designs and Patents Act 1988, s. 12.
[17] *ibid.*, s. 12.
[18] *ibid.*, s. 15.
[19] *ibid.*, s. 12.
[20] *ibid.*, s. 13.
[21] *ibid.*, s. 14.
[22] *ibid.*, s. 163.
[23] *ibid.*, s. 165.
[24] Presumption of Death (Scotland) Act 1977, s. 1.
[25] *ibid.*, s. 5(4).

Delict

An action for damages for wrongous imprisonment prescribes if not pursued within three years after the last day of the wrongous imprisonment, and process being once raised the same shall prescribe if not insisted in yearly thereafter. [26]

A claim for compensation under sections 7 to 11 for breach of duty under the Nuclear Installations Act 1965 must be brought within 30 years from the date of the occurrence giving rise to the claim, or the last event in the course of that occurrence or succession of occurrences, to which the claim relates. [27]

A claim in respect of injury or damage caused by an occurrence involving nuclear matter stolen from, or lost, jettisoned or abandoned by, the person whose breach of duty under sections 7 to 10 gave rise to the claim must be brought within 20 years from the day when the nuclear matter was stolen, etc.[28]

Designs

Copyright in a registered design subsists for five years from the date of registration, but may be extended for four more periods of five years.[29]

Design right in an original design subsists for 15 years from the end of the calendar year in which it was first recorded in a design document or an article was first made to the design, whichever first occurred, or 10 years from the end of the year in which articles made to the design are first made available for sale or hire if that was within five years of that calendar year.[30]

Employment claims

An industrial tribunal may not entertain a complaint by an employee unless presented within three months,[31] or a claim for redundancy payment or as to an equality clause relating to a woman's employment unless presented within six months.[32]

Forestry

Claims for compensation in respect of deterioration taking place after the refusal of a felling licence for trees may be made from time to time but not for deterioration taking place more than ten years before the date of the claim, and, if the trees have been felled, no such claim shall be made after one year from the date of the felling.[33]

Gaming

No charges may be made on premises licensed under the Gaming Act 1968 unless particulars have been notified to the licensing authority at least 14 days before the date on which the charge is made.[34]

---

[26] Criminal Procedure Act 1701 (1701, c. 6).
[27] Nuclear Installations Act 1965, s. 15(1).
[28] *ibid.*, s. 15(2).
[29] Registered Designs Act 1949, s. 8 substituted by Copyright, Designs and Patents Act 1988, s. 269.
[30] Copyright, Designs and Patents Act 1988, s. 216. See also Council Directive (EC) 93/98.
[31] Employment Protection (Consolidation) Act 1978, s. 11.
[32] *ibid.*, s. 101.
[33] Forestry Act 1967, s. 11(3).
[34] Gaming Act 1968, s. 14(4).

Where a person is convicted of certain offences he may be disqualified for not more than five years from holding a licence in respect of the premises in question.[35]

Inhibitions

All inhibitions and notices of litigiosity registered under the Titles to Land Consolidation Act 1868, s. 159, prescribe and are of no effect after five years from the date on which they take effect.[36]

Litigiosity

No summons of reduction, constitution, adjudication, or constitution and adjudication combined, shall have any effect in rendering litigious the lands to which such summons relates, except from and after the date of the registration of a notice.[37] No action relating to land or to a lease or to a heritable security has the effect of making such land, lease or heritable security litigious unless and until a notice is registered in the Register of Inhibitions and Adjudications. No decree in any action of adjudication of land or a lease or a heritable security and no abbreviate of any such decree is to have any effect in making such land, lease or heritable security litigious.[38] All inhibitions and notices of litigiosity registered under the 1868 Act prescribe and are of no effect after five years from the date on which they take effect. In no case is litigiosity pleadable or to be founded on to any effect after six months after final decree in the action creating such litigiosity.[39]

Medicines

A licence under Part II of the Medicines Act 1968, unless renewed or revoked, lapses after five years from its grant or renewal, or after a shorter period specified therein.[40]

A clinical trial certificate or animal test certificate, unless renewed or revoked, expires after two years from the date of issue or renewal, or at the end of a shorter period specified therein.[41]

An order imposing a prohibition on the sale, supply or importation of medicinal products, if made without specified prior consultation, is to lapse after not more than three months from its coming into operation, without prejudice to the making of a further order.[42]

A person convicted of certain offences may be disqualified from using premises as a retail pharmacy for a period specified, not exceeding two years.[43]

---

[35] Gaming Act 1968, s. 24(2).
[36] Conveyancing (Scotland) Act 1924, s. 44(3).
[37] Titles to Land Consolidation Act 1868, s. 159, and Sched. RR.
[38] Conveyancing (Scotland) Act 1924, s. 44(2).
[39] *ibid.*, s. 44(3).
[40] Medicines Act 1968, s. 24(1). It may be renewed for five years or a shorter period: *ibid.*, s. 24(2).
[41] *ibid.* s. 38(1). It may be renewed for two years or a shorter period: *ibid.*, s. 38(2).
[42] *ibid.* s. 62(4).
[43] *ibid.* s. 68(1).

Mines and Quarries

Claims for compensation for damage or disturbance to land resulting from operations on land must be brought within six years from one of stated dates.[44]

Nuclear installations

See DELICT.

Patents

A patent is valid for 20 years from the date of filing thereof.[45]

Plant breeder's rights

Plant breeder's rights may be granted for periods of not less than 15 (in certain cases 18) years and not exceeding 25 years, as prescribed by schemes under the Plant Varieties and Seeds Act 1964.[46]

Pollution by oil

No action to enforce a claim in respect of a liability incurred under section 1 of the Act by reason of the discharge or escape of oil from a ship is to be entertained by any court in the United Kingdom unless the action is commenced not later than three years after the claim arose nor later than six years after the occurrence or first of the occurrences resulting in the discharge or escape by reason of which the liability was incurred.[47]

Postal packets

The Post Office Inland Letter Post Scheme 1989 and Inland Parcel Post Scheme 1989 accept liability for packets and parcels damaged subject to conditions, but without time limit for claims.[48]

Property found

Property found and handed to the police may be offered to the finder after two months.[49]

Race relations

An industrial tribunal may consider a complaint of discrimination only if presented within three months of the act of discrimination.[50]

A sheriff court may consider a claim that a person has committed an act of discrimination only if commenced within six months.[51]

---

[44] Mines and Quarries (Tips) Act 1969, s. 20 and Sched. 3, para. 6.
[45] Patents Act 1977, s. 25.
[46] Plant Varieties and Seeds Act 1964, s. 3.
[47] Merchant Shipping (Oil Pollution) Act 1971, s. 9.
[48] Post Office Act 1969, s. 28.
[49] Civic Government (Scotland) Act 1982, s. 68.
[50] Race Relations Act 1976, s. 68.
[51] *ibid.*

An industrial tribunal may consider certain other claims only if presented within six months.[52]

Registers

The Registrar of the General Medical Register may erase from the register the entry relating to a person if he has no answer within six months from a letter of inquiry whether the person has changed his address.[53]

Roads

A person executing works in or excavating under a public road must make good any damage to the road and maintain such making good for 12 months from the roads authority certifying that the damage has been made good to their satisfaction.[54]

Salvage

See COLLISIONS AT SEA.

Security, standard

A notice calling up the money secured by a standard security ceases to have effect for the purpose of a sale in the exercise of any power conferred by the security on the expiry of five years from the date of the notice or, if the subjects have been offered for or exposed to sale, from the date of the last offer or exposure.[55]

A notice of default, calling on the debtor under a standard security and on the proprietor, if not the debtor, to purge the default, ceases to be authority for the exercise of the rights of sale, repairs and foreclosure on the expiry of five years from the date of the notice.[56]

Sequestration

A petition by a creditor for sequestration of a debtor must be within four months of apparent insolvency.[57]

A copy of the court order awarding sequestration, recorded in the Register of Inhibitions and Adjudications, has the effect of an inhibition and a citation in an adjudication of the estate of the debtor, but such effect expires on the lapse of three years from the date of the order so recorded, but it is competent to, and if the trustee is undischarged he must, record a memorandum before the end of every period of three years renewing the effect of the order.[58]

A debtor sequestrated is entitled to discharge three years from the date of sequestration.[59]

---

[52] Race Relations Act 1976, s. 68.
[53] Medical Act 1969, s. 3(5).
[54] Roads (Scotland) Act 1984, s. 56(4).
[55] Conveyancing and Feudal Reform (Scotland) Act 1970, s. 19(1).
[56] *ibid.*, s. 21(4).
[57] Bankruptcy (Scotland) Act 1985, s. 8.
[58] *ibid.*, s. 14.
[59] *ibid.*, s. 54; *Elliot's Tr. v. Elliot*, 1989 S.L.T. (Sh. Ct.) 46.

Sequestration for rent

A landlord's right to sequestrate for rent is lost unless action is commenced within three months of the date on which payment was due but not made[60] or the last day of the term which includes the date for the payment not made.[61]

Sewers

A claim for compensation for any loss, injury or damage sustained by any person by reason of the exercise by the local authority of any of their powers under the Sewerage (Scotland) Act 1968 is not maintainable unless it is made to the authority within 12 months after the date on which it is alleged to have arisen.[62]

Sex discrimination

Complaint to an industrial tribunal must be presented before the end of three months from the act complained of.[63]

A claim brought in the sheriff court that another person has committed an act of discrimination must be brought within six months.[64]

A sheriff court may not consider an application for enforcement in respect of a discriminatory practice unless made within six months.[65]

Shipping and seamen

A creditor of a deceased seaman is not entitled to obtain payment of his debt out of the seaman's property, if the debt accrued more than three years before his death, or if the demand is not made within two years after the death.[66]

Social security

A person is not entitled to social security benefit unless he satisfies the conditions and makes a claim in writing within the time prescribed for the particular benefit, which is usually 12 months.[67]

Town and country planning

Planning permission granted impliedly includes a condition that the development must be begun not later than five years from the grant.[68]

Trade marks

Registration of a trade mark subsists for seven years, but may be renewed for 14 years from expiry or last renewal of registration. If not renewed registration lapses, but it may be restored.[69]

---

[60] Gloag & Irvine, *Rights in Security,* 431.
[61] *The Laws of Scotland,* vol. 8, para. 383.
[62] Sewerage (Scotland) Act 1968, s. 20(3).
[63] Sex Discrimination Act 1975, s. 76.
[64] *ibid.*
[65] *ibid.*
[66] Merchant Shipping Act 1894, s. 178(2).
[67] Social Security Administration Act 1992, s. 1; Social Security (Claims and Payments) Regulations 1987, reg. 19.
[68] Town and Country Planning (Scotland) Act 1972, s. 38.
[69] Trade Marks Act 1938, s. 20(1) and (2).

Transport

Claims by various departments and authorities to historical records and relics vested in the Railways Board must be made within six months of an offer by the Board to transfer them.[70]

An offer or claim to remove a record or relic vested in the Railways Board must contain a statement of the time, not more than three months, when the claimant proposes to remove what he has claimed, and he removes it within that time or such later time as may be allowed.[71]

See also CARRIAGE.

Trespass

All actions and prosecutions for anything done in pursuance of the Game (Scotland) Act 1832 must be commenced within six calendar months after the fact committed, and subject to conditions.[72]

Wrongous Imprisonment

See DELICT.

---

[70] Transport Act 1968, s. 144(2), (3), (4) and (7).
[71] *ibid.*, s. 144(8).
[72] Game (Scotland) Act 1832, s. 17.

CHAPTER 11

MORA

MORA or delay in pressing a claim or seeking to enforce a right does not by itself have any effect on the claim or right. It is not a kind of prescription or limitation. *"Mora* is not a good *nomen juris.* There must be prescription or not. We are not to rear up new kinds of prescription under different names."[1] *"Mora,* or delay, is not of itself a defence, unless the delay has been for such a period, and the circumstances are such, that prescription applies."[2]

But delay is nevertheless not irrelevant. Delay beyond a stated time or, in any event, a time reasonable in the circumstances is by itself relevant where it is an express[3] or implied[4] term of an obligation that something will be done by a particular date. Thus an acceptance delayed will not bind the offeror where the goods are of such a nature that acceptance at once is called for. Delay in performance beyond the due date or, at all events, a reasonable time for performance, is a breach of contract. A trustee in bankruptcy must elect quickly whether to go on with a contract binding the bankrupt or to cancel it.[5]

MORA, TACITURNITY AND ACQUIESCENCE

Delay short of the prescriptive period is however properly invoked in circumstances where a person has so delayed to press a claim or to seek to enforce a right as to give rise to the reasonable inference that he has abandoned the right or claim; he may then be debarred from pressing it. The proper plea is accordingly that the pursuer is barred by *mora,* taciturnity and acquiescence, and this plea is one aspect of the general doctrine of personal bar, which is to the general effect that a person will not be allowed to act inconsistently with his own prior statements or actings. "It appears to me that the plea of *mora* cannot be successfully maintained merely on account of lapse of time, but that the person stating it must also be able to shew that his position has been materially altered, or that he has been materially prejudiced, by the delay alleged. In other words, mere lapse of time will not, in my judgment, found an effective plea of *mora*.... I do not doubt that, where coupled with lapse of time there have been actings or conduct fitted to mislead, or to alter the position of the other party to the worse, the plea of *mora* may be sustained. But in order to lead to such a plea receiving effect, there must, in my judgment, have been excessive or unreasonable delay in asserting a known right, coupled with a material alteration of circumstances to the detriment of the other party[6] ...

---

[1] *Mackenzie v. Catton's Trs.* (1877) 5 R. 313, at p. 317, *per* Lord Deas.
[2] Maclaren, *Court of Session Practice,* 403, approved in *Halley v. Watt,* 1956 S.C. 370, *per* L.P. Clyde.
[3] *e.g. Gatty v. Maclaine,* 1921 S.C. (H.L.) 1.
[4] *cf. British Motor Body Co. v. Shaw,* 1914 S.C. 922.
[5] *Anderson v. Hamilton* (1875) 2 R. 355.
[6] There follows reference to *C.B. v. A.B.* (1885)12 R. (H.L.) 36 at p. 40 *per* Lord Chancellor Selborne, and to *Mackenzie v. Catton's Trs., supra.*

Accordingly, the usual and proper mode of stating the plea is, that the action is barred by *mora*, taciturnity, and acquiescence, and the facts on which the plea so expressed is founded are set out on the record."[7] Similarly: "Our law ... may I think be stated in these three propositions: (1) that delay *per se*, so long as it is within the years of prescription, does not bar a pursuer's claim; (2) that to avail a defender anything it must be delay in prosecuting a known claim—that is a claim known to the pursuer to exist; and (3) that the delay has been prejudicial to the defender in depriving him of evidence which would or might have supported his defence."[8] On appeal it was observed: "I am not treating *mora* or delay as a plea in law. I do not think it is a plea in law; but I think the lapse of time is a circumstance which ought to be taken into account and ought largely to influence our estimate of and the conclusion we come to upon the facts of the case."[9]

In a later case it was said: "in order to sustain a plea of *mora* and taciturnity 'there must not only be a mere lapse of time, but the whole circumstances must be such as are consistent with the presumption of the claim having been fully satisfied or settled and abandoned as no longer due'".[10]

Plea is on the merits not preliminary plea

Even where *mora*, taciturnity and acquiescence is pleaded, it is not a preliminary plea, like "no jurisdiction" but a plea on the merits.[11] It is not accordingly a matter which, if established, excludes the pursuer's claim; it is rather a matter which if established must be weighed and may be held to be sufficiently strong to justify the view that the claim has been departed from and cannot now be given effect to.

Plea implies capacity and knowledge to challenge

A party can be held barred by delay, silence and acquiescence only where he had, or in the circumstances should reasonably have had, knowledge of the facts entitling him to make the claim in question. If he was disabled from suing,[12] or justifiably ignorant of those facts,[13] delay cannot be pleaded in bar of his claim.

Application of principles

The principles stated have been applied and illustrated in many cases.

Judicial review

A petition for judicial review has been rejected partly because there had been inordinate delay in seeking the remedy.[14]

---

[7] *Assets Co. v. Bain's Trs.* (1904) 6 F. 692 at p. 705 *per* L.P. Kinross (revd. on the facts (1905) 7 F. (H.L.) 104).

[8] *ibid.*, at p. 740, *per* Lord Trayner.

[9] *Bain v. Assets Co.* (1905) 7 F. (H.L.) 104 at p. 109, *per* Lord Davey.

[10] *Lees's Trs. v. Dun,* 1912 S.C. 50 at p. 64, *per* Lord Salvesen, citing Lord Cowan in *Moncrieff v. Waugh* (1861) 21 D. 216 at p. 218; affd. 1913 S.C. (H.L.) 12. See also *Hanlon v. Traffic Commissioner,* 1988 S.L.T. 802.

[11] *Halley v. Watt,* 1956 S.C. 370 at p. 374; Mackay, *Manual of Practice,* 621; MacLaren, *Court of Session Practice,* 403.

[12] *Cassidy v. Connochie,* 1907 S.C. 1112.

[13] *Kintore v. Earl of Kintore* (1886)13 R. (H.L.) 93.

[14] *Atherton v. Strathclyde R. C.,* 1995 S.L.T. 557.

In personal relations

Delay in taking action has repeatedly been held ineffective, if explicable in a way not implying acquiescence or condonation or other acceptance of what has happened.[15]

An action to reduce a decree was dismissed when it had been acquiesced in for 30 years and nearly all parties were dead.[16] But an action for breach of promise was not barred by nine years' delay when there had been intimations during that time that the claim was not abandoned.[17]

In actions of divorce it has been indicated that, to bar an action, *mora* must imply condonation[18] or at least evidence such indifference as amounts to indifference to the other party's conduct.[19] Delay was held to justify dismissal of the action in one case[20] where the pursuer's long-continued silence was held to be such permanent indifference as amounts practically to *remissio injuriae*.

In cases of contract

Delay has been held not to bar a claim in a case of a loan of money acknowledged by holograph writ, though there was no demand for principal or interest for 34 years, and it was said that "to support the plea of *mora* the circumstances must be such as, besides the mere fact of silence, to infer payment, satisfaction or abandonment."[21] Where there is a question of challenging a contract on such a ground as fraud the challenge must be made without delay.[22] In commercial transactions reasonable expedition in business matters is expected but not every delay is fatal.[23]

It has, however, been held a bar in a case of attempted reduction of a decree-arbitral arising out of the dissolution of a partnership, when the position of matters had become entirely changed and the original state no longer existed[24] and where an arbitration clause had not been pleaded until more than seven years after the dispute arose and after an action had been raised.[25]

In cases of delict

Claims of damages have been held barred by delay of 24 years, where it was observed that though in general delay of itself was not enough but abandonment must be implied in the delay, in claims which required constitution mere delay was sufficient to support a plea of *mora* though it

---

[15] *Mackenzie v. Mackenzie* (1883) 11 R. 105; *Holmes v. Holmes,* 1927 S.L.T. 20; *Monahan v. Monahan,* 1930 S.C. 221.

[16] *Lockyer v. Ferryman* (1877) 4 R. (H.L.) 32.

[17] *Colvin v. Johnstone* (1890) 18 R. 115.

[18] *Hellon v. Hellon* (1873)11 M. 290; see also *Mackenzie v. Mackenzie* (1883) 11 R. 105; *Gatchell v. Gatchell* (1898) 6 S.L.T. 218; *Robertson v. Robertson* (1901) 9 S.L.T. 332.

[19] *Johnstone v. Johnstone,* 1931 S.C. 60; *Cocozza v. Cocozza,* 1955 S.L.T. (Notes) 29; *Macfarlane v. Macfarlane,* 1956 S.C. 472.

[20] *A.B. v. C.D.* (1853) 15 D. 976. As to nullity actions see *W. v. W.,* 1933 S.N. 73; *W.Y. v. A.Y.,* 1946 S.C. 27.

[21] *Cuninghame v. Boswell* (1868) 6 M. 890 at p. 895 *per* Lord Cowan. Contrast *Neilson's Trs. v. Neilson's Trs.* (1883) 11 R. 119.

[22] *Gamage v. Charlesworth's Trs.,* 1910 S.C. 257. cf. *Westville Shipping Co. v. Abram,* 1922 S.C. 571; affd. 1923 S.C. (H.L.) 68.

[23] *Gaskell, Deacon & Co. v. Mackay* (1870) 8 S.L.R. 253.

[24] *McKersies v. Mitchell* (1872)10 M. 861; cf. *Stewart v. North* (1893) 20 R. 260.

[25] *Inverclyde (Mearns) Housing Society v. Lawrance Construction Co.,* 1989 S.L.T. 815.

was not alleged that there had been abandonment or acquiescence.[26] A claim for compensation for injuries to property has been held barred by 24 years' delay.[27] A claim for damages for seduction was held barred by 25 years' delay and the pursuer's continuance in the defender's employment.[28]

Delay, however, was held not to bar a claim of damages for slander based on statements in a document issued 10 years earlier when there was explanation for the delay,[29] nor to bar a claim for personal injuries raised 15 years after the accident and despite the pursuer's silence for 12 years.[30]

In cases of heritable property

An action for arrears of feu-duty has been dismissed on the ground *inter alia* that the pursuer's delay in bringing the action had caused loss of evidence to the defender.[31] An objection to the title of heritage bought was deemed departed from and acquiesced in when the titles had been examined and possession had been taken without mention of the objection, which was raised some months later.[32]

In relation to trusts

A plea of *mora* has been rejected where trustees pursued a former trustee for having failed to supervise the trust affairs.[33]

In cases of rights in succession

Mora, taciturnity and acquiescence may no doubt bar a claim for prior rights, legal rights, rights on intestacy or under a will, but can do so only where the claimant knew that he had a claim,[34] and there is evidence indicating intention not to exercise his right to claim.

Consequence of giving effect to plea

Where a plea of *mora*, taciturnity and acquiescence is properly taken, and facts justifying it adequately averred and proved, the effect is to bar the pursuer's claim entirely and require the court to dismiss it.[35] The claim falls to be dismissed because the pursuer has so delayed as to give rise to the inference that he had abandoned his claim and has permitted the defender to alter his position on the faith of that belief.

DELAY AS AFFECTING ONUS AND MODE OF PROOF

Delay not amounting to *mora*, taciturnity and acquiescence may have an effect on the onus and mode of proof. "Where there is a controversy of fact

---

[26] *Cook v. North British Ry. Co.* (1872) 10 M. 513: "It is not mere delay or lapse of time which makes *mora* but delay which leads the other party to believe that the claim has been given up": p. 516, Lord Neaves.

[27] *North British Ry. Co. v. Moon's Trs.* (1879) 16 S.L.R. 265.

[28] *Maloy v. Macadam* (1885) 22 S.L.R. 790.

[29] *Cunningham v. Skinner* (1902) 4 F. 1124.

[30] *Bethune v. Stevenson*, 1969 S.L.T. (Notes) 12.

[31] *Jackson v. Swan* (1895) 3 S.L.T. 149.

[32] *Macdonald v. Newall* (1898) 1 F. 68.

[33] *Lees's Trs. v. Dun*, 1912 S.C. 50; 1913 S.C. (H.L.) 12.

[34] *Kintore v. Earl of Kintore* (1886) 13 R. (H.L.) 93.

[35] *Eliotts Trs. v. Eliott* (1894) 21 R. 858; *Bosville v. Lord Macdonald*, 1910 S.C. 597.

great delay in bringing forward the case increases, in proportion to the length of that delay, the burden of proof which is thrown upon the plaintiff (*sic*); but that there is any definite or absolute bar arising from a certain amount of delay is a proposition which I apprehend cannot be established either by any Scottish or by any English authorities."[36] Similarly where the parties in right of the assets of a bank in liquidation sought to reduce a discharge granted more than 20 years earlier it was held that the delay had transferred to the pursuers the full onus of proving that the contributory had not made a full disclosure of his assets, and that they had failed to do this.[37]

Delay may similarly be held to be special cause justifying the court in ordering proof rather than jury trial,[38] save in cases where the pursuer was statutorily entitled to jury trial in the sheriff court.[39] "Now, the proper estimate and value to be attached to the circumstances which have arisen because of the delay appear to me to be matters that can be more properly dealt with by a judge than by a jury, who are not skilled in estimating matters of that sort, which do not depend upon the credibility of the witnesses who are examined but upon the extent to which the defenders have been prejudiced by being deprived of evidence which would have been available had the action been timeously brought."[40]

---

[36] *C. B. v. A.B.* (1885) 12 R. (H.L.) 36 at p. 40, *per* L.C. Selborne, *cf. Johnston v. Harland and Wolff Ltd.*, 1953 S.L.T. (Notes) 25.

[37] *Bain v. Assets Co.* (1905) 7 F. (H.L.) 104.

[38] *Woods v. A. C. S. Motors, Ltd.*, 1930 S.C. 1035; *McLellan v. Western S.M.T. Co.*, 1950 S.C. 112; *Devine v. Beardmore*, 1955 S.C. 311; *Halley v. Watt*, 1956 S.C. 370; see also *Moyes v. Burntisland Shipbuilding Co.*, 1952 S.C. 429; *McLeish v. Howden*, 1952 S.L.T. (Notes) 73; *Lynch v. Arnott Young & Co.*, 1952 S.L.T. (Notes) 79; *Porter v. Gordon*, 1952 S.L.T. (Notes) 80; *Strawhorn v. Kilmarnock Mags.*, 1952 S.L.T. (Notes) 83; *McKinnon v. Smith & Wellstood Ltd.*, 1953 S.L.T. (Notes) 10; *McKirdy v. Royal Mail Lines*, 1955 S.L.T. (Notes) 63; *Martin v. Palmer*, 1955 S.L.T. (Notes) 79; *Clark v. Pryde*, 1959 S.L.T. (Notes) 16; *Mackinnon v. N.B. Aluminium Co.*, 1960 S.L.T. (Notes) 22; *Davidson v. Chief Constable, Fife Police*, 1995 S.L.T. 545.

[39] *Eccles v. Brown*, 1955 S.L.T. 389; *Halley v. Watt*, 1956 S.C. 370.

[40] *Woods, supra*, 1037, *per* Lord Hunter, approved in *Halley, supra*, 373.

CHAPTER 12

PRESCRIPTION AND LIMITATION IN PUBLIC LAW

THERE are no general provisions as to the application of rules of prescription
or limitation of actions in relation to the Crown, public authorities or other
public bodies. In general the provisions of the Prescription and Limitation
(Scotland) Act 1973 apply, save where special provision is made.

THE CROWN

The Prescription and Limitation (Scotland) Act 1973 by section 24 thereof,
"binds the Crown." Accordingly any provision of the Act may be pleaded
in defence to an action by the Crown or any person or body representing
the Crown, and conversely the Crown may rely on any provision of the Act
as a defence to a claim by a subject. The same applies to all persons,
departments and bodies acting in right of the Crown and entitled to the
privileges of the Crown.

The old rule *nullum tempus occurrit regi* will apply to any case not
covered by the 1973 Act or by a provision to the same effect in the relevant
statute.[1]

JUDICIAL AND COURT OFFICERS

The immunities from action enjoyed at common law by judges and sheriffs
wholly exclude actions against them without regard to time.

Statutory provision is made for certain particular cases. No action
to enforce liability in damages against a judge, clerk of court, or
prosecutor in the public interest in respect of any proceedings taken,
act done, or judgment, decree or sentence pronounced under the
Criminal Procedure (Scotland) Act shall lie, unless the conditions
of the section are satisfied and the action is commenced within two
months after the proceedings, act, judgment, decree or sentence
founded on, or in the case where the Act under which the action is
brought fixes a shorter period, within that shorter period.[2] In this
section "judge" does not include sheriff, but the section is without
prejudice to the privileges and immunities possessed by sheriffs.[3]

No proceedings against any sheriff, J.P., magistrate, sheriff clerk, member
of a licensing board, clerk of a licensing board, procurator fiscal, constable
or other person on account of anything done in execution of the Act are to

---

[1] *Re. J.* [1909] 1 Ch. 574.

[2] Criminal Procedure (Scotland) Act 1975, s. 456.

[3] *ibid.*, s. 456(4). On these immunities see *Harvey v. Dyce* (1876) 4 R. 265. On the application of the section and its
predecessors see *Murray v. Allen* (1872) 11 M. 147; *Ferguson v. McNab* (1885) 12 R. 1083; *Hastings v. Henderson*
(1890) 17 R. 1130; *Lundie v. MacBrayne* (1894) 21 R. 1085; *Walker v. Brander*, 1920 S.C. 840; *Rae v. Strathern*, 1924
S.C. 147; *Graham v. Strathern*, 1924 S.C. 699. On the immunities of the Lord Advocate, his deputes, procurators-
fiscal and their deputes in prosecution on indictment see *Hester v. Macdonald*, 1961 S.C. 370.

lie unless commenced[4] within two months after the cause of such proceedings has arisen.[5]

PROVISIONS APPLICABLE TO PARTICULAR CASES
Customs and Excise

An application by an importer to the Board of Trade for relief from duty to which the section applies may not be made more than six months after the duty has been paid.[6]

A preliminary order imposing a provisional charge to duty retrospectively, lapses, if not revoked after three months from the date it comes into force, unless extended by a further order, in which case it lapses after six months from the date it comes into force.[7]

Elections

Every claim against a candidate or his election agent in respect of election expenses which is not sent in to the election agent within 14 days after the day on which the result of the election is declared is barred.[8]

All election expenses shall be paid within 28 days after the day on which the result of the election is declared.[9]

An election petition challenging an election must be presented within 21 days.[10]

Foreign jurisdiction

An action, suit, prosecution or proceeding against any person for any act done in pursuance or execution or intended execution of the Act, or in respect of any alleged neglect or default in the execution of the Act, does not lie unless commenced within six months after the act, neglect or default complained of, or in the case of a continuance of injury or damage within six months of the cessation thereof, or within six months after the parties came within the jurisdiction of the court.[11]

Social work

Where a local authority receives a child into care another local authority in whose area the child is ordinarily resident may within three months take over the care of the child.[12]

---

[4] See *Alston v. Macdougall* (1887) 15 R. 78; *cf. McNiven v. Glasgow Corporation*, 1920 S.C. 584; *Robertson v. Page*, 1943 J.C. 32.
[5] Licensing (Scotland) Act 1976, s. 130.
[6] Customs Duties (Dumping and Subsidies) Act 1969, s. 2(4).
[7] *ibid.*, s. 8(3).
[8] Representation of the People Act 1983, s. 78(1). Contravention is an illegal practice: *ibid.*, s. 78(3); but the court may grant leave to pay later: ibid., s. 78(4).
[9] *ibid.*, s. 78(2). Contravention is an illegal practice: *ibid.*, s. 78(3); but the court may grant leave to pay later: *ibid.*, s. 78(4).
[10] *ibid.*, ss. 122 and 129.
[11] Foreign Jurisdiction Act 1890, s. 13.
[12] Social Work (Scotland) Act 1968, s. 15(4).

A resolution by a local authority that parental rights shall vest in the local authority lapses 14 days after the service of a notice of objection by a person on whose account the resolution was passed.[13]

A person on whose account a resolution that parental rights shall vest in the local authority is passed has one month after notice of such a resolution is served on him to serve on the authority a notice of objection.[14]

Where a notice of objection to the assumption of parental rights has been served the local authority may prevent the resolution lapsing by applying to the sheriff within 14 days of the receipt of the notice.[15]

A supervision requirement may not remain in force without review by a children's hearing for a period extending beyond one year, and if not reviewed within one year it shall cease to have effect.[16]

The registration of an establishment intended to accommodate persons for the purpose of the Social Work (Scotland) Act 1968 subsists after the death of the person registered for four weeks or such longer period as the local authority may sanction.[17]

Complaint to Parliamentary Commissioner

A complaint to the Parliamentary Commissioner is not to be entertained unless made to an M.P. not later than 12 months from the day on which the person aggrieved first had notice of the matters alleged in the complaint, unless the Commissioner thinks that there are special circumstances which make it proper to investigate a complaint made later.[18]

Post Office

Proceedings against the Post Office in respect of loss of or damage to a registered inland packet must be begun within 12 months beginning with the day on which the packet was posted.[19]

Social Security

Times for claiming various benefits are prescribed.[20]

Times are prescribed for recovery of overpayments.[21]

Taxation

Excess inheritance tax paid is recoverable within six years.[22]

An assessment to income tax can in general only be made within six years of the end of the chargeable period to which it refers.[23]

---

[13] Social Work (Scotland) Act 1968, s. 16(7).

[14] *ibid.*, s. 16(7).

[15] *ibid.*, s. 16(8).

[16] *ibid.*, s. 48(3).

[17] *ibid.*, s. 62(8).

[18] Parliamentary Commissioner Act 1967, s. 6(3).

[19] Post Office Act 1969, s. 30(1).

[20] Social Security Act 1986, s. 51; Social Security (Claims and Payments) Regs. 1987 (S.I. 1987 No. 1968) and 1988 (S.I. 1988 Nos. 522, 1728).

[21] Social Security Act 1986, s. 53; Social Security (Payments on Account) Regs. 1988 (S.I. 1988 Nos. 664, 668, 1725).

[22] Inheritance Tax Act 1984, ss. 240–241.

[23] Taxes Management Act 1970, s. 34.

Claims for relief must in general be made within six years of the end of the chargeable period to which they relate.[24]

An assessment in respect of certain unremittable overseas income must be made within six years of the date specified.[25]

Relief on tax on delayed remittances must be claimed within six years after the end of the year in which the income is received in the U.K.[26]

An adjustment of tax under section 492 may be made not more than six years from the end of the chargeable period in which the payment was made [27]

Wrongful imprisonment

An action for damages for wrongous imprisonment prescribes if not pursued within three years after the last day of the wrongous imprisonment, and process being once raised shall prescribe if not persisted in yearly thereafter.[28]

---

[24] Taxes Management Act 1970, s. 43.
[25] *ibid.*, s. 418(2).
[26] *ibid.*, s. 419(6).
[27] *ibid.*, s. 492(8).
[28] Criminal Procedure Act 1701 (1701, c. 6).

CHAPTER 13

PRESCRIPTION AND LIMITATION IN CRIMINAL LAW

PRESCRIPTION

NEITHER at common law nor under statute is there any rule of prescription extinguishing liability to prosecution or punishment for crime after any particular period.[1]

LIMITATION GENERALLY

There is no general limitation on the time within which prosecutions must be brought or trials concluded.

LIMITS ON DETENTION

A person may be detained by the police[2] or by customs and excise officers[3] to enable them to carry out further investigations. It may not be continued for more than six hours, and the person must then be arrested, or released from detention; if released he may not again be detained on the same grounds.

DELAY IN TRIALS

An accused is not to be tried on indictment for any offence unless the trial is commenced within 12 months of the first appearance of the accused on petition; failing such commencement he is to be discharged and is for ever free from all question or process for that offence. On cause shown a judge may extend the period.[4]

An accused who is committed for any offence until liberated in due course of law is not to be detained for more than 80 days, unless within that period the indictment is served on him, failing which he must be liberated, or 110 days, unless the trial is commenced within that period, failing which he is to be liberated and be free from all process for that offence. A judge of the High Court may extend the period of 110 or 80 days.[5]

The 110 days are calculated from the date of full committal, not from the date of arrest.[6] If the accused is committed successively on a number of

---

[1] *Sugden v. H.M.A.*, 1934 J.C. 103.
[2] Criminal Justice (Scotland) Act 1980, s. 2.
[3] Criminal Justice (Scotland) Act 1987, ss. 48–50.
[4] Criminal Procedure (Scotland) Act 1975, s. 101(2) as substituted by Criminal Justice (Scotland) Act 1980, s. 14; *Rudge v. H.M.A.*, 1989 S.C.C.R. 105. *Black v. H.M.A.*, 1990 S.C.C.R. 609; *Coutts v. H.M.A.*, 1992 S.C.C.R. 87; *Ferguson v. H.M.A.*, 1992 S.C.C.R. 480; *Fleming v. H.M.A.*, 1992 S.C.C.R. 575; *H.M.A. v. Lang*, 1992 S.C.C.R. 642; *Ross v. H.M.A.*, 1990 S.C.C.R. 182; *Young v. H.M.A.*, 1990 S.C.C.R. 315.
[5] *ibid.*, s. 101(2)–(6), as substituted. See *Watson v. H.M.A.*, 1983 S.L.T. 471; *H.M.A. v. Swift*, 1985 S.L.T. 26; *Dobbie v. H.M.A.*, 1986 S.L.T. 648; *Mallison v. H.M.A.*, 1987 S.C.C.R. 320; *Berry v. H.M.A.*, 1988 S.C.C.R. 458; *Brown v. H.M.A.*, 1988 S.C.C.R. 577; *H.M.A. v. Lewis*, 1992 S.C.C.R. 223; *McCluskey v. H.M.A.*, 1993 S.L.T. 897.
[6] *H.M.A. v. McEwan*, 1953 J.C. 55.

charges, they will be computed separately from the date of committal on each charge, though the court may grant an extension of time in respect of the earlier charges to enable them all to be taken together.[7] If an accused is fully committed on one charge and, before being brought to trial, is sentenced to imprisonment on another charge the statutory period does not run during the period of the other sentence.[8] Similarly if an accused already serving a sentence of imprisonment is committed for trial on another charge the statutory period does not begin to run until the expiry of his sentence.[9]

A trial is concluded when the Crown accepts a plea of guilty or the jury returns a verdict or at latest when the Crown moves for sentence. The rule is not infringed by continuing the case for such purposes as obtaining reports before sentencing.[10]

A person charged with a summary offence is not to be detained for more than 40 days after the bringing of the complaint in court unless his trial is commenced within that period, but the sheriff may extend the period.[11] If the trial is not commenced in time the accused is forever freed from that offence.[12]

An accused may plead *mora,* taciturnity and delay, that the Crown has acted oppressively in delaying unreasonably to bring the case to court.[13]

LIMITATION OF TIME FOR INITIATING SUMMARY PROCEEDINGS FOR STATUTORY CONTRAVENTIONS

Proceedings under the Criminal Procedure (Scotland) Act 1975, in respect of the contravention of any statute or order, unless the statute or order fixed any other period,[14] must be commenced within six months[15] after the contravention occurred, or within six months after the last day of a continuous contravention.[16] Proceedings are "commenced" on the date of the granting of a warrant to apprehend or cite the accused, provided it is executed without undue delay.[17] This section applies to statutory offences only, and not to common law crimes, nor to proceedings dealt with under the Criminal Procedure Act but not of a criminal character.[18] In computing the time, the day on which the act was done, or other day from which time is to be reckoned, is excluded, but the day on which proceedings were commenced is included.[19] In some cases preliminary action must be taken before the prosecutor can institute proceedings.[20]

---

[7] *H.M.A. v. Dickson,* 1949 S.L.T. (Notes) 58; *cf. H.M.A. v. Boyle,* 1972 S.L.T. (Notes) 16.

[8] *Wallace v. H.M.A.,* 1959 J.C. 71.

[9] *H.M.A. v. Park,* 1967 J.C. 70; 1967 S.L.T. (Notes) 75; *Hartley v. H.M.A.,* 1970 J.C. 17.

[10] *Wallace, supra.*

[11] Criminal Procedure (Scotland) Act 1975, s. 331A, inserted by Criminal Justice (Scotland) Act 1980, s. 14.

[12] *ibid.*, s. 331A(1). See also *Lockhart v. Robb,* 1988 S.C.C.R. 381.

[13] *Tudhope v. McCarthy,* 1985 S.C.C.R. 76; see also *H.M.A. v. Stewart,* 1980 J.C. 84; *Philips v. Tudhope,* 1987 S.C.C.R. 80; *McGeown v. H.M.A.,* 1989 S.C.C.R. 95; *McFarlane v. Jessop,* 1988 S.C.C.R. 186.

[14] *MacKnight v. MacCulloch* (1909) 6 Adam 144.

[15] Calendar months: Interpretation Act 1978, Sched. 1.

[16] *cf. Hull v. L.C.C.* [1901] 1 K.B. 580; *MacKnight, supra; McLennan v. Macmillan,* 1964 J.C. 1.

[17] Criminal Procedure (Scotland) Act 1975, s. 331. See also *Robertson v. Page,* 1943 J.C. 32; *MacLean v. McMahon,* 1960 S.L.T. (Sh. Ct.) 30.

[18] *Dunlop v. Calder,* 1943 J.C. 49.

[19] *Radcliffe v. Bartholomew* [1892] 1 Q.B. 161; *Frew v. Morris* (1897) 2 Adam 267; *Tudhope v. Lawson,* 1983 S.C.C.R. 435.

[20] *e.g. H.M.A. v. McBurnie,* 1989 S.L.T. (Sh. Ct.) 48.

LIMITATIONS OF TIME UNDER PARTICULAR STATUTES

Numerous statutes prescribe the time within which criminal proceedings under the particular statute must be taken. In each case the precise wording of the statute must be examined to determine its effect. Where a statute requires that a prosecution must be brought within a certain time,[21] the procurator-fiscal cannot, unless allowed expressly or by statutory implication, take such a latitude in his complaint as to extend back outwith the limited period.[22]

---

[21] *e.g.* Road Traffic Offenders Act 1988, s. 1.

[22] *H.M.A. v. Philp* (1890) 2 White 525; *Farquharson v. Gordon* (1894)1 Adam 405; *Creighton v. H.M.A.* (1904) 4 Adam 356.

INDEX

Index